Second Language Performance Testing

L'évaluation de la « performance » en langue seconde

University of Ottawa Press
Éditions de l'Université d'Ottawa
1985

2-7603-0023-7

SECOND LANGUAGE PERFORMANCE TESTING

L'ÉVALUATION DE LA « PERFORMANCE » EN LANGUE SECONDE

**Philip C Hauptman
Raymond LeBlanc
Marjorie Bingham Wesche
Editors/Rédacteurs**

Canadian Cataloguing in Publication Data

Main entry under title:
  Second language performance testing =
L'Evaluation de la performance en langue
seconde

Text in English and French.
ISBN 0-7766-0091-5

1. Language and languages--Examinations--
Addresses, essays, lectures. 2. Language
and languages--Ability testing--Addresses,
essays, lectures. I. Hauptman, Philip C.
(Philip Carl), 1939- II. LeBlanc,
Raymond III. Wesche, Marjorie Bingham,
1941- IV. Title: L'Evaluation de la
performance en langue seconde.

PE53.S33 1985   418'.0076   C85-090106-5E

Données de catalogage avant publication (Canada)

Vedette principale au titre:
  Second language performance testing =
L'Evaluation de la performance en langue
seconde

Textes en anglais et en français.
ISBN 0-7766-0091-5

1. Langage et langues--Examens--Discours,
essais, conférences. 2. Langage et langues--
Tests d'aptitude--Discours, essais,
conférences. I. Hauptman, Philip C.
(Philip Carl), 1939- II. LeBlanc, Raymond
III. Wesche, Marjorie Bingham, 1941-
IV. Titre: L'Evaluation de la performance
en langue seconde.

PE53.S33 1985   418'.0076   C85-090106-5F

© University of Ottawa Press, Ottawa, Canada, 1985
ISBN 0-7766-0091-5
Printed and bound in Canada

Preface

The present collection of articles on Performance Testing represents the first step in a commitment by the Centre for Second Language Learning to produce publications in applied linguistics and second language teaching and learning. We are proud that Second Language Performance Testing is the first in the CSLL Series in Applied Linguistics. We eagerly await future volumes in this series as well as textbooks in the two additional series of English as a Second Language and French as a Second Language.

We are especially pleased to be able to thank the following sources, which helped finance the Testing Conference which took place at the University of Ottawa in March, 1982 and which provided the impetus for this book: The British Council, Office of the Secretary of State, Social Science and Humanities Research Council of Canada, and Wintario.

As a final word of thanks, we wish to express our sincere gratitude to Mrs. Doreen Ready who tirelessly worked on all phases of preparing this volume for publication.

Philip C. Hauptman
Raymond LeBlanc
Marjorie B. Wesche

Préface

Ce recueil d'articles sur le testing de la performance constitue le premier volume d'une série de publications de l'Institut de langues vivantes qui portera sur la linguistique appliquée ainsi que sur l'enseignement et l'apprentissage des langues secondes. Ce premier volume rassemble essentiellement une série d'articles présentés lors du Colloque sur le testing qui a eu lieu à l'Université d'Ottawa au mois de mars 1982. Nous aimerions également signaler qu'il y aura deux autres séries : l'une portant sur l'anglais langue seconde et l'autre sur le français langue seconde.

Nous aimerions remercier, en particulier, les organismes qui ont octroyé des fonds pour la tenue du Colloque sur le testing d'où la publication de ce livre est issue : The British Council, le Secrétariat d'État du Canada, le Conseil de recherches en sciences humaines du Canada et Wintario.

Finalement, nous aimerions remercier Mme Doreen Ready de sa contribution indispensable à la préparation de ce volume.

Philip C. Hauptman
Raymond LeBlanc
Marjorie B. Wesche

Contents / Sommaire

Foreword

This book grew out of a conference on Second Language Performance Testing/Le testing de performance en langue seconde at the University of Ottawa in March, 1983, co-sponsored by the University's Centre for Second Language Learning (CSLL) and Carleton University's Centre for Applied Language Studies (CALS). Language testing is an important focus of activity and research at both Centres, largely in conjunction with their respective teaching programs in English as a second language, and, at the CSLL, in French as a second language and with client groups in other departments and outside the University. Because second language testing, and particularly language testing of older learners, is a relatively neglected topic at conferences in applied linguistics and language education, we wanted to bring together testing specialists and educators with concerns similar to ours, to exchange information and experiences in a focused way.

We selected the topic of performance testing because this approach, borrowed relatively recently from the field of vocational testing, characterizes much current test development in Canada and elsewhere for older learners with specific, real-life second language needs. Little has appeared about it in the literature, however, perhaps because many of the organizations involved in this type of language testing are outside the traditional circles of academic research and communication. Business and government entities which must provide bilingual services on a daily basis tend to be more concerned with accurate decision-making about employee language skills in a particular context (i.e., predictive validity) than about construct validity or statistical properties of tests. While bilingual educational institutions and those admitting non-native speakers to courses of study share this concern with real-life second language abilities, their testing specialists tend to be more involved in theoretical research in language testing and more familiar with one another's work.

The 1983 TESOL convention in Toronto afforded us a special opportunity to bring participants from other parts of Canada and around the world to Ottawa. The result was far beyond our expectation in terms of the more than two hundred participants, the level of interest, and the variety and quality of work reported in this area.

We are happy to present selected papers from the Conference in this book, supplemented with two related papers from the Language Testing Research Colloquium which followed the Conference, and two papers based on presentations at TESOL 1983. We hope that the book will be only a second step in what will become an ongoing exchange on a performance approach to second language testing.

P. Hauptman
R. LeBlanc
M. Wesche

Avant-propos

Le présent ouvrage fait suite au symposium intitulé Le testing de performance en langue seconde/Second Language Performance Testing, tenu à l'Université d'Ottawa en mars 1983 et parrainé conjointement par l'Institut de langues vivantes (ILV) de cette université et le Centre for Applied Language Studies (CALS) de Carleton University. Le testing des langues constitue un domaine important d'activité et de recherche pour ces deux organismes, surtout en rapport avec leurs programmes respectifs d'anglais langue seconde et, dans le cas de l'ILV, de français langue seconde, de même qu'avec des groupes de clients d'autres départements et de l'extérieur de l'université. Le testing de langue seconde, en particulier dans le cas des apprenants adultes, reste un sujet négligé dans les colloques en linguistique appliquée et en didactique des langues; c'est pourquoi il a paru utile de réunir des spécialistes du testing et des éducateurs confrontés à des problèmes semblables aux nôtres pour échanger des connaissances et partager des expériences dans un cadre structuré.

Nous avons choisi le domaine du testing de performance parce que cette approche, empruntée plutôt récemment au champ du testing dans les professions, est représentative des progrès réalisés au Canada et ailleurs dans le testing des adultes face à des besoins spécifiques en langue seconde. Il y a cependant peu de publications sur le sujet, peut-être parce que les organismes qui s'occupent de ce type de testing de langue se situent en dehors des milieux traditionnels de la recherche et de la dissémination de celle-ci. Le monde des affaires et les corps gouvernementaux qui doivent assurer quotidiennement des services bilingues ont tendance à se préoccuper plus de la prise de décision juste au sujet des savoirs langagiers d'une employée dans un contexte précis (validité prédictive) que de la validité du concept hypothétique ou des caractéristiques statistiques des tests. Bien que les institutions d'éducation bilingues et celles qui acceptent des locuteurs non natifs dans leurs programmes d'étude partagent cet intérêt envers les savoirs langagiers authentiques, leurs spécialistes en testing restent plus impliqués dans la recherche théorique et plus familiers avec les travaux de leurs collègues.

TESOL '83, tenu à Toronto, nous a fourni l'occasion de réunir à Ottawa des participants en provenance non seulement d'autres régions du Canada, mais aussi du reste du monde. Les résultats devaient dépasser nos espoirs : plus de deux cents participants, un niveau d'intérêt soutenu et un grand éventail de présentations de qualité. Nous prenons plaisir à présenter dans ces pages quelques-uns des textes choisis parmi l'ensemble des communications présentées au symposium sur le testing de performance en langue seconde, auxquels nous avons ajouté deux textes présentés lors du colloque sur la recherche en testing de langue seconde qui suivait notre symposium et deux autres présentés dans le cadre de TESOL '83. Nous souhaitons que le présent ouvrage ne soit que la deuxième étape de ce qui devrait être un échange continu sur l'approche de la performance en testing de langue seconde.

P. Hauptman
R. LeBlanc
M. Wesche

Introduction

Marjorie Bingham Wesche

This volume represents a collective attempt to define and illustrate what has become known as a "performance" approach to testing second language proficiency (cf. Jones 1979). In performance tests, language knowledge must be demonstrated in the context of tasks and situations which represent or simulate those for which examinees are preparing to use their second language. Such tests are expected to predict how successfully the examinee will be able to communicate using the second language in certain target situations, rather than to establish his or her general proficiency level or to provide diagnostic feedback for the classroom. Performance testing thus finds its applications in achievement testing for specialized second language training programs and in certification testing for life-situations where examinees will use the second language, such as specific occupational or educational settings. Performance tests generally use one of three main techniques: direct assessment, work samples or simulation tasks, the last being the most important in second language testing (cf. Jones 1979, this volume).

PERFORMANCE TESTS AND VALIDITY

Performance-based tests have received increasing attention in recent years for their potential to make better predictions of future second language behaviour than do traditional tests.

A performance approach presupposes that <u>predictive validity</u> will be enhanced when tests reflect a concept of language proficiency that is not only dynamic and interactive, but that is also partly a function of context. The association of performance tests with specific contexts places a major constraint on the selection of test stimulus material and tasks.

Discussion has taken place over whether it is necessary to specify a new category of language tests. Oller has argued that performance tests are "essentially indistinguishable from pragmatic tests" (1983:38). In his view, testing procedures, to be <u>valid</u> measures of language proficiency, must be pragmatic, i.e., they must meet two "pragmatic naturalness" requirements. Pragmatic tests are those which

> cause the learner to process ... temporal sequences of elements in the language that conform to normal contextual constraints (linguistic and extralinguistic); second, they must require the learner to understand the pragmatic interrelationship of linguistic contexts and extralinguistic contexts. (Oller 1979:33)

Clearly, highly contextualized language processing tasks which replicate real-life situations conform to the constraints proposed above; they require examinees to process meaning through contextualized language in real time. Thus performance tests are pragmatic tests. However, given the additional constraint that performance tests must replicate important features of target situations, we believe that such tests should be viewed as a subcategory of pragmatic tests.[1] The content of performance tests, i.e., their subject matter, discourse types and the tasks they require of examinees, must reflect identifiable target situations. Examinees are asked to "understand the pragmatic interrelationship of linguistic ... and extralinguistic contexts" which are directly related to their second language needs or objectives.

The theoretical importance of this distinction between pragmatic tests in general and performance tests as a special case is implied by work in this volume illustrating the effect of background subject matter knowledge on language test scores (cf. Alderson and Urquhart). If, as it appears, it is impossible to select neutral or universally fair subject matter and discourse types for (non-trivial) language processing tasks, these aspects of language test content should be selected in a principled manner and their effect taken into account in the interpretation of results. Less is known about the requirement that the third aspect of test content, the test tasks, reflect in an obvious manner major features of target languages tasks. Does an indirect pragmatic task (e.g., a cloze procedure) which respects target subject matter and discourse type replicate the critical features of the target situation (e.g., being able to understand and take notes on textbook material in the second language) as well as does a performance task actually requiring reading and taking notes on a sample of such material? In other words, are both procedures equally effective in evoking the mental operations critical to being able to carry out the target task? While it would seem intuitively correct to claim increased face and content validity for the latter task the final answer is far from clear on either the practically important question of the predictive validity of performance tasks, or the theoretically important question of their construct validity or, indeed, what they in fact measure. Data are just beginning to appear on the former question (cf. Seaton). In the process of resolving the latter, we will have to refine our notions of the mental operations underlying language processing ability and the features of language use situations which critically influence them.

OTHER ISSUES

In the meantime, the performance approach provides a general operational principle for selecting test content - that of matching it with target language needs. Because of its vagueness, however, this principle raises many new problems - for example:
- How does one go about specifying target language needs (or objectives), assuming that they can be known?
- How detailed a needs specification is required?
- What needs should receive priority in the selection of subject matter, discourse types and tasks for testing purposes?
- How specific must the matching of test content and target situations be?
- How many different tests are required for adequate answers about examinee capabilities for a given purpose?

A performance approach to testing raises other issues as well. Performance testing can be very expensive in terms of test development, administration and scoring. Such expenditure may only be justifiable where wrong decisions about examinee second language abilities carry critical consequences, and where performance tests yield demonstrably better information than less direct procedures. Another issue has to do with the psychometric characteristics of performance tests. At the moment there is relatively little hard statistical data available on either the reliability or the predictive validity of performance testing procedures, or on the relationship between scores on such tests and those on other kinds of second language tests. While all of these and other issues receive considerable attention in this book (see below), it is apparent that much more experience is needed with this approach to language testing to establish its appropriate uses, refine its procedures and properly interpret its results.

While second language performance testing is clearly not without problems, the increasing use of such tests and their popularity with examinee and examiners alike, suggest that this approach can offer advantages over less direct methods. In some situations at least, satisfactory answers are gradually being found to the major problems, and many institutions appear willing to invest in these expensive but presumably effective testing procedures for specific purposes.

THE PAPERS

The papers in this collection deal in detail with most of the major issues which have so far come to light in a performance approach to second language assessment, including the following:

- the rationale for a performance approach, including its potential advantages over more traditional approaches;
- the essential characteristics of such an approach and the consequences for test development, administration and scoring procedures, including the issues of sampling and establishing evaluation criteria;
- the conditions under which performance testing is possible and appropriate, including both theoretical and practical considerations;
- the extent to which examinees may rely on non-linguistic skills and knowledge in performing heavily contextualized verbal tasks, and the related question of generalizability of test results from one context to another;
- problems which may arise in achieving high levels of reliability, particularly when scoring is based on holistic ratings by native speakers;
- technical problems in establishing test validity, in particular predictive validity.

The first five papers, briefly described below, deal mainly with these issues. They are followed by twelve papers which illustrate specific applications of a performance approach to language testing in a variety of situations - academia, the schools, business and governmental organizations. Many of these latter papers also deal in depth with theoretical issues. Taken together they dramatically illustrate how a similar view of language proficiency and parallel test development procedures can lead to very different instruments for different clienteles.

They also provide information on situations in which performance testing has proven worthwhile, and why.

THEORETICAL PAPERS

In the first paper, Randall Jones situates performance
testing in the universe of language testing approaches. He
traces its sources back to an established model in educational
psychology and vocational testing, where it is common to assess
examinees' abilities with respect to specific job-related tasks.
In such tests, "the test stimulus, the desired response, and
the surrounding conditions approximate the reality of an actual
situation drawn from a specific occupational or role-based
content" (Spirer 1980, as cited by Jones). Jones also carefully
distinguishes this use of the term "performance" from its widely
accepted use in linguistic theory as part of a competence/
performance opposition. He goes on to detail a typology of performance tests, and to offer a rationale for a performance
approach in situations where accurate prediction of real-life
second language performance is crucial. Jones also makes a
number of suggestions for test developers regarding reliable
and valid measurement.

The second paper, by J. Charles Alderson and
A.H. Urquhart, while not specifically addressed to performance
testing, deals with an issue vital to this approach. This is the
effect of background knowledge on language proficiency test
scores - in their case knowledge in particular academic disciplines. Alderson and Urquhart report on several studies they
have carried out with ESL university students in Britain to
determine whether these students perform better on reading
comprehension tasks based on texts taken from their own discipline versus texts from other disciplines. Their findings,
which will not surprise second language educators, indicate
such differential performance. They suggest, for example,
that the kinds of general interest social science and humanities
texts which are often selected for second language reading
tests may unfairly bias test results for engineering and science
students, if what one wishes to predict is their ability to use
their second language skills for relatively narrow academic
studies in their own field. This study provides a rationale for
some matching of test content and context with specific needs
when such needs are relatively precise and delimited (and, of
course, known). It also makes clear that many more studies are
needed if we are to develop a better understanding of the
interaction between language proficiency and subject matter
knowledge in test performance.

In the third paper, R.J. Courchêne and J.I. de Bagheera discuss a number of issues in performance testing, with particular emphasis on current theoretical models of communication, language and communicative competence and the questions each raises for test designers. From these, as well as from theoretical work in language testing, they draw a "decision-making checklist" to guide in the development of communicative language tests. An important contribution of this paper is its discussion of the relevance of work in the field of communication theory to the development of second language assessment instruments. As Courchêne and de Bagheera point out, dynamic interactive models of communication, in which the way something is said and its effect on the listener are as important as what is said, suggest a much broader area of concern for second language test designers than has traditionally been considered.

The paper by Jean-Claude Mothe focuses on test design. He makes the important point that test designers must take into account developmental sequences in second language learning; thus native-speaker performance will not necessarily yield appropriate criteria for judging examinee performance. Mothe details a number of techniques used in the testing of employees at the United Nations Headquarters in Geneva, with particular reference to a hierarchy of objectives in second language learning (e.g., the ability to classify). Mothe notes that it is the mental operations required of examinees using the second language in a given situational context which must be the primary consideration of test designers, reminding us that since all aspects of the target situation cannot be simulated in a test, it is vital for test designers to determine which ones are critical with respect to language processing. At the same time, he remarks from a broad base of practical experience on the positive motivating effect of job-related test tasks, surely one of the most important advantages of performance-type testing, which should enhance measurement validity. Mothe discusses a major problem with a performance approach as well, that of defining evaluation criteria which will reflect linguistic behaviour rather than related non-linguistic behaviour. In this way he, like Alderson and Urquhart, expresses concern with the interaction of subject-matter and language knowledge, and, like Courchêne and de Bagheera, with the nature and delimitation of communicative competence in terms of linguistic and other competencies.

Brendan Carroll's paper again reflects wide personal experience with a performance testing approach, in his case in the academic, business and governmental worlds. Carroll, too, discusses the theoretical issues raised by this approach to second language testing, with particular emphasis on reliability and validity. Test design procedures which will lead to instruments which can help his clients to "make good decisions" (i.e., instruments with high predictive validity) must, in Carroll's view, begin with a needs analysis which takes into account stages in the second language process. The latter consideration is vital in tests which have a diagnostic objective, and reflects Carroll's concern with the proper role of tests in the educational process. Carroll also provides practical guidance on principles of task and item development (e.g., use of multimodal, integrative tasks.) While citing his belief that "the manipulation of data must be subordinate to the questions which we wish to answer", Carroll also details some of the procedures he follows to ensure reliable administration and scoring of open-ended test tasks, and the selection or development of appropriate measures on which to base concurrent and predictive validity studies.

APPLICATIONS

The remaining twelve papers in the collection each illustrate the development of one or several performance-based tests for specific client groups. These groups include the following: Indochinese refugees in the United States who need survival English skills, (John L.D. Clark and Allene G. Grognet); foreign students seeking admission to British post-secondary programs (Ian Seaton, Allan Emmett) and similar students seeking admission to regular programs in a Canadian college (Beryl Tonkin); foreign graduate students designated as teaching assistants in an American university (Kathleen M. Bailey); professors in a bilingual Canadian university whose contracts require certification of minimal functional skills in English or French as a second language (Laure Krupka); Dutch school children requiring conversational French, German or English skills for dealing with tourists or for foreign travel (José Noijons); Canadian school children in French immersion programs in which they do much of their academic work in their second language (Daina Green); Hong Kong secondary school students who may need communicative English skills for future employment (Peter Tung); employees at Canada's National Arts Centre in Ottawa requiring adequate French skills for their jobs in the restaurant, the ticket booth, the parking garage or in administration (Marie-Claude Tréville); Canadian civil servants in diverse positions with job requirements for functional second language skills in French or English (Renée Proulx-Dubé et al.); and several other adult client groups representing different facets of bilingualism in Canada, including the civil service, several Crown corporations and a private corporation which must provide bilingual services, the Quebec government in its licensing of professionals for bilingual practice and the University of Ottawa, North America's largest bilingual university (Raymond LeBlanc).

It is significant that each of the performance instruments described can be characterized in terms of its specific target population, unlike many traditional second language tests. Furthermore, all the target groups have describable real-life language needs which can be represented by a limited set of language use situations. In many cases, important decisions such as university admission or getting a job may at least partially depend on examinees' functional second language capabilities. Thus we have present elements of definable real-life needs which can be simulated in testing procedures, as well as a certain criticality of decisions to be based on second language assessment which may justify more individualized and expensive testing procedures. It is also important to note that in all the above cases performance testing procedures are used with examinees who are at a relatively high proficiency level vis-a-vis the target behaviours. Such tests are seldom used with beginners. This may be due to an inherent floor difficulty level of performance type tasks, so that they do not discriminate well at lower proficiency levels. Or it may simply indicate that less direct testing procedures, often far more practical, are more appropriate for many purposes.

A characteristic of many of the instruments described is that they are criterion referenced rather than norm referenced. They are used not to compare an examinee with others, as for placement in a second language program, but rather to indicate his or her readiness to function effectively in a particular second language use environment. A further characteristic of many of the tests described is their use of judgemental, holistic scoring techniques. While there is ample evidence in the literature that such techniques can be made highly reliable through careful criterion descriptions and ongoing training and monitoring of scorers (cf. Clark 1978), they are not automatically so. The achievement of acceptable levels of intra- and inter-rater reliability remains a persistent problem for creators of second language performance tests.

The test development projects described in this collection provide considerable guidance for others dealing with the various problems raised by a performance approach. Several papers offer start-to-finish models for developing such tests. Clark and Grognet present a comprehensive overview of the test development and standardization process, beginning with helpful background information on the target refugee population and the testing needs of user ESL training programs. Techniques used for developing descriptions of the target "survival" tasks of interest, the test design process and resulting draft test, field testing information, and psychometric characteristics of the final form of the test are all covered in detail. Plans for a subsequent predictive validity study are also described. Likewise, Bailey's description of a performance-based ESL test for foreign teaching assistants in American universities provides many useful insights. Her paper traces half a decade of experience with a performance testing procedure designed to select foreign teaching assistants with adequate English skills through the various steps of test development, try-out and use. This article is particularly useful in its discussion of the development of reliable performance criteria and rating procedures, follow-up work on test validation, and its many instructive references to the problem of drawing the line between that linguistic and extra-linguistic knowledge which underlies successful performance. Noijons also describes the many stages of a long-term project, in this case the introduction of performance-based testing into second language programs in Dutch schools. He offers particular detail with respect to development and ongoing refinement of scoring procedures as well as training materials for teacher-scorers.

Other papers are of special interest for the information they present on a particular aspect of the test development process, or for general interest data they present on client populations. Thus Seaton describes the issues which had to be resolved in the organization of a world-wide testing service, the British Council's English Language Testing Service (ELTS), which not only developed but was charged with administration and initial follow-up studies of an ESL performance testing system for foreign students seeking entrance to British universities. This experience, presented in terms of the interplay of concerns of "Researchers", test "Constructor-Validators" and "Managers", provides a useful perspective for organizations involved in large-scale testing. For his part, Emmett focuses on the initial development stages of a performance-based Test of English for Educational Purposes (TEEP) for the Associated Examining Board, also for use with overseas students. He provides a detailed description of the massive project to describe the English language needs of these students in British tertiary education, using observations and questionnaire data in addition to more readily available information. This example of a grass roots needs analysis is of interest both for the procedures which were used, and for the descriptive data generated on this population.

Green's paper on a performance-based test of writing and speaking abilities for students in French immersion programs at the secondary school level focuses on a different aspect of test development - an integrated process of test design and selection/preparation of appropriate materials. Extensive consultation with students in these programs was part of the process which led to an informative, attractive source booklet for the test, thematically organized around an important student concern - summer work. Tréville also provides considerable detail on this aspect of test design and materials development, but in a very different context - the preparation of French tests to screen applicants for various jobs requiring bilingual skills at Canada's National Arts Centre. Similarly, her procedure involved observations of and interviews with current employees in these jobs, as well as with their superiors and personnel officers. This led to the specification of target situations and types of discourse for the test, and focused the subsequent search for appropriate authentic materials. Krupka describes the same kind of procedures applied in yet another context - a faculty of a bilingual university which requires that its professors be able to function adequately in certain work-related second language situations. Again, test design was established through ongoing consultation with administrators and faculty members. The search for appropriate materials for certain individualized parts of the test (e.g., to evaluate the ability to read journal articles related to the professor's area of research) led the test developers into highly specialized material such as aspects of pharmacology and criminal law. Ongoing consultation with subject-matter specialists was not only desirable but necessary in this case. The resulting tests described by Green, Tréville and Krupka illustrate well an important feature of performance-based testing - its perceived relevance and resulting high motivational value for examinees. These tests are also sending very clear messages to examinees, and often, through them, to language trainers, about what kinds of second language abilities and knowledge are important. Green and Tung both emphasize this washback of communicative or performance-based tests on classroom practice. This effect of performance testing can be of particular importance in an "examination oriented context" such as that described by Tung (Hong Kong secondary schools), where students and teachers are reluctant to spend classroom time on anything not in the examination syllabus. Tonkin's description of cumulative assessment during a performance-oriented ESL course for foreign students leading to certification for regular studies carries this relationship between teaching and testing a step further.

The two final papers in this volume differ from the others in that each integrates the work of a number of authors involved in varied testing projects. Both report on performance approaches to testing second language capabilities of adults in

Canadian work contexts. Proulx-Dubé and her colleagues report on diverse aspects of test development for the language training programs of the Public Service of Canada. In her introductory remarks Proulx-Dubé describes the procedures which have been developed to systematically analyze functional second language needs of public servants in work situations as a basis for test development. Gerard Frey and Angie Todesco then describe and illustrate the development of a construct of communicative competence to guide test designers in the Public Service context. Anne-Marie Henrie and Gérard Monfils present the oral interview procedure which is used in the centralized language training program, with particular emphasis on innovative features of the scoring grid. The last two sections of this article present evaluation systems developed for two specialized training programs, the school-work assignment second language training program for highly motivated public servants at advanced proficiency levels, and the highly contextualized second language course, Francomer, for Coast Guard officers in training. In the former, Huguette Laurencelle and William Cahill detail the variety of self-assessment, observation and testing instruments developed for use at different stages of the highly individualized Advanced Training Program. Lise Séguin-Duquette then describes the series of criterion-referenced performance tests developed for each teaching module in the Francomer programme. As a whole, this paper provides a wealth of information on the complex problems of developing assessment systems and instruments in a bureaucratic environment in which "bilingualism" is sometimes a politically sensitive issue as well as an important job qualification.

The final paper by LeBlanc and his collaborators views the role of second language performance testing in a wider context, the world of bilingual work. The paper again reports on language testing within the training programs of the federal government of Canada (Proulx-Dubé) but also within the Quebec government's organism for promoting the French language in various aspects of provincial life, l'Office de la langue française (Diane Pruneau); several Crown corporations involved in air and railroad transport, Air Canada and Canadian National (Mireille Voyer); a private airline, Canadian Pacific (Pascal-André Charlebois); and at a bilingual university, the University of Ottawa (Marjorie Bingham Wesche). In all these situations a performance approach has proven desirable for the certification of individuals as meeting functional, work-related second-language requirements.

As a whole, the papers in this volume provide a rich definition of the performance approach to second language testing, including the test development procedures which typify it, the special characteristics of performance tests, and problems which arise during the development and operational use of such tests. They offer many examples of situations in which performance testing is proving to be appropriate. They suggest tentative procedures to resolve some of the problems of needs analysis, sampling and reliable task administration and scoring which are posed by such tests. With a few notable exceptions, these papers do not pay as much attention to the statistical properties of the tests as one might wish, including demonstration of their presumed strong point, predictive validity. However, the next generation of work in performance testing will surely bring us more information of this nature, some of it from work already under way. We are encouraged by the rapid development to date of this area of language testing, and look forward to its future.

NOTES

1. Oller has recently expressed the view (personal correspondence 1984) that he finds nothing objectionable in the definition of performance tests as a subcategory of the broader class of pragmatic tests.

REFERENCES

Clark, John L.D. (ed.). 1978. Direct Testing of Speaking Proficiency: Theory and Application. Princeton, N.J.: Educational Testing Service.

Jones, R. 1979. Performance testing of second language proficiency. In Briere, E., and F. Hinofotis (eds.), Concepts in Language Testing, pp. 50-57. Washington: TESOL.

Oller, John W. 1979. Language Tests at School. London, Longman.

Oller, John W. Jr. 1983. Language testing: where to from here? Unpublished manuscript. University of New Mexico.

THEORETICAL PERSPECTIVES/ ASPECTS THÉORIQUES

1.
Second Language Performance Testing: An Overview

Randall L. Jones

As I think back on my own personal experience with regard to language testing, I am reminded of my first German test. It was in 1954 and I was in my first year in high school. I found the class to be quite difficult, and I was not at all looking forward to the test. To the best of my recollection, some of the items were as follows:

- In the following sentences underline the subject and draw a circle around the verb.
- List the accusative prepositions.
- Write the nominative and accusative personal pronouns.
- State the rule concerning the word order of subject and verb.

I do not recall how well I did on this test. I do recall, how-ever, that George Holt, the boy who sat in front of me, had the German word <u>gut</u> written at the top of his test paper and I did not. Furthermore, I had no idea then - nor would I now - what the German teacher learned from the test about the abilities of the students in the class.

That was, of course, back in the era referred to by Bernard Spolsky as "pre-scientific." What I experienced was probably not much different from what millions of students were experiencing elsewhere. It was fairly standard procedure. Although I was too young and inexperienced to know, I seriously doubt that my teacher was very concerned about such matters as validity and reliability.

A great deal has happened in the profession since then. We have developed a rather impressive methodology for designing, administering, scoring and evaluating language tests. In fact, there is really a sub-profession within language teaching that is dedicated to the science of language proficiency measurement. The level of sophistication has become so great that an understanding gap has emerged between the testing specialists and their colleagues in other areas of language teaching.

PERFORMANCE TESTING

One of the more recent directions that has been developing in language testing is that of performance testing. The very name seems to be self-explanatory, but apparently there exist differing perceptions among those who use the term. Anyone who is familiar with Chomsky's competence/performance dichotomy may interpret performance testing to be the measurement of language performance in his sense. There are, however, some problems associated with this interpretation. First, in Chomsky's model competence is a person's potential to use language. It is a system of rules which cannot be directly observed or measured. Performance is any manifestation of this competence. Second, in educational jargon the term competence or competency has already been pre-empted, giving rise to possible misunderstandings. I have even heard the expression "competency-based performance."

I use the term performance testing just as I did in my 1978 TESOL paper, Performance Testing of Second Language Proficiency (Jones 1979). It is based on an established model which already exists in psychological testing, especially in the area of vocational testing. Its purpose is usually to assess the ability of an examinee in relation to some kind of job-related task. The following definition based on Sanders and Sachse (1977) provides an example: an applied performance test measures performance on tasks requiring the application of learning in an actual or simulated setting. Either the test stimulus, the desired response, or both are intended to lend a high degree of realism to the test situation. The identifying difference between applied performance and other types of tests is the degree to which testing procedures approximate the reality of the situation in which the actual task would be performed. A similar definition is proposed by Janet Spirer. She says that performance tests

refer to tests in which the test stimulus, the desired response, and the surrounding conditions approximate the reality of an actual situation drawn from a specific occupational or role-based content.... They assess a portion or all of an actual work setting by attempting to approximate the reality of the actual work setting. (1980:185)

There are numerous work situations for which proficiency in language is desirable or even essential. In some cases these positions are occupied by workers who are not fluent speakers of the local language. The difficulty encountered in communication may not always be critical, e.g., with a waitress in a restaurant or a desk clerk in a hotel, but more serious cases can exist, e.g., with a doctor or policeman. A language performance test can assist employers in screening applicants for these kinds of positions. By observing examinees using the language within the context of a specific task, it is possible to predict how well they can perform under real conditions. Unfortunately, most traditional language tests are not good predictors. It is possible to obtain a high score on a multiple-choice language proficiency test and still not be able to function well in a real situation. Performance tests are at the opposite extreme from the German test I described earlier. For some testers, especially those who insist on strict standards for reliability, performance testing is looked upon with a great deal of skepticism. But times and needs are changing. According to Stephen Slater,

While once the standardized, norm-referenced objective achievement test modeled after Binet's, Cattell's and others' instruments [was] held in high regard, that unquestioned acceptance is eroding. Today we are witnessing a broadening of testing options that is raising issues at a faster rate than they are being resolved. A common thread running through these options is the complexity of human competency - and the inadequacy of the ubiquitous multiple-choice examination as a measure of competence. (1980:3)

TYPOLOGY OF PERFORMANCE TESTS

Slater goes on to suggest a typology of performance tests in which he identifies the following three main types.

1. Direct Assessment

The highest fidelity that can be achieved in assessing behavior required for success in a real life setting is through direct observation of behavior (or its outcomes) in that setting. Stimulus and response characteristics of the test and the surrounding conditions are assumed to be equivalent to those present in naturally occurring situations. (1980:5)

In a direct assessment the examiner observes, perhaps surreptitiously, the work of the examinee. There is no concealing the fact that observations are being made, but examiners want to remain as inconspicuous as possible so that their presence does not affect the performance of the examinee.

A common type of direct assessment is the observation of apprentice teachers in a classroom. The task is very real and approximates almost exactly what the performance would be in a typical teaching situation. Unfortunately, assessing second language proficiency in a direct manner such as this is not as simple, especially if it is related to a specific task. In a direct assessment situation the examiner would not be involved in the conversation, but rather would observe the examinee interacting with other people. Language behavior is very complex, and it would be necessary to make observations over a relatively long period of time before one could be satisfied that an adequate sample had been obtained.

2. Work Sample Methods

Evaluation of work samples is distinguished from direct assessment techniques primarily on the basis of where the performance is observed. Whereas direct assessment takes place in the setting where the behavior is normally displayed, work samples can be obtained in more controlled settings. (Slater 1980:6)

The principal feature that distinguishes the work sample method from direct assessment is the degree to which the examiner manipulates the tasks performed by the examinee. In direct assessment there is virtually no manipulation. In the work sample method, on the other hand, an attempt is made to standardize the tasks in order to make the evaluation more consistent and efficient. The types of tasks and even the location may be very similar in both cases, but the work sample method is more controlled.

Slater mentions the Plymouth Trouble Shooting Contest as a good example of a work sample method. All examinees are asked to locate the problem in an automobile that will not start, then make the necessary repairs. Other examples might include similar types of tests for bricklayers, stenographers, hairdressers, etc.

A variety of language-related work sample testing methods suggest themselves. For example, a medical assistant might be

asked to obtain information from a patient in order to make a
preliminary diagnosis. The language proficiency of prospective
secretaries could be assessed by having them respond to a
variety of telephone calls. Prospective teachers could teach a
few mini-classes and respond to students' questions. The
situations are controlled but they are essentially authentic.

3. Simulation Techniques

As the term is currently used in educational measurement, simulation refers to the process of abstracting some
aspect of reality and concretely representing it in the
form of a specific task that examinees are expected to
perform. Simulation accounts for an enormous spectrum
of performance testing approaches, varying in their
degree of "abstraction" from real life situations. (Slater
1980:7)

Slater uses the famous in-basket exercise as a good example
of a simulation technique. The examinee performs a task that is
similar but not identical to a real life situation. The task is
supposed to predict how well the examinee will perform on the
job.

Simulation techniques are the next logical point on the
spectrum after direct assessment and work sample methods.
Not only is there manipulation on the part of the examiner, but
the entire situation is essentially contrived. Be that as it may,
this type of approach is perhaps the most feasible for language
testing. The examinee engages in conversation with the
examiner (or another person), and the language revolves
around a specific task or set of tasks that are typical of the job
under consideration. Maatsch and Gordon point out that

the use of simulations to evaluate student performance
occupies the vast middle ground between highly reliable
and practical multiple-choice tests and the more valid
but frequently impractical individual assessment during
real clinical encounters.(1978:5)

In other words, the multiple-choice test is not a valid test of
real language performance, but real language performance is
virtually impossible to measure efficiently with any degree of
accuracy. The simulation technique thus offers the logical
compromise between the two.

Perhaps the best known language testing simulation technique is role playing. The examiner describes a situation and
ask the examinee to play a part in it. For example, the

examinee is told that he or she works in a hotel and must handle a dialogue with a prospective guest. The situation can be very routine, or it might include some unexpected turns, e.g., dickering about the price of a room or dealing with someone who insists a reservation has been made when in fact there is no record of one. There is almost no limit to the number of simulation techniques that can be used with language situations. The examiner must be skilled in controlling the situation while at the same time making it appear as real as possible. It is helpful if the situation is written out on a small card or piece of paper so that the examinee can read it.

With regard to second language performance testing it must be kept in mind that language is only one of several factors being evaluated. The overall criterion is the successful completion of a task in which the use of language is essential. A performance test is more than a basic proficiency test of communicative competence in that it is related to some kind of performance task. It is entirely possible for some examinees to compensate for low language proficiency by astuteness in other areas. For example, certain personality traits can assist examinees in scoring high on interpersonal tasks, even though their proficiency in the language may be substandard. On the other hand, examinees who demonstrate high general language proficiency may not score well on a performance because of deficiencies in other areas.

CRITERIA FOR GOOD TESTS

As language performance tests are developed and used, it is important to keep in mind the three main criteria for a good test: validity, reliability, and practicality. Unlike a standardized objective examination which can be pretested, analyzed statistically with a high degree of accuracy, modified, then re-analyzed, a performance test exists only as a model in the minds of the testers. It is possible, however, to achieve a high degree of validity and reliability, and to do this within an acceptable time frame, as long as certain conditions are met. The role of the examiner(s) in a performance test is basically two-fold. First, it is necessary to elicit from the examinee a ratable sample of performance. The degree to which this task is successfully accomplished largely determines the level of validity. The second role of the examiner is to rate the sample and to quantify it into some kind of useful score. The reliability of the test rests mainly on the successful completion of this task.

The test is valid if the elicited performance is representative of what actually takes place on the job. Richard Stiggins suggests the following three steps for developing the description for a performance test:

> 1) conduct systematic observations of practitioner work samples and identify the relevant skills (i.e., conduct a job analysis), 2) involve experienced practitioners in an in-depth discussion of the knowledge and skills that form the basis of their profession, and/or 3) generate potential lists of relevant skills. (1981:5)

It is, of course, not possible in most cases to evaluate all of the requisite skills associated with a task. Thus, an important responsibility of the tester is to sample these skills and determine a generalized judgment on that basis.

Reliability in performance testing requires that the scorer match the performance of the examinee against a standard set of criteria. According to Stiggins,

> If those who are to judge performance have the desired performance criteria clearly in mind (as a result of careful training) and if they are evaluating performance on the basis of those criteria, then two or more judges simultaneously observing the same examinee in a practical examination context should arrive at similar conclusions regarding examinee competence. (1981:6)

There have, of course, been several significant studies of inter-rater reliability in oral testing, for example Adams (1978) and Clifford (1978). We are reasonably certain that a high degree of consistency can be achieved if the raters are properly trained. There have, however, been few studies of "inter-eliciter" reliability, i.e., how consistent oral examiners are in obtaining language samples during the course of an oral interview. A notable exception is work done by Shohamy (1981).

I should perhaps emphasize that even though I have mentioned only oral language testing, performance tests can exist for the other modalities as well. A look at the Conference program shows that papers on the testing of reading, listening and writing are also being read. Indeed, there are numerous situations requiring various combinations of language skills. It is important that all of these skills be tested in a way that reflects the real tasks associated with the situations.

During the past few years there have been some interesting and innovative attempts to develop performance tests involving language proficiency. Perhaps the most ambitious one is the project at UCLA under the direction of Frances Hinofotis (Hinofotis, Bailey, and Stern 1981). (Editor's note: See also article by Bailey in this volume.) There is not sufficient time here to explain the project in detail, but let me briefly describe it. As is the case at many American universities, some of the graduate teaching assistants at UCLA do not speak English as a native language. They are graduate students in a variety of disciplines, e.g., biology, computer science, mathematics, sociology, etc. and teach classes in their respective majors as part of their program requirements and to earn part of their living expenses.

In a few cases, however, students in these classes have complained that they were not able to understand the foreign teaching assistants in class because the English proficiency of these assistants was inadequate for teaching the subject matter. In some cases it was reported that the assistants were not able to understand students' questions.

Hinofotis undertook to devise a method of assessing the English proficiency of foreign teaching assistants before they were allowed to teach. Although the project is still in progress, preliminary reports indicate that a performance test can be very useful in screening applicants in this kind of situation. Similar types of language-related performance tests have been described by van Naerssen and Davies (1978).

I feel that we have made good progress in language performance testing during the past few years. The field is interesting and very challenging. The Foreign Service Institute is now in the process of modifying its testing criteria in order to include more work samples, i.e., in order to be more performance oriented. The Defense Language Institute has developed an oral language testing training film to demonstrate the types of language performance that can be expected at various proficiency levels. Under the direction of Pardee Lowe, the United States Government Inter-Agency Language Roundtable is compiling an extensive document on the administration and scoring of oral proficiency tests. And it is obvious that some of the most interesting work in language performance testing is taking place here in Canada.

This is the first symposium totally devoted to language performance testing; I am certain that it will not be the last. I am equally certain that much of the information which results from this symposium will serve for many years to come as the basis for future work.

REFERENCES

Adams, M. 1978. Measuring foreign language speaking proficiency: a study of agreement among raters. In Clark, J. (ed.), Direct Testing of Speaking Proficiency: Theory and Application, pp. 129-149. Princeton, N.J.: Educational Testing Service.

Clifford, R. 1978. Reliability and validity of language aspects contributing to oral proficiency of prospective teachers of German. In Clark, J. (ed.), Direct Testing of Speaking Proficiency: Theory and Application, pp. 191-210. Princeton, N.J.: Educational Testing Service.

Davies, A. Personal communication, 1982.

Hinofotis, F., K. Bailey, and S. Stern. 1981. Assessing the oral proficiency of prospective foreign teaching assistants: instrument development. In Palmer, A., P. Groot, and G. Trosper (eds.), The Construct Validation of Tests of Communicative Competence, pp. 106-126. Washington: TESOL.

Jones, R. 1977. Testing: a vital connection. In Phillips, J. (ed.), The Language Connection, pp. 237-265. ACTFL Foreign Language Education Series, 9. Skokie, Ill.: National Textbook Co.

Jones, R. 1979. Performance testing of second language proficiency. In Briere, E., and F. Hinofotis (eds.), Concepts in Language Testing, pp. 50-57. Washington: TESOL.

Maatsch, J., and M. Gordon. 1978. Assessment through simulation. In Morgan, M. and D. Irby (eds.), Evaluating Clinical Competence in the Health Professions, pp. 123-138. St. Louis, Mo.: C.V. Mosby.

Sanders, J., and T. Sachse. 1977. Applied performance testing in the classroom. Journal of Research and Development in Education 10 (3): 92-104.

Shohamy, E. 1981. The stability of oral proficiency assessment on the oral interview testing procedures. Paper delivered March 1st at the Third Colloquium on Validation of Oral Proficiency Tests, Ann Arbor, Michigan.

Slater, S. 1980. Introduction to performance testing. In Spirer, J. (ed.), Performance Testing: Issues Facing Vocational Education, pp. 3-18. Columbus, Ohio: The National Center for Research in Vocational Education.

Spirer, J. 1980. Performance Testing: Issues Facing Vocational Education. Columbus, Ohio: The National Center for Research in Vocational Education.

Spolsky, B. 1975. Language testing: art or science? Paper delivered August 27, 1975 at the Fourth AILA World Congress, Stuttgart, Germany.

Stiggins, R. 1981. Strategies for optimizing and documenting the quality of oral and practical examinations in medical education. ERIC Document Reproduction Services: ED 206 634.

van Naerssen, M. 1978. ESL in medicine: a matter of life and death. TESOL Quarterly 12:193-203.

2.
This Test is Unfair: I'm not an Economist

J. Charles Alderson and A.H. Urquhart

The studies reported in this article[1] were designed to test the hypothesis that an English foreign language (EFL) student's background discipline - that is, his knowledge of a particular academic field - would affect his performance on tests of reading comprehension. In other words, we hypothesized that a student of, for example, engineering, would perform better on an engineering text than would a student of economics, even though the general level of EFL proficiency of the two students was equivalent.

In what might be considered the traditional position towards the selection of texts for testing purposes, the aim is to select texts which are sufficiently "general" so as to avoid favouring any particular group of students. It can be seen that underlying this position is a belief that certain texts will favour particular groups, presumably because of the background knowledge available to these groups. To this extent, the traditional position is in line with the hypothesis being investigated here. Where we differ is in our view of the possibility and desirability of using general texts.

The traditional view depends crucially on the following assumptions:

(a) that it is possible to find truly "general" texts, that is, texts which are so neutral in content and cultural assumptions that they will not in any significant way favour any particular group.

(b) That in English for Academic Purposes (EAP), at least, performance on such texts can be used as predictive of students' performance on texts in their academic field; that, for example, the performance of a would-be post-graduate student of dentistry on a text about piracy in the seventeenth-century Caribbean can be used to predict his or her ability to read research material in dentistry. Both the above assumptions are open to doubt.

Recent work on comprehension has tended to stress the reader's contribution to the process, and the way that background knowledge is used to interpret text information. As Steffensen and Joag-Dev put it,

> Recent TESL and foreign-language pedagogy has moved away from the idea that comprehension involves abstracting meaning that is in some sense present on the page and is recognizing the creative contribution made by the reader.
> (Steffensen and Joag-Dev, in press.)

Thus, increasingly, background knowledge, the information which the reader brings to the comprehension process, is seen not just as an aid in comprehension but as an integral part of the process and product. If readers bring their background knowledge to the comprehension process, and this knowledge is bound to vary from reader to reader, then there can be no single text-bound comprehension, but rather a host of inter-pretations. This may not be a problem when all the readers, together with the tester, belong to the same cultural back-ground and share a large number of cultural presuppositions. In EFL, at least at the tertiary level, this situation cannot be expected to occur often. Hence we may expect markedly different interpretations of the same text. Steffensen and Joag-Dev (in press) have shown that comprehension can be radically affected by the reader's cultural background. In general, the increased recognition of the importance of back-ground knowledge may lead us to doubt the existence of any text which is "neutral" across a wide range of readers. Cer-tainly we may suspect the "generality" of themes popular with recent text-book writers - pollution, the women's movement etc. Paradoxically, in the EFL context, it is the more special-ized texts to which we might expect a relatively homogeneous response. A popular magazine article may activate a wide range of differing schemata among a group of students; a physics text, on the other hand, will presumably be interpre-ted in similar ways by a group of physicists, regardless of their L1. Widdowson (1979) has argued that subject areas such as physics constitute sub-cultures of their own.

Thus the very existence of general texts can be doubted. Even if they existed, however, the second traditional assumption, that performance on such texts can be used to predict performance on more specialized texts, is very questionable. In part, this is because it seems to involve a belief in a very generalized reading ability, a belief that if one' can read one English text, one can read them all. However, the skills involved in responding to a novel by Dickens are likely to be very different from those used in extracting information from an economics text. Still, the skilled reader may have a wide repertoire of skills, which testers may sample using general texts. Thus it is possible that success on general texts can be used to predict performance in other fields. Many L2 readers, however, whose use of English texts is much narrower, may have acquired a much more limited set of skills appropriate only for extracting particular kinds of information from a specialized range of texts. And these skills, successful in the contexts for which they were developed, may not be sufficient for dealing with general texts. Thus it may not be possible to use inability to perform successfully on texts to predict performance on texts more relevant to the student's field of interest. There is plenty of anecdotal evidence, for example English-speaking engineers able to read German texts related to their own speciality but not an article from a German newspaper, to suggest that such an extrapolation is likely to be invalid.

Doubts such as these, and associated fears that suitable students may be denied the possibility of studying in English-speaking countries because of their inadequate performance on traditional proficiency tests, have led to the development of English for Specific Purposes (ESP) tests, the best known of which in the U.K. is the British Council English Language Testing Service (ELTS) test. There is no doubt that such tests have a number of disadvantages compared to the traditional "general" test. They are inevitably more expensive and more difficult to administer. The number of specialist modules is very debatable: do we have a test for all engineers or one for chemical engineers, one for electronic engineers, etc? Then there is the problem of cross-disciplinary studies. If the ESP test contains at least three modules - law, economics, and technology - and a student wishes to study urban studies, with classes in law, economics and technology, which module should the student take? Problems like these are not, on the whole, encountered with general tests.

Should it be found, however, that general tests were discriminating against a major group, say engineers, or that they were having the effect of denying further study to students who were quite competent readers in their own academic area, then these practical advantages would not be enough to ensure the survival, in tertiary ESP, of general tests. The decision thus rests on empirical evidence. However, although we have presented above theoretical objections to the concept of general or neutral texts, together with opinions, based partly on anecdotal evidence, against using general comprehension tests to predict performance in specialized subject areas, it must be said that so far, hard empirical evidence in favour of either the general or the specific approach has been lacking. The two studies reported below were designed to gather such empirical data.

We hypothesized that students reading texts in a familiar content area, that is, related to their area of study, would perform better than students unfamiliar with that subject. The latter, it might be argued, would lack familiarity not only with the content of the subject area, but also with such aspects as genre effect, rhetorical organization, forms of argumentation, and linguistic and non-linguistic relations.

DESIGN OF STUDY ONE[2]

Four groups of students from different academic disciplines were tested at Aston University at the end of a pre-sessional English and Study Skills (ESS) course. The groups were as follows:

1. Fifteen students about to do courses in either development administration or development finance. With one exception, they all had experience in administration or finance. Most had first degrees in economics.
2. Eleven engineers about to study in a variety of postgraduate engineering fields, e.g., chemical, civil and electrical engineering. All had first degrees in engineering.
3. Six post-graduate students of mathematics and/or physics.
4. Five students of liberal arts, whose first degrees included education, psycholgy, and language and linguistics.

At the beginning of the ESS course, students had taken, for placement purposes, a 100-item pseudo-random cloze test, made up of nine short texts on various topics. Mean scores for the four groups, which may be taken as a rough guide to each group's linguistic proficiency, are presented in Table 1.

TABLE 1 Group Means on Placement
Test

GROUP	1	2	3	4
SCORE	48.2	48.8	46.0	57.4

It can be seen that, on this measure, the first three groups were virtually equal. Group 4, the Liberal Arts group, was somewhat more proficient.

Five texts were selected, each between 250 and 280 words long. Two were on engineering topics, of which one, dubbed Electrolytes, was from an academic monograph, (Gregory 1972), and the other, Turbines, was from an engineering periodical (Hulme 1981). Two more texts were related to economic development and finance: Polanyi and Malaysia, which were taken from the same university text-book (Latham 1978). The fifth text, Quixote, designed to be the general text, was taken from the top level of the Science Research Associates 1963 (SRA) 3B Ratebuilder cards, intended, according to the publishers, for American junior-high and high-school students, and not infrequently used with L2 students. Electrolytes and Malaysia included a diagram and a table respectively.

As a very rough measure of linguistic complexity, the Fog Index (Gunnings 1952) for each text was calculated. The indices were all very similar, ranging from 17.5 to 18.5. Thus in terms of sentence length and word length in syllables, all five texts were closely comparable.

From each text lexical items were deleted which, in the judgement of the authors of this study, were restorable from information in the text, i.e., their restoration was not intended to depend on students' knowledge of the subject area. Particular attention was paid to the selection of items whose restoration depended on understanding of the text as a whole, rather than short chunks of language. In the case of Electrolytes and Malaysia, some items required information from the diagram or table for successful restoration.

Example

In principle, the electrolyte is simply an ionically conducting layer which serves to prevent the two electrodes from coming into electronic contact, and allows the passage of ions from one .... where they are generated, to the

.... where they are discharged. This ....
takes place by diffusion, and does not involve physical
movement of the .... itself. Indeed, fuel cells have
been .... using solid-phase electrolytes.

Extract from <u>Electrolytes</u>

All texts were scored twice, once taking only exact word
replacement as correct, then accepting any word which in the
judgement of the investigators was suitable in the overall
context.

RESULTS

Mean percentage scores for all five texts, using both the
exact and acceptable scoring methods, are presented in
Table 2.

TABLE 2   Mean Percentage Scores by Two Scoring
Methods

Group/Text	N	ECONOMICS Polanyi		Malaysia		ENGINEERING Turbines		Electrolytes		GENERAL Quixote	
		Ex	Acc	Ex	Acc	Ex	Acc	Ex	Acc	Ex	Acc
Development Administration/ Finance	15	13.2	42.7	29.4	44.7	34.3	44.0	20.4	34.2	12.2	33.3
Engineering	11	8.7	19.0	25.1	34.2	35.9	54.1	32.7	52.1	7.0	22.5
Science & Mathematics	6	6.1	21.2	23.5	33.3	30.8	40.0	26.7	42.2	14.7	22.5
Liberal Arts	5	15.5	38.2	28.2	34.1	38.0	49.0	26.7	36.0	14.1	30.6
All Groups	37	10.9	30.3	26.6	36.6	34.8	46.8	26.6	41.1	12.0	27.2

Ex =Exact   Acc= Acceptable

Comments

1. The Engineers as a group performed better on engineering texts than did Administration/Finance
   students:

Exact Scoring: Turbines   35.9 vs 34.3
                           Electrolytes 32.7 vs 20.4

Acceptable Scoring: Turbines   54.1 vs 44.0
                           Electrolytes 52.1 vs 34.2

2. Administration/Finance students performed better on administration/finance texts than did the Engineers:

Exact Scoring: Polanyi 13.2 vs 8.7
                           Malaysia 29.4 vs 25.1

Acceptable Scoring: Polanyi 42.7 vs 19.0
                           Malaysia 44.7 vs 34.2

3. It is noticeable from the above scores that the effect of acceptable scoring is to increase the differences between the groups.
4. The Liberal Arts group performed similarly on all texts to the Adminstration/Finance group. The Administration group (as expected) had a slight advantage on administration texts. The Liberal Arts group performed better than the Administration group on engineering texts. This may have been due to their superior linguistic proficiency.
5. The Science and Mathematics group behaved in a very similar fashion to the Engineering group, doing best on the two engineering texts, although (again as expected) their performance on those texts was somewhat inferior to the Engineering group.
6. There was a marked text by method effect. Thus on exact scoring, Turbines was the easiest text for all groups, and on aggregate, it was easiest on both scoring methods. The most difficult texts were Quixote and Polanyi. It should be remembered that Quixote was selected as being a general text, and was, moreover, the only text to be chosen from pedagogic English language material. On the basis of the results here, such texts appear to discriminate particularly against engineers and mathematics/physics students.

CONCLUSIONS: STUDY 1

The hypothesis was supported that students from a particular discipline would perform better on tests based on texts taken from their own subject discipline than would students from other disciplines. That is, students appear to be advantaged by taking a test on a text in a familiar content area.

For the Engineering and Mathematics/Physics groups in particular, tests in familiar content areas were easier than tests in unfamiliar areas. It will be noticed that on Quixote, the administration students performed at least as well as the Liberal Arts group, even though one would be inclined to place it in the academic area of the second group.

For the Engineering and Mathematics/Physics groups in particular, tests in familiar content areas were easier than tests in unfamiliar areas. It will be noticed that on Quixote, the administration students performed at least as well as the Liberal Arts group, even though one would be inclined to place it in the academic area of the second group.

It is interesting that, with minor differences, engineering and mathematics/physics students can perhaps be regarded as forming two closely related groups. Similarly, there are close resemblances between the Administration/Finance group and the Liberal Arts group. Should this be confirmed by wider testing, it would seem to be relevant to the problem of how specialized tests should be.

DESIGN OF STUDY TWO

Study One was intended as a pilot experiment. The numbers of students involved were very small, particularly in the cases of the Liberal Arts and Mathematics/Physics groups. Thus we decided the following year to replicate and extend only minimally the first experiment.

The second study was in two parts. The first was an attempt to replicate exactly the study of the previous year, i.e., the same tests on the same texts were given to a highly comparable group of students on the same pre-sessional course at Aston University one year later. Many of the students would later be studying the same courses as the previous year's students. To these subjects were added a number of comparable students studying on the University of Lancaster's pre-sessional course.

The second part was an attempt to extend the first study by changing the nature of the test task - from gap-filling to short answers. However, where possible, the same range of supposed skills and language abilities were covered - the ability to interpret tables, diagrams and associated texts and relate them to each other, the ability to interpret anaphoric reference, to process cohesive items, to identify main ideas, etc.

At Aston, students fell into very similar groups as in the previous year, namely:

1. Development Administration and Finance. To this group were added a number of Economics students (DAFE).
2. Engineering.
3. Science and Mathematics. This was a broader group than the previous Mathematics/Physics group.
4. Liberal Arts.

For these students, the same measure of linguistic proficiency was available, the 100-item Placement Test. Scores are presented in Table 3.

TABLE 3 Group Mean Scores on Placement Test

GROUP	1	2	3	4
SCORE	46.0	41.3	43.3	57.8

It can be seen that these scores are quite similar to the group scores of the previous year.

At Lancaster, the groups were very similar, namely:
1. Economics
2. Engineering
3. Science and Mathematics
4. Liberal Arts

For these groups English Language Battery (ELBA) scores were available, and they are presented in Table 4.[3]

TABLE 4 Group Mean Scores on ELBA

GROUP	1	2	3	4
SCORE	57.8	48.25	42.3	64.6

It can be seen that, as at Aston, the Liberal Arts group were the most linguistically proficient. Unlike Aston, the Economics group was markedly superior in proficiency to both the Engineering group and the Science and Mathematics group.

At this point it seems appropriate to comment on the difficulties encountered when placing a student in a particular group. For example, how does one place a student who has a Masters degree in a liberal arts subject, is going to study librarianship, but works in her national institute for national planning, is concerned daily with reading texts on economics, and who, at the same time as the pre-sessional course, takes an optional course, A Refresher Course in Economics? More generally, there is the problem caused by the fact that many engineers enrol for management courses; thus one cannot conclude that because a student intends to study management, he is not an engineer. On the other hand, in our experience all students entering post-graduate courses in engineering have undergraduate degrees in the same subject. As mentioned earlier, this is a general problem in ESP testing, and faces the tester with the problem of whether students should be tested according to their previous academic experience, or according to the course they are about to enter. It is hoped that the present study and subsequent ones will throw some light on this difficulty.

Students at both universities performed the gap-filling task first. The short-answer test on the same texts was performed a week later. The numbers of students involved in (a) the gap-filling test, (b) the short-answer test, and (c) both tests are set out in Table 5.

TABLE 5 Numbers of Students Completing Texts by Either or Both Answering Methods

	Gap filling		Short Answer		Both	
	Aston	Lancaster	Aston	Lancaster	Aston/Lancaster	Total
DAFE	18	8	24	9	16/8	24
Engineering	17	4	16	4	16/4	20
Science & Mathematics	32	6	28	6	24/6	30
Liberal Arts	13	9	10	16	10/9	19

DAFE= Development Administration, Finance, Economics

RESULTS

A. **Gap-filling**: mean percentage scores for all the groups are presented in Table 6. On this occasion, all tests were scored three times, taking (a) only exact word restoration as correct, then (b) taking synonym replacement as correct, and finally (c) taking any word considered acceptable in the overall context.

TABLE 6 Group Means and Standard Deviations for Each Text Using the Gap-Filling Technique Scored by 3 Different Methods

Group**		Polanyi			Malaysia			Turbines			Electrolytes			Quixote		
		*a	b	c	a	b	c	a	b	c	a	b	c	a	b	c
DAFE	M	9	31	43	17	33	39	33	47	56	19	34	40	10	28	33
	SD	9	23	22	8	16	22	14	20	21	12	18	16	9	18	20
Engineering	M	3	14	27	10	23	24	32	49	52	21	40	47	5	18	25
	SD	4	12	18	9	17	19	11	19	19	12	16	16	7	12	14
Science &	M	6	17	27	20	31	33	30	42	47	28	47	54	7	20	22
Mathematics	SD	6	13	17	7	11	14	15	21	20	11	13	15	6	11	14
Liberal	M	13	30	54	21	33	34	43	61	63	22	37	44	16	38	44
Arts	SD	12	19	24	14	23	21	13	17	23	16	21	21	11	20	21

* a = exact   b = synonym   c = acceptable   ** Variable $\underline{N}$
DAFE = Development Administration, Finance, Economics

Significant differences between mean scores are presented in Table 7.

36

TABLE 7 Significant Differences between Mean Scores for Each Text According to Scoring Method**

Text	Group	Engineering			Science & Mathematics			Liberal Arts		
		*a	b	c	a	b	c	a	b	c
Polanyi	DAFE	NS	p≤05	p≤05	NS	p≤05	p≤01			
	Engineering							p≤05	p≤05	p≤05
	Science & Mathematics							p≤05	p≤05	p≤001
Malaysia	Engineering				p≤01	NS	NS	p≤05	NS	NS
Turbines	Science & Mathematics							p≤05	p≤05	p≤05
Electrolytes	DAFE				NS	p≤05	p≤01			
Quixote	DAFE				NS	NS	.05			
	Engineering							p≤01	p≤01	p≤01
	Science & Mathematics							p≤01	p≤01	p≤001

```
  * a = exact       b = synonym       c = acceptable
 ** Only the results yielding significant differences have been reported
    DAFE = Development Administration, Finance, Economics
```

Comments

1. Students of Development Administration, Finance and Economics (DAFE) performed significantly better on Polanyi than did the Engineers or the Science and Mathematics group. They also performed better than the Engineers, though not the Science and Mathematics group, on Malaysia.
2. In contrast, the Engineers on this occasion did not perform better than the other groups on either of the engineering texts. However, the Science and Mathematics group performed better than the DAFE group on Electrolytes.
3. The Liberal Arts did well on most texts, being much better than the Engineering and Science and Mathematics groups on Polanyi and Quixote and better than the

Science and Mathematics group on <u>Turbines</u>. Presumably this was due to their superior linguistic proficiency, although even this did not enable them to perform better than the Engineers on the two engineering texts.

B. Short Answers: Mean scores are presented in Table 8. Significant differences between groups are set out in Table 9.

TABLE 8 Group Means and Standard Deviations for Each Text Using the Short Answer Technique

Group		Polanyi	Malaysia	Turbines	Electrolytes	Quixote
DAFE	M	47.1	56.1	53.8	42.0	55.4
	SD	25.1	22.3	17.1	28.7	22.0
Engineering	M	24.5	42.3	58.1	45.1	48.5
	SD	22.7	23.7	24.1	25.9	21.9
Science &	M	34.9	46.1	58.0	47.5	40.8
Mathematics	SD	22.3	20.8	16.4	18.6	21.3
Liberal	M	55.7	54.4	60.3	46.6	70.8
Arts	SD	22.8	20.0	20.2	19.4	14.3

DAFE = Development Administration, Finance, Economics

TABLE 9 Significant Differences between Group Means
(t test) for Each Text*

Text	Group	Engineers	Science & Mathematics	Liberal Arts
Polanyi	DAFE	p≤.01	NS	NS
	Engineering		NS	p≤.001
	Science & Mathematics			p≤.01
Malaysia	DAFE	p≤.05	NS	NS
Quixote	DAFE	NS	p≤.05	p≤.01
	Engineering		NS	p≤.001
	Science & Mathematics			p≤.001

* Only texts yielding significant differences have been
reported
DAFE = Development Administration, Finance, Economics

Comments

1. The DAFE group did better than the Engineers on both
the DAFE texts. They did not, however, outperform the
Science and Mathematics group.
2. On the other hand, there was no significant difference in
means between the DAFE group and either the Engineers or the Science and Mathematics group on the two
engineering texts.
3. The Liberal Arts group did well on Polanyi, outper-
forming the Engineers and the Science and Mathematics
group, though not the DAFE group, and, as expected,
outperformed all groups on Quixote.

DISCUSSION

On the whole, the results support the hypothesis. On both
test methods, the DAFE group performed significantly better on

DAFE texts than did the Engineers. The Liberal Arts group did best on the general text. However, with one exception, the Engineers and Science and Mathematics groups did not outperform the other groups on the engineering texts. Possible reasons for this will be discussed later; at the moment, though, it looks as if these two groups would be disadvantaged by the use of texts outside their own fields of study.

Before we return to a discussion of why some groups performed better than others, it is worthwhile looking at some points of interest which emerge from an examination of scores on both test methods.

1. There is evidence of a strong method effect. Although the overall correlation between the gap-filling test and the short answer is fairly high (.78) when results are summed across texts, correlations for individuals and groups vary widely. Moreover, the rank order of text difficulty does not remain stable across methods. On the gap-filling test, Electrolytes is ranked second in overall difficulty, that is, it is comparatively easy. Quixote, on the other hand, is ranked fourth, i.e., a difficult text. On short answers, however, the ranks are reversed, with Quixote ranked second and Electrolytes ranked fourth.

2. In spite of this, the text effect mentioned earlier remains reasonably constant. With both methods Turbines emerges as the easiest text and Polanyi the most difficult.

3. The suggestion made in Study 1 that we have, in effect, not four groups but two is supported by the results of Study 2. Taking both test methods into account, there are no significant differences between the Engineers and the Science and Mathematics group, and only one significant difference between DAFE students and the Liberal Arts group (short answers - Quixote). As said before, this result has relevance to the question of how many specialized tests are required.

Finally, we return to the problem of explaining the results. The "background knowledge" hypothesis was only partially confirmed: DAFE students did better on DAFE texts than did Engineers, but the converse was not the case.

Linguistic proficiency would clearly seem to be one factor involved. The fact that on both test methods the Liberal Arts group performed better than any other group on Quixote can be explained in terms of the hypothesis. The same explanation is not available when we try to account for the fact that the group also did best on Polanyi and Turbines. For the Lancaster students, scores on ELBA and ELTS were available, and correlations between the students' performance on these language tests and the present tests are presented in Table 10.

TABLE 10   Test Correlations with ELBA and
ELTS*

Short Answer

	ELBA			ELTS		
	1	2	Total	G1	G2	M1
Malaysia	.45	.38	.43	.45	NS	.38
Polanyi	.52	.52	.56	.68	.63	.69
Turbines	.42	.50	.50	.55	.41	.49
Electrolytes	NS	NS	NS	.44	NS	NS
Quixote	NS	.45	.40	.61	NS	.49

ELBA $\underline{N}$ = 35   **ELTS** $\underline{N}$ = 20

Gap Filling (Acceptable Scoring Method)

	ELBA			ELTS		
	1	2	Total	G1	G2	M1
Malaysia	NS	.34	NS	.55	NS	.54
Polanyi	.53	.61	.63	.67	.51	.71
Turbines	.57	.66	.66	.73	NS	NS
Electrolytes	NS	NS	NS	NS	NS	NS
Quixote	.50	.46	.51	NS	NS	NS

  ELBA N = 21/25   **ELTS** $\underline{N}$ = 11/13
* **ELBA** $\underline{1}$ = Listening Skills   **ELTS** $\overline{G}1$= Reading Skills
        2 = Reading Skills   G2= Listening Skills
                         M1= Study Skills

Editor's Note: For a more detailed description of the **ELTS**,
see B. Carroll in this volume.

As can be seen from the table, the highest correlations between
the tests occur in the case of Polanyi and Turbines. This is,
then, quite strong evidence that it was linguistic proficiency
that enabled the Liberal Arts group to do well on these two
texts.
    We are left with the problem of why the Engineers did not
do better than the DAFE group on the engineering texts. It

may be that this is again a matter of linguistic proficiency –
it will be remembered that the Lancaster economists were more
proficient than the Engineering or Science and Mathematics
groups. This does not explain, however, why the Engineers
did at least as well as the DAFE group on the Electrolytes text
(both methods) and on Turbines (short answer method). What
we need is an explanation which combines the effects of linguistic proficiency and of background knowledge so as to
account for the totality of the results. An examination of the
gap-filling scores might lead one to the following explanation.
Turbines and Electrolytes are overall the easiest texts, ranking
first and second respectively. That is, the two engineering
texts are, on average, the easiest texts. It might be possible
to claim that below a certain level of text difficulty (of neces-
sity undefined), a certain score could be arrived at by means
of (a) linguistic proficiency and (b) general knowledge of the
world. Thus on an easy text, all groups could be expected to
get roughly the same score, with the possible exception of
Liberal Arts, who might score higher. And Table 6 seems to
bear this out: for example, on Turbines, exact scoring, the
groups scored as follows: DAFE 33, Engineering 32, Science
and Mathematics 30, and Liberal Arts 43.

Beyond a certain level of linguistic difficulty, the argument
continues, more specialized background knowledge would
become more important, being used to "top up" linguistic proficiency scores. Thus on the two economics texts, which on
gap-filling are ranked overall third and fifth, the DAFE group
were able to use their background knowledge to gain an
advantage over the Engineers.

Such an explanation has a certain superficial attraction.
Admittedly the idea of a "pure" linguistic proficiency base,
added to by means of background knowledge, is probably the
antithesis of the schema based view of comprehension. However, gap-filling is not a "natural" comprehension task, and it
might be argued that in the context, such an explanation might
be appropriate.

The explanation does not, however, stand up to further
data analysis. In the gap-filling test, Electrolytes was a
comparatively easy text; in the short answer test, however, it
was a difficult text, yet this did not prevent the DAFE group
from doing as well on it as the Engineers.

Secondly, if on the gap-filling test, Electrolytes was a
genuinely easy text linguistically, then one would have
expected the Liberal Arts students to do well on it. However,
if one compares their performance with that of the other
groups, it can be seen that this was not the case.

Thirdly, if Electrolytes was a linguistically easy text, one would expect a high correlation between performance on it and scores on language tests. However, examination of Table 10 shows that this was not the case: there was virtually no correlation between Electrolytes and the two language tests.

This explanation having apparently failed, we can at present see no obvious alternative explanation. Probably the best way forward would be to replicate the study using a wider range of texts, in order to get rid of what may be the idiosyncratic effects of particular texts.

CONCLUSIONS

The studies described in this paper have shown that academic background can have an effect on reading comprehension. They are thus a contribution to research into the nature of comprehension in general. They have also shown that particular groups of students may be disadvantaged by being tested on areas outside their academic field. If these findings are supported by further studies, then they will represent important evidence in support of the need for ESP proficiency tests.

NOTES

1. A version of this paper was presented at TESOL Toronto, March 1983.

2. An account of STUDY 1 has appeared in Hughes, A., and D. Porter (eds.), Current Developments in Language Testing. London: Academic Press, 1983.

3. ELBA is a post-graduate admissions test for foreign students used until recently by the University of Edinburgh.

REFERENCES

Gregory, D. 1972. Fuel Cells. London: Mills and Boon.

Gunning, R. 1952. The Technique of Clear Writing. New York: McGraw-Hill.

Hulme, B. 1981. Development of off-shore turbine packages for power generation and mechanical drive. General Electric Company Journal of Science and Technology 47.

Latham, A. 1978. The International Economy and the Underdeveloped World, 1864-1914. London: Croom Helm.

Steffensen, M.S., and C. Joag-Dev. In press. Cultural knowledge and reading. In Alderson, J., and A. Urquhart (eds.), Reading in a Foreign Language. London: Longman.

Widdowson, H. 1979. Explorations in Applied Linguistics. Oxford: Oxford University Press.

3.
A Theoretical Framework for the Development of Performance Tests

Robert J. Courchêne and Jean I. de Bagheera

The new emphasis in language testing on what someone can do with the language as opposed to what one knows about the language has had important ramifications for L2 test construction. In designing tests researchers are now focusing on a subject's active performance. They want to prepare tests that will enable L2 specialists to predict how subjects would perform in real communicative situations. They want to construct tests that force an L2 learner to actively perform his competence and not just give a pencil-and-paper account of it.

Before test designers can begin to develop such performance tests, however, many important theoretical and practical decisions have to be made concerning factors such as content, skill parameters, judges, and method. In this paper we will examine those decisions with a view to providing a type of checklist for test designers working in the field. Throughout the paper, reference will be made to theories and tests currently described in the literature.

PERFORMANCE TESTS: THEORETICAL AND PRACTICAL DECISIONS

The fundamental decisions that test designers have to make will be discussed in detail under the following headings:

1) underlying theories to be respected
2) the content to be selected and evaluated
3) how this content is to be evaluated while respecting the previously chosen underlying theories

1.0 Underlying Theories

1.1 Communication

As concerns L2 theorists, very little has been done (Canale and Swaine 1980; Canale 1981a-d; Canale 1983; Morrow 1979; Hymes 1972) to relate theories of communicative competence (CC) to communication theory in general. This is important for testing. A designer has the choice of adopting either a dynamic or a static model with static or dynamic test designs based on the respective models. Researchers in speech and human communication research are much more concerned about and conscious of the relationship between theories of communication and theories of CC. Interactive models such as that proposed by Wiemann and Backlund (1980) could provide valuable information for test designers. In such models, communication is always seen as a dynamic-interactive process where the way someone says something and its effect on the listener are as important as what is said. In the past, these aspects of communication were often not considered, as our discrete point tests were based on static models of communication.

Integrating a theory of CC in a general theory of communication would allow test designers to have a more consistent approach to test design and avoid leaving out some important aspects of the communicative process.

1.2 Theory of Language

The underlying linguistic theory will, by definition, influence the way a researcher views language. Structuralists see language as a decomposable-composable system of tiny parts that can be analyzed in minute detail. They also place a strong emphasis on phonology. Testers adopting such a theory would also see the oral aspects of language as being extremely important (Chomsky 1965).

If one adopted a tranformational-generative approach to language theory more emphasis would be placed on the rule-governed nature of language, on its innate features and the primordial importance of syntax.

One could also adopt a more functional approach as outlined by Halliday (1975). In such a perspective, language is seen as being composed of a series of functions that the learner must acquire if he is to perform different speech acts in various contexts and situations. Semantic and sociolinguistic theory play an important role in this theory of language. The tests that have been produced based on this theory of language are at the other end of the spectrum from the discrete point tests based on structural linguistics as performing implies the marshaling of both skills and knowledge to perform the task in question. The emphasis is not on discrete units but on performance units of CC.

The view that a test designer holds of language will influence not only what will be chosen but how it will be tested. As well, test designers must be certain that their view of testing is in line with the views of the curriculum designer, teachers and learners as concerns language theory. If not, the people involved will be working at cross purposes and the results obtained will not be valid (Upshur 1979).

1.3 Theories of Competence

It is both ironic and interesting that the researchers in L1/L2 and those in communication-related fields have had many of the same discussions, and have reached many of the same conclusions without being aware of each others' activities. In both fields, the common mentors have been Chomsky, Hymes, Labov, Halliday, Bernstein, Brown, Bruner, to mention only a few. After the early 1970s, however, one finds only rare mention of what the other group is doing. Even the major reviews of the literature (Canale and Swain 1980; Larson et al. 1978; Wiemann and Backlund 1980) contain no important references to work going on in the other field.

Wiemann and Backlund (1980; cf. Larson et al. 1978) categorize theories of communicative competence as (1) cognitive, (2) behavioral and (3) cognitive-behavioral. The "cognitive" category is what is frequently known as the "descriptive" view of CC (Chomsky 1965); i.e., it describes in detail what a learner must know to be considered competent, but it does not state what he must be capable of doing (performance). In the cognitive view of CC, the emphasis is on the underlying knowledge that one needs to operationalize this competence, to perform it. Cognitive theorists make a definite distinction between competence and performance. They also maintain, as did Chomsky (1965), that performance is the only way to measure competence. Critics of this position point out, however, that one can demonstrate performance without being able to give an account of one's underlying competence, and one can be competent without being able to perform (Larson et al. 1978; Pylyshyn 1973). According to Wiemann and Backlund (1980), definitions of CC that provide a description of only the underlying knowledge necessary to perform but do not tie this knowledge to actual performance are inadequate. "Knowledge of" is an important but partial explanation of CC. No theorists in the communication field adhere to the cognitive view, as such.

The second type of theory of CC is behavioral. By definition, such descriptions emphasize action, performance. Such theories are not limited to describing a set of rules the competent communicator must know but rather try to account for communicative behavior. In such a perspective, one tries to explain how a communicator uses both "knowledge of" and "knowledge how" (communicative skills) in attempting to achieve his communication goals (cf. Larson et al.'s [1978] discussion on whether, to be considered competent, one must always be effective as regards the achievement of one's goals). In the behavioral perspective, competence is closely tied to performance; the emphasis is on the actual overt behavior that the communicator demonstrates. Explaining or being able to account for such behavior in terms of underlying systems of knowledge is less important. As well, to be judged competent, a communicator would have to demonstrate his knowledge of appropriate behavior in ongoing interaction (Allen and Brown 1976; Wiemann 1977). Many theorists in the field of communication research have theories that are behavioral in emphasis (Wiemann 1977; Wang et al. 1973; Allen and Brown 1976; Norton 1978; Larson et al. 1978; Bochner and Kelly 1974; Simon 1979; Parks 1976; Miller and Steinberg 1975). It is important to note here that these theorists are not purists: they also realize the importance of underlying knowledge and skills. To take the behavioral perspective to its logical conclusion, dealing only with overt manifestations of behavior without trying to account for such behavior, would not advance theory or provide an adequate explanation of CC.

A third perspective suggested by Wiemann and Backlund (1980) is the cognitive-behavioral approach that encompasses the two previous ones. The definition of this dual theory is very close to that proposed by Canale and Swain (1980). The cognitive-behavioral theorists state that the competent communicators will have the necessary underlying knowledge and communicative skills to carry out their communicative acts in an appropriate manner. The competent communicator will have to demonstrate this knowledge in real language situations. What is not clear, however, is whether to "demonstrate" should be taken to mean to "accomplish". Certain theorists maintain that effectiveness is a necessary characteristic of being communicatively competent (i.e., Wiemann 1977; Allen and Brown 1976); others maintain that it is enough to manifest the behavior (Larson et al. 1978); they maintain that people can be competent without being effective and vice-versa. One major difference between this perspective and that suggested by Canale and Swain is that Wiemann and Backlund (1980) do not distinguish between competence and performance (cf. Halliday 1973). Performance is seen as part of competence. The "knowledge of" and the "knowing how" are closely related. The dual-perspective view of CC is process oriented: the central focus is the ongoing relationships that exist between the people who are communicating. It is dynamic and interactive. Wiemann and Backlund (1980) in their review of the literature suggest that only by using this dual approach can one adequately account for CC. A test designer's choice of one of these three perspectives will have important ramifications for test construction (see Figure 1).

2.0 Content to be Selected and Evaluated

One of the most important decisions testing theorists have to make is what to include in their definition of CC. They must provide an answer to the question "What must a learner know (in general and in the specific testing situation) to be considered to be competent?". To do so, they must answer four sub-questions:

1) What components (if any) constitute CC?
2) What is the realtionship among the components?
3) Does competence imply both knowledge and skill?
4) Is there a hierarchy concerning teaching, learning, acquisition and, therefore, testing?

2.1 Components of Communicative Competence

In the literature today, there are many theories concerning what one must know to be considered competent (Chomsky 1965; Widdowson 1978; Munby 1978; Oller 1979; Canale and Swain 1980; Canale 1981a-d; Canale 1983). Chomsky (1965) in his original statement equated competence with linguistic competence. In the most developed definition, Canale and Swain (1980) and Canale (1981a-d)) state that CC includes knowledge of and the underlying skills to be able to use the following content areas: linguistic, sociolinguistic, discourse and strategic competence. Oller (1979), though he never uses the term, talks in terms of grammars of expectancy at all levels (phonology, grammar, etc.). Other specialists also mention affective and behavioral content (Wiemann and Backlund 1980). If test designers want to be able to state that an interactant is competent, they must first define what competence includes for their specific situation.

FIGURE 1   Checklist of Theoretical and Practical Decisions

Content	View of Competence	Theory of Communication	Theory of Language	Judges	Methodological Factors
Dimensions	Cognitive	Static	Behavioral (structural)	Expert	Selection Criteria and Weights
Linguistic	Behavioral	Dynamic	Cognitive	Naive	Discrete—Global Evaluation Grid
Sociolinguistic	Cognitive—Behavioral	Static—Dynamic	Functional/ Sociolinguistic	Peers	Method/Trait Effect
Discourse		Implicit &/or non-stated	Information—Processing	1) Aspects of CC evaluated by each	Multiple vs Unity View of Language Proficiency
Strategic			Other	2) Weight given by each group to each factor	
Other					
Affective					
Behavioral					
Flexibility					
Interaction					
Management					
Relationship Among Dimensions					
1) Componential					
2) Dynamic					
3) Orthogonal (Independent)					
Parameters					
1) Passive—Active Knowledge/Skills					
2) Non-speaker Native speaker Level of skills					
Hierarchy					
1) Equal Weight					
2) Different Weights					

2.2 Relationship Among the Components: Integrated or Componential?

Researchers must answer for themselves whether they believe the relationship is componential or integrated. If several components are involved (Canale and Swain 1980), what is the relationship that exists among them? It could be that: (1) the different components have been isolated but no precise indication of their relationship exists;[1] or (2) the relationship is dynamic as the elements act together as a dynamic unity and the individual parts cannot be measured separately (cf. Oller's grammar of expectancy 1979: 16-33). The researcher's choice of model will certainly influence not only the design of the test but also the evaluation grid.

2.3 Competence: Knowledge and Skill?

Once the content has been decided, test designers must still stipulate whether learners are to have an active or passive knowledge of it. What degree of skill must the interactants demonstrate to be declared competent? As skill and knowledge are often a question of degree, they are best represented as continua rather than equally graduated intervals along a scale (see Figure 2).

FIGURE 2   Content: Parameters

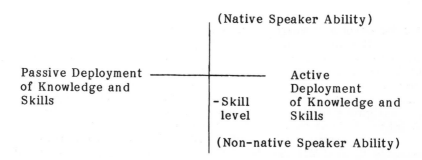

According to one's theory of testing, competency along these continua would be measured using discrete point tests, global tests or some combination of the two. These two continua are complementary; they enable the theorist to determine the possible relationship between how one possesses the required knowledge and skills and the skill level at which one possesses

them. It also enables test designers to specify which knowledge and skill areas are being considered. For example, a
theorist in a given situation could equate competence with one's
ability to speak and understand English and exclude both
reading and writing. Unless the theorist specifies type of
knowledge and skill level, it will be very difficult to construct
a test and to measure accurately an interactant's performance.

2.4 Hierarchy

Depending on whether one adopts an integrated or a componential approach, one has to decide what weight to give to
each of the subcomponents (i.e., sociolinguistic, linguistic).
A theorist would have a choice of setting up a hierarchy in
which all had equal weight, one in which components had different weights, or one in which only a global score would be
given because of the impossibility of assigning weights. This
decision would certainly be tied to one's view of competence
as being either componential or integrative in nature.

3.0 Methodological Aspects

In this section we will examine mostly methodological
aspects of listing, but certain theoretical facets of testing will
also be discussed as they are often closely tied to methodological questions.

3.1 Selection and Weight Values for Criteria

In establishing an evaluation grid, decisions must be made
concerning what facets of the communicative act will be evaluated and how weight will be accorded to each. In the Foreign
Service Interview (FSI), for instance, fluency, grammar,
pronunciation, etc., have been selected as evaluation criteria
in assigning a level to prospective candidates. In the
weighting, however, pronunciation has been assigned a "0"
value. In examining the performance of a candidate, what one
chooses to evaluate can be considered from different points of
view. If one looks at performance from the point of origin (the
speaker), the emphasis might be grammar, content, pronunciation, vocabulary; if one examines it from the point of view
of the receiver (the listener), one would examine affective
factors, such as empathy, politeness, the appropriateness of
the message, the effect of the message, its comprehensibility;
or, if one examines it within the speaker-hearer dynamic, one

might look at appropriateness, affective factors, behavioral management factors, interaction management skills. What the individual test designer will choose to emphasize, will be, as mentioned above, closely related to his or her view of what communication is.

In some of the current frameworks for performance tests (Royal Society of Arts [RSA] Tests 1981; Carroll's Band System 1980; the Clément-DesBrisay Test 1983;[2] tests from the Federal Language Training Branch),[3] what is measured is expressed in terms such as size independence, range, accuracy, appropriateness. Such terms are radically different from those used by the discrete-point testers and encompass different aspects of the communicative process.

To summarize, test designers must decide which aspects of a subject's performance they are going to evaluate and what value they will give to each (see Figure 1).

3.2 Discrete-Global Evaluation

In setting up an evaluation grid, designers must choose a discrete approach, a global one, or some combination of the two. The most common examples of the global approach are tests developed by the Foreign Service Institute and its adaptations by the Interagency Roundtable, Carroll's band system 1980, the Royal Society of Arts RSA Tests and some tests from the Federal Language Training Branch. With the global evaluation system, the idea is to set up a continuum from incompetent to competent speaker (cf. Clément-DesBrisay Test). The subjects are placed along the continuum for each of the parameters being evaluated. Performance scores can then be arrived at by designating people as moderate speakers, competent readers, native-like writers etc.

There is some discussion whether discrete point-evaluation grids can be used with real performance tests as the latter involve the deployment of an ensemble of skills and knowledge. In the discrete point test, the task is broken up into small related units (pronunciation, grammar, vocabulary) and a score is assigned for each. A global score is attained by summing the scores for the individual units. The question that remains is, "Is the whole more than the sum of its parts?"

3.3 Method

The method (test design) used to evaluate a candidate's performance significantly affects the results of the test. In recent research carried out by Bachman and Palmer (1981a and b) using sophisticated statistical procedures the authors demonstrated that the choice of the method (interview, translation, or self-report) significantly affected the results obtained on reading and speaking traits.

Bachman and Palmer's findings should force test designers to ask themselves why they have chosen one test format as opposed to another. It should, also, force them to include method control groups in order to evaluate the effect of different methods on the results obtained. In the long run, it should also result in test designers arriving at the best choice of method for measuring each type of language trait (see Figure 1).

3.4 Unitary versus Multiple Trait Models

Recent research by specialists such as Oller (1983) and Bachman and Palmer (1981a and b) has resulted in the rejection of the strongest form of the unitary trait hypothesis for language proficiency. Oller, who was the major proponent of the unitary hypothesis, has since recanted and opted for a general "g" factor of language proficiency in addition to other factors, such as speaking. Cummins (1981) in his formulation of cognitive and academic language proficiency (CALP) and basic inter-communication skills (BICS) has also given support to the multiple trait hypothesis. There may be some evidence for equating Oller's "g" factor and speaking factor with Cummins CALP and BICS.

Whether designers adopt a unitary or multiple trait model will have consequences for their test design. If they adopt the unitary model, they assume that CC can be measured using one test (i.e., it will account for all the variance). If they adopt the multiple-trait model, they will have to use a battery of tests to completely measure CC (see Figure 1).

3.5 Judges

Prior to designing tests, theorists must ask themselves another important question, "Who is going to be the ultimate judge of the subjects who are being tested?" If I choose experts (i.e., language teachers, trained raters) will the results be the same as if I were to choose naive judges or peers? Researchers (Ludwig 1982; Clifford 1981; Backlund 1977; Tardif and d'Anglejan 1981) have demonstrated that expert and naive judges differ in at least two important ways: first, they do not look for the same thing; second, they rate the same thing in different ways. For example, in some cases, naive judges are more interested in what was said than in how it was said. Test designers must be acutely aware who the ultimate judges of their subjects will be and what criteria these judges will use to conclude that someone is competent. If the criteria used by the user-public are significantly different from those used by the trained judges, one would certainly have to question the usefulness of such a test in preparing candidates for the work world.

SUMMARY

We have examined many of the practical and theoretical decisions that can affect test construction. Our intention here has not been to take a definite position on these issues; rather, it has been to provide designers with a decision-making checklist. We believe that if theorists make such decisions for the contexts in which they are working, the final product will enable them to evaluate their candidates' communicative performance in a more reliable and valid way. The theoretical and practical decisions test-designers must make have been summarized in Figure 1.

NOTES

1. Researchers at The Ontario Institute for Studies in Education (OISE) are presently conducting research based on Canale and Swain's model to ascertain the type of relationship that might exist.
2. More information may be obtained from Richard Clément, School of Psychology, Univeristy of Ottawa.
3. Personal Communication. See also Proulx-Dubé, this volume.

REFERENCES

Allen, R., and K. Brown (eds.). 1976. Developing Communicative Competence in Children. Skokie: National Textbook Company.

Bachman, L., and A. Palmer. 1981a. The construct validation of the FSI oral interview. Language Learning 31.1: 67-86.

Bachman, L., and A. Palmer. 1981b. The construct validation of tests of communicative competence. Paper read at the Colloquium on the Validation of Oral Proficiency Tests, University of Michigan. To appear in the Proceedings.

Backlund, P. 1977. Speech Communication Correlates of Perceived Communicative Competence. Unpublished Doctoral Dissertation, University of Denver.

Bochner, A., and C. Kelly. 1974. Interpersonal competence: rationale, philosophy, and implementation of a conceptual framework. Speech Teacher 23:279-301.

Canale, M., and M. Swain. 1980. Theoretical bases of communicative approaches to second language teaching and testing. Applied Linguistics 1.1.

Canale, M. 1981a. From communicative competence to communicative language pedagogy. In Richards, J., and R. Schmidt (eds.), Language and Communication. London: Longman.

Canale, M. 1981b. A communicative approach to language proficiency assessment in a minority setting. Paper presented at the Language Proficiency Assessment Symposium, Airlie House, Virginia. To appear in the Proceedings.

Canale, M. 1981c. The method effect in communicative testing. Medium 6.2. Special issue on evalution in foreign language programs, J. Ricciardi (ed.).

Canale, M. 1981d. Communication: how to evaluate it. Bulletin of the CAAL 3.2: 77-94.

Canale, M. 1983. On some dimensions of language proficiency. In Oller, J. (ed.), Issues in Language Testing Research. Rowley, Mass.: Newbury House.

Carroll, B. 1980. Testing Communicative Performance. Oxford: Pergamon Press.

Chomsky, N. 1965. Aspects of the Theory of Syntax. Cambridge: MIT Press.

Clifford, R. 1981. Testing oral language proficiency: a dynamic model. EDRS ED193666.

Cummins, J. 1981. The cross-lingual dimensions of language proficiency: implications for bilingual education and the optimal age issue. TESOL Quarterly 14.2:175-187.

Halliday, M. 1973. Explorations in the Functions of Language. London: Edward Arnold Publishers Ltd.

Halliday, M. 1975. Learning How to Mean: Explorations in the Development of Language. London: Edward Arnold Publishers Ltd.

Hymes, D. 1972. On communicative competence. In Pride, J., and J. Holmes (eds.), Sociolinguistics. Harmondsworth: Penguin Books.

Larson, C., et al. 1978. Assessing Communicative Competence. Falls Church, Va.: Speech Communication Association and ERIC.

Ludwig, J. 1982. Native speaker judgements of second language learners' efforts at communication: a review. Modern Language Journal 66: 274-83.

Miller, G., and M. Steinberg. 1975. Between People. Chicago: Science Reseach Associates.

Morrow, K. 1979. Communicative language testing: education or revolution. In Brumfit, C., and K. Johnson (eds.), The Communicative Approach to Language Teaching, pp. 143-159. Oxford: Oxford University Press.

Munby, J. 1978. Communicative Syllabus Design. Cambridge: Cambridge University Press.

Norton, R. 1978. Foundation of a communicator style construct. Human Communication Research 2:50-67.

Oller, J. 1979. Language Tests at School: A Pragmatic Approach. London: Longman.

Oller, J. 1983. A concensus for the eighties? In Oller, J. (ed.), Issues in Language Testing Research. Rowley, Mass.: Newbury House.

Parks, M. 1976. Communication competency. Paper presented at the annual convention of the Speech Communication Association, San Francisco.

Pylyshyn, Z. 1973. The role of competence theories in cognitive psychology. Journal of Psycholinguistic Research 2.1.

Royal Society of Arts, Inc. 1981. Communicative Use of English as a Foreign Language. London: Royal Society of Arts.

Simon, C. 1979. Communicative Competence: A Functional Pragmatic Approach to Language Therapy. Tucson: Communication Skill Builders Inc.

Tardif, C., and A. d'Anglejan. 1981. Les erreurs en français langue seconde et leurs effets sur la communication orale. The Canadian Modern Language Review 37.4: 706-723

Upshur, J. 1979. Functional proficiency theory and a research role for language tests. In Brière, E., and F. Hinofotis (eds.), Concepts in Language Testing: Some Recent Studies. Washington: TESOL.

58

Wang, M., et al. 1973. The Development of the language communication skills task. Pittsburgh: Learning Research and Development Centre, University of Pittsburgh. (ED 087000.)

Widdowson, H. 1978. Teaching Language as Communication. London: Oxford University Press.

Wiemann, J. 1977. Explication and test of a model of communicative competence. Human Communication Research 3.3: 195-213.

Wiemann, J., and P. Backlund. 1980. Communicative competence. Review of Educational Research 50.1:185-199.

4.
Les tests de savoir-faire en langue seconde : l'expérience européenne

Jean-Claude Mothe

Dans le cadre de ma présentation, je voudrais faire état de quelques types d'épreuves de savoir-faire comme on en trouve maintenant un peu partout en Europe, en me limitant 1) à des épreuves de français langue étrangère (FLE), 2) à deux seulement des différentes fonctions d'évaluation :   celle de l'efficience, pour la mesure d'une qualification professionnelle, et l'évaluation formative, intégrée à l'apprentissage, et 3) à des épreuves auxquelles j'ai pu personnellement contribuer, car il aurait été présomptueux et vain de ma part d'essayer de dresser un tableau, nécessairement partiel et partial, des expériences européennes dans leur ensemble.

Je commencerai par énoncer deux principes directeurs, les hypothèses de travail qui ont conduit à l'élaboration d'épreuves de ce genre, pour donner ensuite, en les commentant, quelques exemples de réalisations concrètes, dont les caractéristiques découlent de ces principes directeurs.

Certains de ces exemples seront tirés d'épreuves qui ont été conçues depuis 1977 pour mesurer les compétences de travail en français des fonctionnaires internationaux non francophones de l'ONU de Genève et de l'UNESCO à Paris.   D'autres seront extraits d'épreuves destinées à l'évaluation formative d'apprenants débutants ou moyens.

AUTHENTICITÉ

L'idée directrice essentielle est de tirer les conséquences, pour l'évaluation, de la notion de hiérarchie des objectifs. De même que la connaissance d'une règle de grammaire, par exemple, ne constitue qu'un objectif intermédiaire, pédagogique, par rapport à un objectif plus lointain et hiérarchiquement supérieur qui est la capacité d'appliquer cette règle à bon escient en cas de besoin, de même l'apprentissage de la langue ne constitue en général qu'un objectif intermédiaire par rapport à l'objectif terminal qui est, dans la plupart des situations d'apprentissage d'une langue étrangère, l'acquisition d'une compétence de communication au moyen de cette langue, c'est-à-dire d'une capacité de s'en servir dans des situations langagières réelles, lorsque l'apprentissage est terminé. La principale conséquence de cette évidence sur les techniques d'évaluation est la recherche de l'authenticité dans les tâches qui sont demandées aux apprenants ou aux candidats, sans, bien sûr, se faire d'illusions excessives sur cette authenticité.

La situation d'évaluation comporte en effet une part d'artifice irréductible, dont la moindre n'est pas la nature des enjeux. Mais il est clair que les épreuves qui font appel à des opérations mentales qui n'existent que rarement ou pas du tout dans l'utilisation authentique d'une langue en situation réelle seront plus artificielles encore que celles qui s'efforcent de simuler ces situations réelles. Ce sera, bien entendu, le cas des épreuves qui isolent les composantes de l'analyse linguistique, comme les épreuves spécifiques de grammaire ou de vocabulaire, puisque la quasi-totalité des situations langagières réelles intègrent l'ensemble de ces composantes, dont la distinction est purement linguistique ou pédagogique.

Les épreuves de ce type ont peut-être leur place dans l'évaluation formative, qui est orientée vers l'apprentissage: ici, la recherche de l'authenticité à tout prix et en toutes circonstances nuirait probablement à la précision du diagnostic, même en cas de combinaison entre évaluation externe et auto-évaluation.

Mais, même en évaluation formative, les épreuves de connaissances linguistiques sont insuffisantes, et sans doute les moins utiles.

Et dans les tests de qualification, on doit pouvoir affirmer qu'elles n'ont pas du tout leur place : dans ce type d'évaluation, tourné non plus vers l'apprentissage mais vers la vie réelle extra-scolaire, tout comme dans les examens de fin d'études, par exemple, la précision du diagnostic n'a plus d'intérêt, ni la façon dont l'apprentissage s'est déroulé. Seul compte le résultat, c'est-à-dire la capacité de résoudre efficacement les problèmes posés par des situations réelles de communication.

Comme, de plus, dans ce genre d'évaluation, le problème d'économie, donc de choix et de représentativité de ce choix, est beaucoup plus draconien que dans l'évaluation formative, il paraît évident qu'il faut y préférer les épreuves de savoir-faire simulant des situations réelles, à l'exclusion d'épreuves moins authentiques et mesurant l'atteinte d'objectifs plus secondaire.

DIVERSIFICATION

Une autre idée essentielle, tout à fait liée à la précédente, est celle de la diversification des techniques. Elle est nécessaire, d'abord en raison de l'extraordinaire diversité des compétences langagières, diversité qui n'est que le reflet de l'infinie variété des situations de communication de la vie réelle, ensuite en raison de la diversité non moins grande des objectifs globaux d'apprentissage selon les apprenants ou selon les types de besoins.

Il semble que l'évaluation en langues doit s'efforcer, par sa flexibilité, de tenir compte le plus possible, quoique d'une façon nécessairement partielle, de ces diversités-là. Elle manquera de validité si elle se contente de quelques techniques, toujours les mêmes, qui privilégieront nécessairement certaines facettes, toujours les mêmes, de la compétence langagière.

Sans doute existe-t-il pour chaque type d'apprenants, pour chaque sous-compétence digne d'être évaluée, des techniques plus adaptées, plus efficaces, plus valides que d'autres, qui seront peut-être plus appropriées pour d'autres apprenants et d'autres sous-compétences.

ÉVALUATION DE LA COMPRÉHENSION

Je vais essayer de développer un peu et d'illustrer ces notions d'authenticité et de diversification, en commençant par l'évaluation de la compréhension.

Il n'est pas question de proposer le rejet pur et simple de techniques éprouvées comme les questions à choix multiples (QCM) ou les tests de closure. Mais leur systématisation ne me paraît pas souhaitable pour au techniques éprouvées comme les questions à choix multiples (QCM) ou les tests de closure. Mais leur systématisation ne me paraît pas souhaitable pour au moins deux raisons : la première est qu'elles sont relativement éloignées de l'authenticité. Certes, elles reposent sur des mécanismes mentaux qui font partie de l'activité langagière réelle, à savoir l'anticipation en lecture et la formulation d'hypothèses en interprétation. Mais il faut reconnaître que, dans l'usage quotidien d'une langue, on se trouve rarement en situation d'avoir à combler les lacunes d'un texte à trous ou à choisir entre quatre ou cinq interprétations différentes, et de plus formulées dans la langue-cible, comme il arrive quand on subit un QCM de la forme la plus répandue, celle que j'appelerai QCM à distracteurs fabriqués par le constructeur.

Le second reproche qu'on peut adresser à la systématisation de ces techniques est bien évidemment leur uniformité. Tout se passe alors en effet comme si on supposait que la compréhension est une fin en soi, au lieu de n'être qu'un moyen d'atteindre une autre finalité, qui peut être linguistique (réponse à une question) ou non linguistique (prise de décision). C'est ainsi que, pour s'en tenir provisoirement à l'exemple de la compréhension écrite chez les fonctionnaires internationaux, on négligerait d'évaluer des capacités importantes comme celles de la compréhension sélective ou de la compréhension globale rapide.

Les QCM classiques de compréhension d'un texte ambitionnent en effet presque uniformément de mesurer la compréhension détaillée et approfondie d'un texte, quelles que soient sa nature et sa fonction, et ne constituent pas toujours une technique fonctionnelle d'évaluation.

Or, même la compréhension détaillée peut être évaluée par d'autres techniques, qui peuvent se révéler plus appropriées. Par exemple, pour l'ONU de Genève, on avait imaginé l'épreuve suivante.

On fournit au candidat : 1) la photocopie d'un texte de référence authentique : en l'occurrence, une circulaire administrative extraite du règlement du personnel et définissant en détail les conditions d'octroi au personnel de l'Organisation d'une indemnité pour frais d'études des enfants à charge; 2) toute une série de textes de nature variée (lettres personnelles, notes officielles, messages téléphonés), tous simulés, qui étaient censés émaner de divers ayant-droit (ou se croyant tels) et dont le traitement correct supposait une compréhension exacte du texte de référence.

La consigne était de classer ces demandes en trois catégories : "recevables", "irrecevables" et "douteuses fautes d'informations suffisantes", et de justifier de façon succincte le classement dans les deuxième et troisième catégories, en fournissant selon le cas la raison (ou l'une des raisons) du caractère irrecevable de la demande, ou la liste complète des informations manquantes.

Une épreuve de ce genre me paraît réunir une foule d'avantages avec un minimum d'inconvénients : d'abord, la situation d'évaluation simule de la façon la plus exacte possible une situation authentique où peuvent se trouver réellement ces fonctionnaires. Ensuite, il s'agit d'un savoir-faire à la fois spécialisé (car qui a besoin de comprendre le détail d'une circulaire administrative sinon les fonctionnaires chargés de l'appliquer?) et purement langagier, car il ne comporte pas de composantes extra-langagières, comme c'est le cas d'autres types de savoir-faire professionnels complexes où la compétence linguistique n'est qu'un élément parmi d'autres. De plus, la dimension de la compréhension écrite n'est pas évaluée pour elle-même, mais à travers son résultat: l'accomplissement d'une tâche nécessitant une compréhension pertinente. En outre, le problème de la compréhension du stimulus secondaire par exemple (la souche et les options d'une QCM traditionnelle, qu'il faudrait d'ailleurs, à mon avis, rédiger, dans la plupart des cas où c'est possible, en langue maternelle) est ici résolu puisque ce qui en tient lieu, ce sont les demandes simulées dont la compréhension mérite d'être évaluée au même titre que celle de la circulaire. Enfin, ce genre d'évaluation, qui n'a pas l'apparence d'une tâche scolaire, se révèle motivante pour des adultes tout en restant parfaitement objective et rigoureuse.

Je dois reconnaître qu'il s'agit ici d'un exemple assez privilégié, et qu'on trouvera peut-être difficilement des techniques, applicables à d'autres types de sous-compétences et à d'autres types d'apprenants, qui réunissent autant d'avantages.

Je voudrais pourtant donner, pour la compréhension orale cette fois, l'exemple d'une technique sensiblement différente, qui comporte un peu plus d'inconvénients que la précédente, mais conçue dans le même esprit. Cette épreuve a été administrée à la session 1982 de l'examen d'aptitudes linguistiques pour le français des personnels de l'UNESCO.

Les candidats recevaient, d'une part, la photocopie d'une page d'agenda vierge divisée en 7 colonnes représentant les journées d'une semaine donnée, et en une douzaine de lignes représentant les tranches horaires de 8 heures du matin à 21 heures; et, d'autre part, une feuille de papier avec les consignes suivantes :

> Vous êtes chargé(e) d'organiser, dans la semaine du lundi 31 mai au dimanche 6 juin, une réunion d'environ deux heures entre trois personnes : le professeur ALVAREZ (A), Madame BERGER (B) et Monsieur COSTA (C). Chacun d'eux vous a donné, enregistré sur répondeur automatique, son emploi du temps pour cette semaine. Vous allez entendre leurs réponses deux fois, avec des pauses. Vous pouvez prendre des notes pendant l'audition, et utiliser la page d'agenda ci-jointe. Faites dans le tableau ci-dessous la liste complète des moments où cette réunion de deux heures sera possible, en indiquant chaque fois : 1) le jour, 2) l'heure, 3) éventuel-

lement à quelles conditions (exemple de condition :
demander à A ou à B ou à C de changer quelque chose qui
peut être changé dans son emploi du temps).

Les candidats entendaient alors un enregistrement qui
comportait, après l'énoncé oral des mêmes consignes, la
description, naturellement simulée, par chacun de ces trois
personnages imaginaires, de ses prévisions d'emploi du temps
pour la semaine en question, avec des contraintes impératives
et des préférences négociables. Le croisement de ces différentes données aboutit, à condition qu'elles aient été comprises, à faire ressortir une série de tranches de 2 heures où
aucun des trois personnages n'a d'empêchement majeur, la
décision du choix définitif du meilleur rendez-vous étant censée
appartenir à quelqu'un d'autre dans une phase ultérieure.

Ici encore, la situation simulée est plausible dans le contexte professionnel des candidats. Ici encore, la compréhension n'est pas évaluée directement, mais à travers l'action
qu'elle permet. Ici encore, la forme du test est relativement
motivante et tout à fait objective.

Mais on tombe cette fois-ci dans un défaut que l'exemple
précédent évitait et qui est l'intervention de savoir-faire autres
que langagiers, à savoir, dans ce cas, une technique très
particulière de prise de notes, mettant en jeu la capacité de
transposer dans une visualisation spéciale, synthétique et
claire des données temporelles, analytiques et hiérarchisées.

Cet inconvénient pourrait cependant, il faut le noter, être
réduit par une présentation informatique de cette épreuve,
puisqu'il est tout à fait possible de construire un programme
qui laisserait l'ordinateur se charger de tout le travail extra-
langagier de synthèse et de visualisation à partir des instructions, justes ou fausses, fournies par l'apprenant. Il est vrai
qu'alors l'évaluation de la compréhension serait encore quelque
peu biaisée par la capacité, à la vérité assez rapide à acquérir
pour cet exercice, de se servir du clavier de l'ordinateur.

Autre inconvénient, mais dont il ne faudrait pas à mon sens
exagérer l'importance : l'énoncé qu'on soumet à la compréhension des apprenants est ici artificiel, entièrement fabriqué par
le constructeur, ce qui peut paraître contradictoire avec la
recherche d'authenticité dont nous parlions tout à l'heure. Je
pense que cette contradiction n'est qu'apparente. En effet,
cette authenticité concernait davantage, dans mon propos, le
contexte situationnel et surtout les opérations mentales mises
en jeu chez l'apprenant, que les énoncés eux-mêmes.

Cela n'empêche pas, bien entendu, de proposer des textes
authentiques pour évaluer la compréhension, dans tous les
types d'exercices qui s'y prêtent.

Mais le problème se pose en termes complètement différents
lorsqu'il s'agit d'énoncés à destinataire individuel, comme c'est

le cas dans notre exemple actuel, ou dans l'exemple précédent en ce qui concerne les lettres des postulants à une indemnité, ou dans tous les cas quotidiens d'échanges verbaux personnels, et lorsqu'il s'agit d'énoncés à destinataires multiples et indéterminés, comme c'est le cas pour les circulaires administratives, mais aussi pour tous les messages véhiculés par les différents médias, écrits ou parlés.

Autant, dans le second cas, il est facile de s'identifier à l'un des innombrables destinataires de l'énoncé, pourvu qu'on fasse partie de sa cible potentielle, autant, dans le premier cas, l'énoncé est tellement dépendant des différents paramètres de la situation d'énonciation que son authenticité devient d'une extrême fragilité : cette authenticité serait certainement tout à fait illusoire si elle se bornait à la seule forme de l'énoncé, tandis que la situation d'énonciation serait, elle, complètement modifiée par la situation d'évaluation.

On a donc tout avantage, pour évaluer la compréhension, à utiliser des textes authentiques de presse, de publications diverses, de radio, de télévision, mais s'il s'agit de "messages personnels", l'authenticité présente de telles difficultés et de tels risques qu'il est sans doute préférable d'y renoncer.

Il est d'ailleurs remarquable de constater, d'une façon tout empirique, que, dans l'usage quotidien de notre langue maternelle et probablement aussi pour la majorité des usagers d'une langue étrangère, la proportion de ces deux catégories d'énoncés que nous avons besoin ou envie de comprendre n'est pas du tout la même pour l'oral et pour l'écrit. Parmi les textes écrits que nous somme amenés à lire, l'énorme majorité a été rédigée non pas pour nous personnellement, mais pour des ensembles plus ou moins vastes et plus ou moins définis de lecteurs plus ou moins anonymes. Pour l'oral, sauf cas marginaux d'asociaux installés en permanence devant leur télévision ou retranchés sous leur walkman, la différence est loin d'être aussi écrasante, et même souvent inversée. Aux enseignants et aux évaluateurs d'en tenir compte.

Pour passer un peu plus rapidement sur des exemples d'évaluation d'autres types de compréhension, je peux mentionner des techniques moins spécialisées, donc plus généralisables.

La compréhension sélective peut se mesurer entre autres par des épreuves du genre de celle-ci : à partir d'un document authentique assez long de type informatif, ou d'un dossier composé de plusieurs documents de sources variées, articles de presse, extraits de rapports, etc., on propose un questionnaire dont les réponses ouvertes sont censées être l'ossature d'un futur exposé (qu'on ne demande pas de rédiger) et sont fournies, en totalité ou en partie, par les sources documentaires proposées.

Ou encore, à partir d'articles ou de rapports ou d'exposés oraux de type argumentatif ou récapitulatif, on remplit, par des réponses ouvertes ou fermées, les cases d'un tableau dont les entrées ont été préparées par l'examinateur dans une optique identique ou différente de celle de la source.

C'est une compréhension globale rapide qui sera mise en jeu par des épreuves comme celle qui consiste à repérer dans un texte informatif long, divisé par exemple en paragraphes numérotés, à quels endroits se trouvent les réponses à certaines questions posées sur le contenu du texte.

Ou celle dont la consigne est de répertorier, selon les entrées d'une classification par exemple thématique, des documents de natures, sources, thèmes, styles et longueurs variés, chacun d'eux pouvant être classé sous une ou plusieurs entrées, la difficulté de l'épreuve pouvant être modulée à volonté par la finesse de la classification, la richesse des entrées, l'abondance et la diversité des documents, la limitation du temps de passation, etc.

Beaucoup des types d'épreuves que je viens de citer peuvent être rangés dans la catégorie des QCM, quand il s'agit de questions à réponses fermées. Mais ce ne sont pas ici des QCM à distracteurs fabriqués par le constructeur du test mais des QCM de classement, variété qui est loin de présenter autant d'inconvénients : ce sont ceux qui demandent aux intéressés de répartir en un certain nombre de classes des textes, des fragments, des éléments quelconques, en fonction de critères bien définis qui peuvent être très naturels et très proches de l'authenticité, s'ils sont adaptés à la fonction des énoncés en question.

L'épreuve de compréhension de circulaire administrative que j'ai mentionnée est un exemple de QCM de ce type, avec, il est vrai, une petite complication supplémentaire, mais facultative, consistant à demander la justification de certaines classes de réponses. Mais le principe de base est de classer les demandes en trois catégories.

Ce modèle permet de générer très facilement des épreuves de compréhension adaptées à toutes sortes de types d'énoncés et à toutes sortes de niveaux, y compris les débutants. Des modes d'emplois, par la répartition d'une liste d'opérations en "obligatoires", "interdites" ou "possibles". Des petites annonces, à classer entre "adaptées", "douteuses" ou "inadaptées" à telle exigence définie. Ou, encore plus simple, des séries d'énoncés brefs, écrits ou oraux, destinés à vérifier les capacités d'interprétation de différentes réalisations d'actes de parole de type binaire, comme l'expression de l'accord ou du désaccord, de l'acceptation ou du refus, de l'opinion favorable ou défavorable, etc. Il s'agit bien ici d'une interprétation en situation authentique, d'un savoir-faire pragmatique simple.

Les épreuves de ce genre conservent, me semble-t-il, les avantages théoriques et pratiques qu'on s'accorde généralement à reconnaître aux QCM (évaluation spécifique de la compréhension, objectivité, rapidité de correction) sans en avoir les inconvénients : ni la difficulté de construction (car ici pas de distracteurs à imaginer), ni le rôle du hasard (car la simplicité de l'exercice autorise la multiplication des items, qui réduit ce rôle), ni la schématisation excessive (car les oppositions accord/désaccord ou acceptation/refus ou recevable/irrecevable sont elles-mêmes schématiques).

Dans d'autres cas, avec d'autres types de textes, ce seront les questions à réponses ouvertes qui seront les plus appropriées ou, comme nous l'avons vu dans notre premier exemple, un mélange des deux formules.

L'inconvénient du procédé des réponses ouvertes est avant tout pratique, car il diminue la rapidité de correction et la perfection de l'objectivité, mais ce n'est pas une raison suffisante pour l'exclure de l'éventail des techniques utilisables, si l'authenticité, la diversité et la validité peuvent y gagner.

ÉVALUATION DE L'EXPRESSION

L'éventail des techniques utilisables semble malheureusement moins vaste pour l'évaluation de l'expression, toujours plus délicate et plus problématique que celle de la compréhension. L'une des raisons de cette difficulté est certainement le rôle, bien différent de ce qui se passe en compréhension, que jouent respectivement la liberté et la contrainte dans l'activité langière de l'expression.

En situation authentique de compréhension, en effet, l'énoncé qu'il s'agit de comprendre nous est donné tel quel, nous est en quelque sorte imposé, et dans son contenu et dans sa forme. Certes, il y a presque toujours une marge de liberté d'interprétation qui est laissée à l'auditeur ou au lecteur, mais cette marge est relativement étroite.

Au contraire, en situation authentique d'expression, l'énoncé que nous produisons est le résultat d'un libre choix, tout au moins dans sa forme, sauf cas de production stéréotypée. D'où le caractère hautement artificiel et même scolastique de nombreuses épreuves traditionnelles, encore hélas! très répandues en Europe, qui imposent aux apprenants des contraintes formelles, au prix, bien souvent, de consignes métalinguistiques diamétralement opposées à l'authenticité.

Mais on peut penser que les non moins traditionnelles épreuves d'expression "libre" tombent, elles aussi, pour des raisons inverses, dans l'artifice : les récits sur consignes vagues, les descriptions d'images, les commentaires de textes correspondent à des activités langagières peu fréquentes dans la réalité et, surtout, laissent au locuteur, dans le contenu même de son énoncé, une liberté anormalement grande, dont on ne bénéficie que rarement dans la vie réelle.

Car, dans l'énorme majorité des cas réels, le contexte énonciatif et surtout l'intention de communication (même si cette intention résulte elle-même d'un libre choix) fournissent des contraintes impératives qu'ignorent totalement les épreuves d'expression libre. Quand on parle ou qu'on écrit, c'est naturellement avec une intention de communication précise, pour traduire en mots l'idée qu'on a dans la tête, et non pas n'importe qu'elle idée.

Or, dans les épreuves traditionnelles d'expression libre, il est impossible d'évaluer la pertinence du contenu, sauf précisément dans des cas où cette pertinence relève d'autre chose que des compétences langagières en expression : une rédaction "hors du sujet", un commentaire de texte mal approprié révèlent surtout des déficiences dans la compréhension du sujet à traiter ou du texte à commenter, non dans les capacités d'expression. Autrement, en vertu de quoi pénaliserait-on un candidat qui, par exemple, raconterait des événements hautement improbables qu'il prétendrait, contre toute vraisemblance, avoir vécus? La pertinence du contenu de l'expression échappe donc bien complètement, dans ce cas, à l'évaluation, alors qu'il s'agit d'une qualité essentielle de la communication.

Quels critères d'évaluation reste-t-il donc dans ces épreuves? L'évaluation scolaire traditionnelle prend souvent en compte des critères comme l'originalité ou l'imagination. Mais s'agit-il de compétences langagières? Et ces compétences ont-elles la moindre pertinence dans un usage professionnel de la langue? Au contraire, la langue administrative, par exemple, ou la langue commerciale sont déterminées non seulement par leur fonction strictement utilitaire, mais encore par l'existence de stéréotypes et de modèles. L'imagination, la richesse d'invention, l'originalité, l'expressivité, la créativité y ont vraiment peu de place.

Et, en définitive, il ne reste plus guère, dans ce genre d'épreuves, qu'un critère unique, celui de la conformité aux normes linguistiques, de la correction. C'est bien là le critère essentiel et souvent exclusif de l'évaluation traditionnelle de l'expression : peu importe, à la limite, ce qu'on écrit, pourvu que ce soit correct.

Pour évaluer cette dimension essentielle qui consiste à exprimer, de façon à la fois exacte et compréhensible, une intention de communication bien définie, il faut en fait des épreuves à consignes contraignantes simulant les contraintes d'une situation authentique c'est-à-dire portant uniquement sur la signification, non sur la forme. Et, pour que ce genre de tâche ait un sens et soit autre chose qu'une simple copie ou une répétition mécanique, il est nécessaire que le mode d'expression de la consigne et celui de la tâche attendue soient différents, et qu'il y ait transposition.

Une première sorte de transposition possible est celle de l'oral à l'écrit par la transmission écrite d'un message oral. Il est facile d'imaginer des exercices de ce genre adaptés à l'âge, au niveau, aux intérêts, aux besoins de n'importe quels apprenants. Voici un exemple de consigne possible pour une situation de relations civiles, non professionnelles, pour des apprenants presque débutants.

"Vous êtes chez votre ami X, qui est francophone dans un pays francophone. Le téléphone sonne. Vous décrochez. C'est Y, qui veut vous laisser pour X un message urgent que vous allez entendre. Mais vous devez partir tout de suite. Alors vous laissez le message par écrit à X, qui le trouvera quand il rentrera."

On peut donner alors n'importe quel type de message, très simple ou plus complexe, avec des pauses ou avec un débit rapide, avec le contenu qu'on voudra, et on aura la possibilité d'évaluer une capacité langagière tout à fait authentique, qui présente la particularité de combiner compréhension et expression, qu'une tradition relativement récente exige, abusivement me semble-t-il, de séparer systématiquement dans l'évaluation.

Il est vrai que, dans le cas d'une évaluation formative, le diagnostic risque de manquer de précision, mais ce genre d'épreuves est plutôt utile pour tester des savoir-faire langagiers en cours d'acquisition. C'est le résultat final d'une association très naturelle entre compréhension orale et expression écrite qui est évalué, la compréhension orale l'étant ici encore par l'acte, linguistique cette fois, qu'elle permet, et l'expression écrite pouvant être évaluée d'une façon tout à fait fonctionnelle, puisque l'important ici est de transmettre de façon à la fois exacte, complète et intelligible le sens du message entendu. Ce qui permet une évaluation analytique aussi rigoureuse que possible et utilisant le critère de pertinence, beaucoup plus important que celui de correction linguistique, le tout se plaçant dans une situation de communication tout à fait plausible.

Il existe un autre type de transposition, plus riche encore de possibilités, c'est le passage d'une langue à une autre, c'est-à-dire, puisqu'il s'agit d'expression écrite ou orale en langue étrangère, la transposition de la langue maternelle, ou d'une langue seconde bien maîtrisée, à la langue-cible.

On assiste actuellement en Europe à une réhabilitation de ce procédé dans l'évaluation. Il ne s'agit pas vraiment de la traduction au sens strict du terme - qui exige, qu'il s'agisse d'interprétation simultanée ou de traduction de textes littéraires, ou de spécialité, des capacités très sophistiquées et professionnelles, que la plupart des apprenants n'auront jamais besoin d'acquérir -, mais d'une simple transposition de sens d'une langue à l'autre, par exemple à partir de consignes détaillées qui ne sont contraignantes que sur la signification de ce qu'on a à dire, non sur l'aspect formel.

Certes, cette technique n'est pas toujours possible. Elle est exclue de fait quand, par exemple, le groupe des apprenants ou des candidats est linguistiquement hétérogène. C'est d'ailleurs précisément le cas, et pour cause, dans les organisations internationales, où la multiplicité des langues maternelles et la diversité des langues de travail constituent des obstacles insurmontables.

L'usage de la langue maternelle est sans doute à manier avec précaution dans l'apprentissage et même en évaluation : il heurte, en tout cas, certains principes hérités des méthodes directes et structuro-globales. Mais pourquoi se priver, dans les cas où elle est utilisable, d'une technique d'évaluation à la fois commode, efficace et proche de l'authenticité puisque, dans l'usage réel d'une langue étrangère qu'on ne maîtrise pas encore, c'est bien souvent dans la langue maternelle, ou dans une autre langue étrangère mieux maîtrisée, que l'intention de communication se verbalise d'abord.

De plus, un bilingue, même s'il s'agit d'un bilinguisme encore embryonnaire, peut se trouver très plausiblement dans toutes sortes de situations où il pourra utiliser sa double compétence. Et ces situations ont toutes les chances d'être motivantes puisqu'elles sont valorisantes pour celui qui s'y trouve, même si une face de cette double compétence est encore très limitée. Enfin, pour l'évaluateur, elles constituent une mine inépuisable de simulations tout à fait opératoires pour une évaluation réellement communicative.

Je dirai pour conclure que ces considérations très partielles ne prétendent pas proposer une solution à tous les problèmes, dont beaucoup ne sont pas près d'être résolus. Je pense, par exemple, à celui de l'objectivité de l'évaluation directe de l'expression, tout au moins en situation d'évaluation certificative puisque, dans l'évaluation formative, l'auto-évaluation, dont l'importance et l'efficacité sont bien démontrées, résoud la question d'une autre manière; ou encore, toujours dans l'évaluation certificative, au problème de la simulation d'une situation d'expression orale, ou à celui de l'arbitraire du seuil de réussite, ou encore à celui de la conciliation des exigences contradictoires d'économie et de représentativité.

Mais le fait que l'évaluation en langue étrangère ou seconde mette désormais davantage l'accent sur les savoir-faire langagiers, après l'avoir mis un peu trop sur les connaissances linguistiques, constitue très certainement un progrès en lui-même, même si beaucoup d'autres progrès restent à accomplir.

II
APPLICATIONS

5.
Second Language Performance Testing for University and Professional Contexts

Brendan J. Carroll

INTRODUCTION

In this paper, I wish to follow through the design and development of linguistic-communicative tests to the operational end where decisions are made about individuals or groups of testees. My primary task as a test consultant has always been to help my clients to make better decisions about their employees, trainees or students. Just as passengers would be nervous about a pilot whose pre-occupations were engine design and aerodynamics rather than guiding the plane and its passengers safely to their destination, so would my clients feel uneasy if they considered that my priority lay in uncovering the nature of language or devising new methods of statistically analyzing human communicative behaviour rather than in providing them with practical, intelligible guidance about their own testees.

It is unfortunate that we do not at present have a comprehensive, detailed theory of the nature of language communication. From my attendance at TESOL colloquia over five years, it seems to me that some experts say one thing and some another; in short, they have not come up with a generally accepted leakproof theory of language necessary for measuring linguistic behaviour. In this partial vacuum, those of us whose

responsibility it is primarily to devise and operate test systems
for real human beings will be excused if we look, in the first
instance, at the communicative settings in which our testees
will operate, structure those settings by means of a communicative needs specification and devise tests which pick up salient features of the specifications as economically as possible,
the resulting instrument then being subjected to scrutiny
under such criteria as relevance, stability, acceptability and
practicality.

One major consideration is, of course, validity.   But
where is the criterion which can validate our criteria?   The
answer - again in the absence of a foolproof conceptual framework for validation - must at present be that validation rests
on a constellation of objective correlational measures and subjective operational judgements ultimately based on the exercise
of human common sense. For me, two features of this constellation of special import are, first, the measure of agreement
between the subjects' test results and the judgement of
experienced language teachers familiar with those testees and,
secondly, the extent to which the results provide accurate
guidance to the making of decisions about the testees.   In
these ways I believe it is possible to introduce quality control
and teaching programme direction in a way sadly lacking in
most language teaching contexts.

In several projects, I and my collaborators have been able
to realize the above ideas in practice.   In 1980 the British
Council and the Cambridge Examinations Syndicate launched
the English Language Testing Service (ELTS), which has now
tested some 20,000 overseas scholarship applicants in over 100
centres around the world   (Carroll 1981). A steady stream of
data is being amassed to provide an assessment of the
measurement characteristics and practicality of this testing
system   (Seaton 1983).   In 1981, the Royal Society of Arts
introduced its examination in the use of Communicative English
(Royal Society of Arts Examinations Board 1980), and in Qatar
a new communicative system of tests and examinations was
started for the children using a new functional, communicative
language course.[1]   In 1982, the tests devised for NATO/
SHAPE,[2] closely job-related, were put into operation and the
Pergamon General and Specific Test Publications began to be
released.[3]   And, very recently, the training programme for
Aramco Oil Company executives was equipped with a full test
system for placement, progress and accreditation purposes as
well as the groundwork for developing aptitude tests to predict
future rates of language learning.[4]

Those who need the fortifying wine of statistical analysis
will be comforted to know that the above projects in communi-

cative testing are systematically providing data to indicate how far this type of test is a genuine and practical instrument. Without releasing premature statistics, it can be said that the prognosis is excellent - reliability figures being often higher than for existing tests and validation indices very considerably higher. The tests also prove, because of their authenticity, much more acceptable, and even enjoyable, to the testees, to me possibly their most significant advantage.

PRINCIPLES OF COMMUNICATIVE TESTING

Before discussing the actual tests I have been working on, I would like to touch on a few points of principle bearing on their design and use.

Replication

In devising my tests, I have given special attention to what I call the principle of replication - the need to incorporate in my tests as many as can sensibly and economically be included of the communicative features of the settings which the testee is likely to encounter. Although this is a "direct" approach to testing it is neither a wholly "ad hoc" nor a pragmatic one but a model-based approach deriving from, as it were, a functional map. That is, we have to consider constructs. For example, it is rare in job settings to find separated the skills of listening, speaking, reading and writing. Arriving at the office, one reads a memo, speaks and listens on the phone, converses with a colleague face-to-face, dictates a letter, studies a report, meanwhile answering personal or telephone enquiries from time to time, all as a preparation for an inter-departmental meeting or crucial annual report. To test merely listening and the other skills one by one, even deliberately to isolate them for testing purposes, seems to me to strip the tests of a very important integratory skill, to fall into the "objectivity trap" lying in wait for those who hanker for atomizing and counting facets of human behaviour. I believe that the manipulation of data must be subordinate to the questions which we wish to answer.

Functional Specification

I think the initial consumer resistance to communicative needs analysis has by now been well overcome, and needs analysis is an activity requiring little defence. Nevertheless, there remain at least two areas of controversy worth mentioning. First, the needs analysis emphasis on the product, i.e., target behaviours, can tend to overshadow process, i.e., the mechanisms of learning or behaving which contribute to the product. We need a diachronic as well as a synchronic section. I do not believe, however, that to form a clear picture of target behaviour whilst devising language tests and programmes is of itself undesirable and, in any event, ignorance of such an important area can hardly earn one any extra points. Any insights provided during the course of a specification exercise must surely give us the opportunity of making more enriched tests.

The second point concerns the degree of detail necessary for forming a test design basis - a full Council of Europe or Munby analysis is a painstaking, time-consuming business as it may take several weeks to examine one job (Van Ek 1975; Munby 1978). I think the answer is one of practicality rather than principle. In my first test specifications (Carroll 1980, 1981), my colleagues and I followed the full analysis procedures primarily to give the new specification model a fair wind - that is, arbitrarily to cut out certain parameters on a priori, intuitive grounds would not give the model the serious consideration it deserved. In due course, I found that for academic English we could afford to de-emphasize several specification areas such as attitudinal tones, social relationships and many aspects of the physical and psychological environment, and still produce highly valid and reliable tests. This is not to say that the personal relationship between teacher and student could be ignored in certain contexts; however, there were strong reasons on discriminatory grounds why we did not test the skills of our overseas students in cultural matters which grew from our Western (and to them foreign) cultural standards. "Thank God it's Friday" would have a very different connotation for a Muslim! Such considerations could be relevant for problem diagnosis but improper for initial selection purposes.

Statistical Treatment

Compared with the usual wide-spectrum samples of traditional general purpose proficiency tests, the specific-purpose samples are, naturally, much more restricted in both size and range. Indeed, from a statistical point of view we could in English for Specific Purposes (ESP) have a sample of one person representing a population of one as against a general proficiency sample group of five thousand representing a population of five million. The more specific a sample is, the less appropriate becomes the use of the statistics of probability.

From the practical point of view, the restriction of numbers and range of my ESP testees makes it more difficult to carry out item analysis, establish indices of internal consistency, assess the significance of correlation coefficients and establish acceptable norm-referenced standards of performance. There is also a fair wastage of one's efforts in test production in that we could put weeks of work into devising a one-off test for a given person or group. In other words, when we opt, on wider educational grounds, for specific-purpose testing we give ourselves several statistical headaches. But it would be educationally just as wrong for us to constrain our test strategies to fit the statistical procedures available as it would be for a teacher to restrict his or her teaching just to those areas which he can easily test.

I am using certain devices to meet this problem of sample/population constriction and hope in due course to comment on them, but whatever we do, we will, I think, be forced more towards content/construct and intuitive/subjective validations and less to mechanical, numerative statistics; overall, to rely on subjectivity rather than objectivity in test construction and appraisal.

Now, to say this must be a great provocation to the devotees of scientific human behaviour measurement. How many times have I been told, "Ah yes, that test looks quite nice but it is subjective," as if the test were thus worthy to be consigned to the scrap heap. I myself would go in the other direction to an extent and query the applicability of a very objective measurement process to a field so complex as human communicative behaviour where we impose a superstructure of measurement on an extremely complex mechanism. In practice, what I do is to establish performance profiles which combine "hard" (or objective) and "soft" (or subjective) elements so as to optimize the particular advantages of each type of measurement. I find that I give a lot of attention to this psychometric balancing act between hard and soft procedures in developing my test systems and hope that some method can be seen in my madness.

The Curriculum-Test Relationship

As an educationist, I see the test primarily as part of a learning/teaching process and not as an entity in itself. Clearly, any measuring instrument worthy of the name must have certain basic characteristics, but the role of the test in the educational process is to operate at a higher level of significance than measurement. It has always been my objective to ensure that the test is a benign influence on educational programmes and that is partly why I do not like to see a test of human skills put in a mechanical, inhuman format. This issue is too big for statistics to guide us. The most gratifying experience in my testing projects over the last five years has been to devise tests which are also a wholesome influence on programme directions and on teaching strategies even if, in the process, I have occasionally caused raised eyebrows in the community of testers and examiners. I look for tests which vitalize teaching, not lay a dead hand on it.

One outstanding example of subjectively assessed performance has been the value of the Group Oral test in our recent test batteries. This test usually has been the single best predictor of both performances on the test as a whole and of subsequent performance in the programme as indicated by independent teacher estimates. In spite of possibly justified criticisms on measurement grounds, we find that the group task encapsulates on-job experiences to a high degree and, given coordinated and monitored multiple assessments, is a stable assessment instrument.

The Test and Decision-Making

After all the academic research and statistical analysis, the important thing is how far the test can help us in making decisions about our testees. The principal questions needing to be answered are, in my experience: (1) Has the testee the linguistic mastery to do a particular job? and/or (2) What sort of tuitional course would be needed to bring him to that level of mastery? Unless we have made a close study of the communicative demands of a job and unless we have techniques for matching a testee's performance to those demands, we cannot answer these two questions. In fact, I think that few language tests I know can do so. The question they can answer is: Given a group of testees how can we rank them in order of general linguistic competence? Unfortunately this is not a question my clients usually ask of me. In other words, in my experience, existing language tests give the answer to a question which few people ask and fail to give the answers which everyone seems to expect.

MODELS FOR LANGUAGE TESTING

To focus on decision-making via the use of language tests we will now discuss several working outlines: the English Language Testing Service (ELTS) (Seaton 1983), a diagnostic

English test system, a professional English language test system, and management by a nine-point performance scale.

The ELTS

Figure 1 shows the main elements of the test framework by the ELTS, the disciplinary areas, test pattern options and possible target levels in terms of a 9-band performance scale (cf. Appendix 1). From experience in some 100 countries worldwide, we find that the target levels accepted by British institutions range between Bands 5 and 7, with 6 being the most common level, the lower bands being acceptable for courses in technology, mathematics and the physical sciences, and the higher bands being required by such courses as social and political science. Many institutions require minimum performance in particular areas (such as listening comprehension) and also use the performance profile to identify a student's particular strengths and weaknesses. Bio-data are collected for all examinees, and tests for non-academic purposes are also under development.

Reliability indices for the objective tests range from 0.84 to 0.92 with a median of 0.88 (KR20).[5] Full monitoring, including long-term validation, is in progress using the RAMIS computer programme and a new Test Report Form.[6] The ELTS is thus an exemplar for a diversified test system derived from detailed specifications of the communicative needs of a range of academic programmes followed by wide-scale trials and use and a detailed and continuing monitoring process.

Complimenting the ELTS, which serves a variety of British institutions, are other testing systems designed to prescribe pedagogical programmes for students based on their individual needs. These are described below.

FIGURE 1   The English Language Testing Service
(ELTS) Outline

General

```
G1  Reading

    40 Multiple Choice
       Questions
    Test Length:  40 minutes

G2  Listening

    35 Multiple Choice
       Questions
    Test Length:  30 minutes
```

Disciplinary

DISCIPLINARY AREAS

```
M1   Study Skills

     40 Multiple Choice
        Questions
     Test Length: 55 minutes

M2   Writing

     2 Topics
     Test Length:  40 minutes

M3   Oral

     3-Phase Interview
     Test Length:  10 minutes
```

Life Sciences
Medicine
Physical Sciences
Social Studies
Technology
General Academic
Non-Academic

TEST OPTIONS

All Tests (5)
Disciplinary Only (3)
G1, G2, and Oral
G1 and Bio-data
Non-Academic
(Total Test Length:
   50-180 minutes)

Diagnostic English Test System

In cases where universities accept applicants on their academic track record without specific reference to English language competence, it often happens that certain students are "at risk" because of weaknesses in their communication skills. A detailed diagnostic system is being developed with several such universities to identify the strengths and weaknesses of students likely to have communication problems and to give appropriate remedial treatment to help them reach adequate levels of mastery.

In Table 1 is shown the diagnostic framework for the system with an example of a student "at risk" in several skill areas. Further workshops to develop this test system are planned and should result in further useful instruments for decision-making about students and remedial English courses.

Professional English Language Test System

One of the most comprehensive language test systems with which I am concerned is that of a large oil company (Aramco) which gives high priority to the English language training of Arabic-speaking mid-level executives. The full test system incorporates placement, progress and final accreditation tests. Diagnostic and aptitude test batteries are also under development.

The professional English programme consists of 900 hours of tuition divided into three 300-hour levels and preceded, where necessary, by a basic preparatory course. The test content (source booklets, course tapes and test tasks) is drawn from the company's work setting and is directly related to the content of the language course which itself was constructed on the basis of a detailed needs analysis. The tests themselves, as the course develops, are increasingly based on authentic tasks and become increasingly thematic and project-oriented. The tests at the final level are in fact two projects, one based on a parking and traffic problem (the "Traffic Congestion File"), the other on the problems of an expanding manufacturing company (the "Shelco File").

Trainees are given the source materials the day before the test and are given a guided tour through them. They can then work singly or in groups to gain insight into the background of the project. The tests themselves consist of wide-ranging reading tasks, listening comprehension, paired and grouped discussion of problems and a final written report of each individual's conclusions and recommendations.

TABLE 1 Diagnostic Academic English Test
Sample Profile of "At Risk" Student X

Levels of Skill Analysis	Macro-Level		Transcode	Style	Meta-Level			Micro-Level		
	Message	Ideas			Logic	Strategies	Reference	Stress	Vocabulary	Graphology/Phonology
Graphic	3*	3	2	2	3	2	1	4	4	4
Oral	4	3	2	2	4	4	2	4	4	5
Mixed	4	4	2	3	3	2	2	4	4	5
Totals	11	10	6	7	10	8	5	12	12	14

Diagnostic Band (5-point scale)	Approximate Equivalent On 9-band scale
5 – competent	7
4 – marginal	6
3 – sub-marginal	5
2 – very deficient	4
1 – rudimentary	3–

* Areas of concern are all those with values less than 4.
Pedagogical prescription for Student X: five programmes of 30 hours, including macro and meta-level graphic and oral skills, meta-level mixed skills.

A performance profile for each trainee is then constructed based on the various objectively and subjectively assessed activities elicited by the project (see Table 2).

TABLE 2   Trainee Language Performance Profiles

Name	ID #	R	W	L	I	G	All
A	085	4	4	5	4+	5	4+
B	229	5	5	4+	5	4+	5
C	229	4+	6	5+	6+	6+	6
D	236	7	6	7+	6+	7	7
E	250	6	5	5+	5+	5	5+
F	290	6+	7+	6+	7	7	7
G	007	6+	5	5	5+	6	5+
H	008	6+	6	5+	4+	6	6
I	013	4+	4	5	5+	5+	5
J	029	5+	5	4+	5	5	5
K	031	5	5	6+	7	6	6
L	040	4+	4+	4+	6+	5+	5
M	055	6+	5+	6	5	--	6
N	099	4+	--	4	5+	4	4+

KEY: Scale: (1 to 9)
R = Reading   I = Interview   9 = Complete Mastery
W = Writing   G = Group Task   1 = Non-user of English
L = Listening   All = Overall

At the basic preparatory level, intensive diagnostic work is done on the trainees' linguistic enabling skills. The common linguistic problems arising at each of the three programme levels are also being listed for individual remedial work using "Apple" computers. A parallel study is being made to identify characteristics likely to assess aptitude for language learning in terms of rate of progress from band to band on the 9-band scale in terms of the number of hours per band. For all tests, reliability and validity indices are being calculated on an expanding data base; initial indications based on limited numbers are so far extremely promising.

Management by Performance Scale

The 9-band performance scale is sufficiently flexible and precise to be used in a work-related language training programme. There are very few test systems comprehensive or explicit enough to establish accountability, proper quality control and programme management. By using the 9-band performance scale, it is possible to express, in common terms and in a way comprehensible to both managers and trainees, the main operational features of language performance from initial placement through to final accreditation. One current application of this system is described below and in Table 2 and Figure 2. Each trainee is first given a profile based on his performance in each test (Table 2). These profiles form the basis for placement and promotion (Figure 2) and remedial teaching until they attain Band 4, then they join the mainstream course.

FIGURE 2   Management by Performance Scale: Example

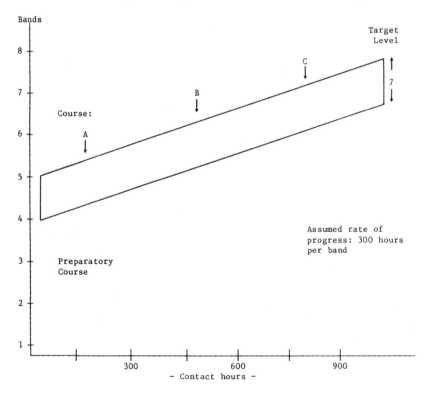

Their progress is then monitored at 150-hour intervals. On achieving Band 5, they may join Course B and then, at Band 6, join Course C. Completion of the course comes at Band 7 - a high performance standard for any non-native speaker and now being achieved quite widely under the impetus of a well-designed and conducted communicative language programme supported by appropriately designed management instruments in the shape of the test system described above.

CONCLUSION

In this paper, I have outlined the recent progress made in moving from the typical discrete-item language centred tests of yesterday to the project-based, job-related test system as exemplified in the "Shelco File" test. I have tried to rationalize this development in theoretical terms but make no claim to theoretical purity or completeness. At present my basic criteria for test validity are, first, parallel assessments by experienced teachers and, secondly, operational effectiveness as managerial instruments.

At a deeper level, our validation will eventually lie in a full, coherent description of linguistic behaviour and our tests will be valid insofar as they realize this description and apply it effectively in specific instances.

NOTES

1. The actual tests are not released by the Ministry of Education, but there are descriptions in the Oxford University Press publications: 1980, Teacher Training Manual for the Crescent English Course, ELTA/OUP. 1981, London Workshop (for the Crescent English Programme), ELTA/OUP.

2. These tests are not available because of the close security of these organizations.

3. The background to much of these tests can be found in: Carroll, B. 1980. Testing Communicative Performance. Oxford: Pergamon Press.

4. Like NATO, these tests are treated as secure and are not available.

5. These figures are taken from the British Council/ Cambridge Syndicate, First Report on the ELTS, p. 4, February 1982.

6. This is taken from the British Council/Cambridge Syndicate, Second Annual Report, p. 1, November 1982.

REFERENCES

Canale, M., and M. Swain. 1980. Theoretical bases of communicative approaches to second language teaching and testing. Applied Linguistics 1.1.

Carroll, B. 1980. Testing Communicative Performance. Oxford: Pergamon Press.

Carroll, B. 1981. Specifications for an English language testing service. In Alderson, J., and A. Hughes (eds.), Issues in Language Testing. ELT document 111. London: The British Council.

Carroll, B. 1982a. Is there another way? In Heaton, B. (ed.), Language Testing. Oxford: Modern English Publications.

Carroll, B. 1982b. Communicative testing. In Lutjeharms, M. and T. Culhane (eds.), Practice and Problems in Language Testing. I.U.S.

Carroll, B. (In press a). The English Language Testing Service. In Jordan, W. (ed.), Case Studies in ELT. London: Collins.

Carroll, B. (In press b). Issues in the testing of language for specific purposes. In Hughes, A., and P. Porter (eds.), BAAL Language Testing Seminar, December 1981. New York: Academic Press.

Munby, J. 1978. Communicative Syllabus Design. Cambridge: Cambridge University Press.

Royal Society of Arts Examining Board. 1980. Examinations in the Communicative Use of English as a Foreign Language. London: Royal Society of Arts.

Seaton, I. 1983. Issues in the development and operation of the English Language Testing Service (ELTS) 1976-1983. Paper presented at the TESOL Seventeenth Annual Convention, Toronto.

Van Ek, J. 1975. The Threshold Level in a European Unit/Credit System for Modern Language learning by Adults. Strasbourg: Council of Europe.

Wesche, M. 1981. Communicative testing in a second language. Canadian Modern Language Review. 37.3.

APPENDIX 1   From: Carroll 1980

1. General assessment scale

Band

9	Expert user. Communicates with authority, accuracy and style. Completely at home in idiomatic and specialist English.
8	Very good user. Presentation of subject clear and logical with fair style and appreciation of attitudinal markers. Often approaching bilingual competence.
7	Good user. Would cope in most situations in an English-speaking environment. Occasional slips and restrictions of language will not impede communication.
6	Competent user. Although coping well with most situations he is likely to meet, is somewhat deficient in fluency and accuracy and will have occasional misunderstandings or significant errors.
5	Modest user. Although he manages in general to communicate, often uses inaccurate or in appropriate language.
4	Marginal user. Lacking in style, fluency and accuracy, is not easy to communicate with, accent and usage cause misunderstandings. Generally can get by without serious breakdowns.
3	Extremely limited user. Does not have a working knowledge of the language for day-to-day purposes, but better than an absolute beginner. Neither productive nor receptive skills allow continuous communications.
2	Intermittent user. Performance well below level of a working day-to-day knowledge of the language. Communication occurs only sporadically.
1/0	Non-user. May not even recognize with certainty which language is being used.

(Editor's Note: More detailed versions exist for oral
                              assessments, etc.)

6.
Development and Validation of a Performance-Based Test of ESL "Survival Skills"

John L.D. Clark and Allene G. Grognet

The recent arrival in the United States of large numbers of non- or limited-English-speaking refugees from Indochina and other regions created the need for development of performance-based testing procedures to assess the refugees' ability to accomplish basic "survival" tasks in English, including, for example, giving basic autobiographical information orally, telling time, asking for and giving directions, shopping for food and clothing, describing emergency situations, dealing with health and housing matters, reading printed caution signs, and filling out simple data forms. This paper describes the development, trial administration, statistical analysis, and initial validation of an English proficiency test battery designed for use with this examinee population, and concludes with a discussion of further validation studies that are being planned for these instruments.

BACKGROUND

Between 1975 and mid-1983, nearly one million refugees entered the United States from the countries of Indochina: Cambodia, Laos, and Vietnam. Of these, only a very small percentage came already speaking English, or accustomed to Western culture and values. To cope with this situation, massive resettlement efforts were mounted which included, as major components, the development of English as a Second Language (ESL) and Cultural Orientation (CO) courses designed specifically for refugee needs. These activities have had a profound effect on both the ESL and cross-cultural training fields.

The language learning and cultural orientation needs of the Indochinese refugees differed considerably from those of the typical adult English language student. Besides having little English ability, many refugees had received little or no formal education in their native country; thus, classes oriented towards refugees were often faced with the task of teaching basic literacy and numeracy in addition to developing English proficiency per se. The functional language requirements of refugees - involving for the most part acquisition of the survival or coping skills needed to obtain basic necessities such as food, clothing, shelter, and transportation; perform adequately in entry-level employment; and interact on an elementary social level with native English speakers - constituted quite different instructional goals from those typical of more traditional ESL instruction.

Faced with these new instructional needs, adult ESL programs addressed to refugee populations began to change their emphases and techniques. Special intensive and semi-intensive ESL programs for refugees were funded by both federal and state governments, and competency-based, functionally oriented curricula stressing survival skills were developed. Corresponding textbooks were written and published, including ESL texts for learners illiterate in any language. The locales for ESL instruction also expanded beyond the school or college classroom to include factories, church basements, community centers, and a variety of other learning sites. Curriculum guides, training programs, and other materials and procedures began to be developed to assist the refugee class teacher, often a volunteer with little or no prior training or experience.

By mid-1981, as a result of large-scale funding and manpower investment, as well as the diligent efforts of ESL/CO specialists and others, the refugee training programs that had been developed could be generally perceived as doing a rather creditable job of guiding students to the desired linguistic performance and cultural familiarity.

However, such an appraisal could be made only on the basis of impressionistic or anecdotal information, since there were not available, within the testing field, reliable and valid measures of either survival English proficiency or cultural knowledge/performance at a level or in a form appropriate to the refugee training situation. In recognition of the crucial need to develop and make available appropriate assessment instruments for use in the refugee context, in early 1981, Region I (Northeastern United States) of the Office of Refugee Resettlement, Department of Health and Human Services (ORR/ HHS) contracted with the Center for Applied Linguistics (CAL) to develop a competency-based test of survival-level English for use with Indochinese and other refugees receiving basic ESL instruction in the United States.[1]

Test Content and Format Planning

Initial planning of test content, as well as overall test format, involved the close collaboration of CAL project staff and a group of approximately 20 ESL teachers and administrators representing each of the Region I refugee training centers funded by ORR/HHS. The first activity in this regard was the holding of a two-day working conference to discuss and come to agreement on (1) the particular language-use tasks considered crucial for survival in situations routinely faced by refugees (for example, giving personal information upon request, telling time, shopping for food and clothing, dealing with health problems or emergencies); (2) the communicative functions implicit in each situation (for example, imparting information, seeking information, and seeking clarification); and (3) the syntactic or morphological structures at issue in each instance (for example, simple present and present progressive tenses, "yes", "no", and "wh" questions, and negation). Although a detailed experimental study of the kinds of language situations actually encountered by refugees in daily living contexts would have been a quite desirable preliminary activity, both time constraints and funding limitations precluded this approach. However, the informed, collective judgment of the project participants, which together reflected many years of intensive experience in the refugee resettlement context, was considered to constitute a very high level of expertise in and suitability for the content specification work. The high degree of unanimity among the participants concerning the language-use situations recommended for inclusion in the test was also considered corroborative of close familiarity with refugee language needs.

In addition to developing the overall content specifications, the planning conference members established a number of rather stringent technical performance requirements for the test, as summarized below.

(1) The test should be usable with all refugees to the United States, regardless of native language, age, sex, amount of previous education, degree of urbanity or rurality, or

degree of literacy in the native language. From a test development standpoint, this meant that, among other things, the
examinee's native language could not be used to present the
test stimuli at least without the use of separate versions of the
test for each native language, an operationally unfeasible
approach. In addition, many of the ordinary testing procedures, such as use of a separate answer sheet or multiple-
choice space marking, were not appropriate for examinees who
in most instances have no prior experience with these
techniques.

(2) The test should include those language situations
which have face validity. It was anticipated that teachers,
program coordinators, funding agency supervisors, legislative
bodies, and others would understand and endorse the developed
instruments, as well as give credence to the measurement
information provided, in direct proportion to the extent to
which the tasks presented in the test itself could be viewed as
having face and content validity and thus being examplars of
the tasks they were intended to reflect. Also, since there
were no other known face-valid or otherwise validated tests of
proficiency at the survival level for use with this population
(and against which the test to be developed could in principle
be compared), it was considered essential for the new instrument to be able to stand on its own on face/content validity
grounds.

(3) The test should assess all four language skills: listening comprehension, speaking, reading, and writing. Listening
comprehension and speaking, especially in a conversational
setting, were considered the predominant survival skills in
terms of frequency and extent of use, but it was also recogni-
zed that rudimentary reading and writing tasks (for example,
understanding common public signs such as "no smoking",
"emergency exit", etc., or filling out a simple biographical
data form) were also important components of adequate performance at this level. It was therefore recommended that the
basic instrument to be developed (which eventually became
known as the core test) contain these types of reading/writing
tasks in addition to tasks addressing listening comprehension/-
speaking. To assess reading comprehension and writing at a
level somewhat higher than survival (up to about that required
for entry-level employment of further educational pursuits), a
separate literacy skills section devoted to these two skills was
also planned and developed.

(4) The test should be easy to administer and to score
reliably by volunteers who could not be presumed to have any

specialized training in ESL teaching techniques or in language testing. Numerous implications for test format and administration procedure arose from this consideration, including the following: (a) Total testing time needed would be kept as short as possible consistent with satisfactory content coverage and scoring reliability (no more than 15 minutes envisioned for the individually-administered core section and no more than 60 minutes for the group-administered literacy skills section). (b) The test had to be administerable without the use of specialized equipment, including tape recorders, which were not always available at many of the anticipated testing sites. (c) Test administration instructions, as well as the procedures for scoring, would need to be couched in very straightforward, nonspecialized terms. Even knowledge of basic English grammatical terminology such as present progressive tense or "wh" questions could not be presumed on the part of all potential test administrators.

(5) In addition to yielding general proficiency information, the test should provide diagnostic feedback concerning individual examinee or classroom group results with respect to relative performance on each of the language skill areas tested (e.g., listening comprehension versus reading), as well as even more detailed information concerning examinee group performance on those items comprising a particular language-use task within a given skill area (for example, reading price labels).

TEST DEVELOPMENT

Based on the format, content, and test administration considerations outlined above, an overall framework for what was eventually formally named the Basic English Skills Test (B.E.S.T.) was adopted. This consisted of two physically separate test sections: the Core section, which embodied primarily listening comprehension and speaking tasks but also included a limited number of elementary reading comprehension and writing activities; and the Literacy Skills section, which presented a wider variety of reading and writing tasks in a format amenable to group administration. Figures 1 and 2 summarize the content areas included in both sections of the test, classified by the communicative situation/topic represented in each instance (e.g., "time/numbers", "health and parts of body", "emergencies/safety") as well as the language skill area (listening, speaking, etc.) involved.

FIGURE 1   Test Content Specifications: Core Section

Topic Areas	Speaking	Listening	Reading	Writing
Greetings, Personal Information, Employment	Greets, gives name, spells name, states where from, how long in U.S.		Reads "Name" and "address" on form	Fills out simple data form
Time/Numbers	Tells time on clock	Understands spoken time	Reads time on clock	
Money/Shopping for Food, Clothing	Asks "How much...?", "where is...?" Compares shopping in U.S. & native country	Understands spoken price; shows correct coins	Reads price sign	
Health and Parts of Body	Describes ailment, condition	Shows understanding of parts of body		
Emergencies/ Safety	Describes accident scene		Matches signs, e.g., NO SMOKING, STOP, etc., with appropriate photographs	
Housing/Kinship	Identifies family members, rooms of house, household activities			
Directions	Asks for, gives directions	Understands spoken directions	Reads map	

FIGURE 2 Test Content Specifications: Literacy
Skills Section

TOPIC AREAS	Reading	Writing
Greetings, Personal Information, Employment	Reads job want ad	Fills out more complex data form
Time/Numbers	Locates given dates on calendar; finds telephone numbers in directory; reads train schedule	Writes date of birth on form
Money/Shopping for Food, Clothing	Reads price, price per lb., and other information on food labels; reads price, size, etc. on clothing labels	
Health and Parts of Body		
Emergencies/Safety	Reads excerpts from driver's manual	
Housing/Kinship	Reads ad for apartment	Fills out rent check; addresses envelope to landlord
Directions	In addition to the above, the Literacy Skills section tests understanding of tense and number in reading, and comprehension of general reading materials (newspaper articles, school catalogs)	

Core Section

For the core section, it was decided to use face-to-face conversation between examiner and examinee as the basic testing format, supplemented by a booklet containing photographs and simple line drawings about which questions were to be asked by the examiner at specified points in the test. In addition, the examiner was provided with a test administration/scoring booklet (see Figure 3 for sample page) containing, in side-by-side columns for each of the test questions: a brief description of the administration procedure to be followed (e.g., the examiner instructed to "Point to [photograph of a] baby"); the specific test question to be asked ("What's the

96

FIGURE 3 Sample Page from Administration/Scoring Booklet

Procedure	Test Questions	Response		Score			
				0	1	2	3
Turn the page, please.							
Sometimes people get sick, and sometimes they get hurt in accidents and have to go to a doctor.							
Point to the doctor.							
	35. Who's this?	"A doctor".	35.	☐	☐	☐	
Point to baby.							
	36. What's the matter?	"sick, crying, sad," etc. "Her hand is broken."	36.	☐	☐	☐	
	37. Where's her arm?	points	37.	△	△		
	38. Where's her stomach?	points	38.	△	△		
	39. What do you do when you get sick?	explains	39.	○	○		○

Subtotal

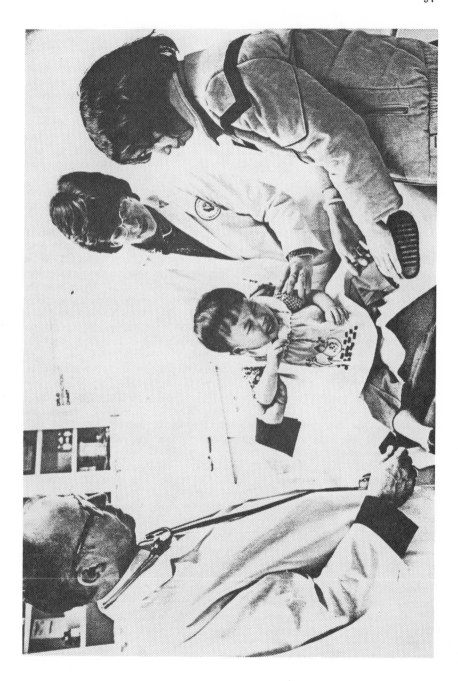

matter?"); the response(s) to be considered correct ("sick, crying, sad,...etc."); and a space for scoring and marking the examinee's response. Small triangles, squares, and circles in the score area designate questions addressed, respectively, to Listening Comprehension, Communication, and Fluency; these symbols were designated to facilitate later totaling of diagnostic sub-scores for each of these performance categories. The two further scoring categories for the Core section were a combined reading/writing scale and an informal three-point rating for Pronunciation, based on a global assessment of the examinee's speech production throughout the test (see Appendix 1).

As finally developed, the initial questions in the Core section involve polite conversation on autobiographical topics (examinee's name, country of origin, length of residence in the United States), with the last question in the series ("What do you like about the United States?") allowing the examinee to give a somewhat more elaborated response. Then follow a number of other sub-sections, each dealing with a particular topical area as specified in the content outline. In general, items within a given topical area follow a progression from highly contextualized questions requiring only a very brief and focused reply (e.g., "Where are these people?", asked about the photograph of a family seated around a television set) to broader and linguistically more challenging questions requiring descriptions of relevant personal experiences or opinions ("In [native country], what did your family like to do in the evening?"). Further sub-sections deal with time-telling (reading of digital and analog clock faces); following directions on a map in response to spoken instructions (e.g., "Go two blocks and turn left"); handling American currency ("It costs two-sixty-seven. Show me how much...[by selecting the correct bills and coins]"); reading comprehension of simple informational or cautionary signs ("Closed", "No Smoking", etc. [by pointing to an appropriate photograph, such as a person extinguishing a cigarette]); and communicating in health care/emergency situations by describing and answering questions about, respectively, photographs depicting a "doctor's office visit" and an automobile accident. As a measure of elementary writing ability, the examinee is asked, as the final activity for the Core section, to fill out a simple information form with basic biographical information (e.g., name, age, current address).

One important aspect of real-life communication, use of the telephone, was unfortunately not amenable to effective representation within the administrative and other technical constraints of the testing program.

An assessment of the examinee's ability to communicate on the telephone which would have both face and operational validity would presumably involve both (a) a test setting in which the examiner and examinee are in separate rooms or in some other way isolated from visual cues, and (b) degradation of the acoustic signal to the degree typically encountered in telephone communication. The non-availability of handsets and extension lines at the testing sites precluded actual use of the telephone equipment, and possible alternative arrangements (for example, use of a previously made tape recording of one side of a telephone conversation, with which the examinee is asked to interact) were considered highly artificial and seriously lacking in face validity.

Literacy Skills Section

As previously indicated, the Literacy Skills section comprised a separate booklet of reading comprehension and writing exercises, with examinees making all of their responses in the booklet itself. Reading tasks within this section include:

- Comprehension of printed dates in both fully-written and abbreviated numerical form (e.g., October 31, 1981; 10/31/81).

- Understanding of weight, size, price, and other information as shown on facsimiles of supermarket labels and clothing store tags.

- Literacy for various types of reference materials, as represented by a telephone directory page in which the examinee locates the telephone numbers of given individuals and by a portion of a train schedule from which the examinee determines specified arrival and departure times (e.g., "When does the train leave Washington, D.C.?").

In addition to these basic literacy tasks, somewhat higher-level materials are provided, including:

- A short excerpt from a driver training manual, in multiple-choice cloze format (e.g., ...To get a license you [need, must, wanted] take an eye examination, a written test, and a [answers, driving, try] test...). A series of multiple-choice questions based on excerpts from newspaper articles, want ads, catalogs, and other types of reading material with which examinees would be expected to come in contact in typical nonspecialized daily contexts.

One further question type addressed to reading comprehension was also included: short printed sentences for which the examinee was to indicate, by circling the appropriate word, the "time" or "quantity" implication of the sentence (e.g., We went to a movie last night [circle one: before, now, after]; Mrs. Thompson likes a cup of coffee in the morning [none, one, many]). Although more artificial and consequently having appreciably less face and content validity than the other reading comprehension formats, this question type was considered to reflect the examinee's ability to use available lexical or morphological cues to determine basic temporal or quantity aspects of the texts involved and to merit inclusion on this basis.

Writing activities in the Literacy Skills section included both context-specific, highly formulaic tasks (e.g., filling out a check, addressing an envelope) and more open-ended assignments (e.g., "What do you want to do in the United States? Please write 3-4 sentences"), the latter intended for examinees somewhat beyond the rote level of writing performance (for scoring method, see Appendix 2).

TRIAL ADMINISTRATION AND ANALYSIS OF DRAFT TEST

In keeping with the above descriptions, preliminary versions of both the Core and Literacy Skills sections were developed for initial administration. For both sections, the total number of items (62 for the Core section and 104 for Literacy Skills) was, intentionally, appreciably greater than the number to be included in the operational test so as to allow flexibility in selecting final form items with close attention to the statistical performance of individual items, the range of question difficulty represented in the final test, and the content coverage of the completed test.

Beginning in November 1981, the preliminary test versions were administered at each of ten Region I training centers, with all administration and scoring activities being carried out by teachers and program supervisors at these centers. Examiner training for both test administration and scoring involved an approximately three-hour training session for one or two representatives from each site; this process included observation and administration of sample tests and study and discussion of a detailed administration/scoring manual. On return to the sites, some participants were responsible for training other members of their staff in both administration and scoring, as necessary to accommodate the testing volumes involved in particular instances.

Native language backgrounds of the examinees tested in the initial administration included Vietnamese, Hmong, Lao, Cambodian/Khmer, Chinese, Spanish, and Japanese. Total number of subjects for the Core section was 217 and, for the Literacy Skills section, 101, the latter representing that sub-group of examinees whose scores on the reading/ writing questions of the Core section were considered sufficiently high (9 or more of a possible 14 points) to suggest at least some degree of success on the Literacy Skills section.

For both the Core and Literacy Skills sections, selection of items for inclusion in the operational form of the test was based for the most part on the statistical results of the SCALAR analysis program, an interactive computer program for scale development and analysis of test item performance developed at Educational Testing Service. For the present study, input data included (1) student performance on each test item, with each item assigned, according to its primary measurement intent, to one of four analytic scales: Listening Comprehension, Communication, Fluency, and Reading/Writing; (2) a code representing the student's native language (to check on possible test bias attributable to native language background); and (3) an independent, external rating of the student's general level of English proficiency at the time of testing, based on a six-point scale ranging from lower-level beginning to higher-level advanced. These ratings were provided by the individual instructors or program coordinators at the testing sites and were based on overall student language performance as demonstrated in classwork and informal contacts in the course of the instructional program.

For the Core section, based on a 67 x 67 variance-covariance matrix consisting of the above variables, the reliability, mean, and standard deviation of each specified scale were determined. The correlation of each scale with the student native language code and with the instructor's overall rating of examinee language proficiency was also determined, as was the correlation of each item with (1) its own scale (correcting for the item itself); (2) the other three scales; and (3) the native language code and instructor overall rating. Items that exhibited low correlations with their own scale or with the external proficiency scale or that, in a few instances, showed undesirable patterns of correlation with other scales (for example, a communication item - "Where are you from?" - correlated .41 with the total communication scale but .52 with the fluency scale) were deleted on an iterative basis and the resulting new reliabilities, means, and correlations computed. This process was continued until subsequent changes yielded little or no additional statistical improvement. Final item selection also involved some deletions based on considerations of content coverage and item sequencing.

Of the 62 items in the initial Core section, 49 were retained for the operational Core test. A similar process of statistical analysis using the SCALAR program, together with item content review, was used to analyze the preliminary administration data for all items in the Literacy Skills section. For this section, of 104 items initially administered, 70 were retained in the operational test form.

RELIABILITY AND VALIDITY ESTIMATES FOR FINAL TEST FORM

Because in the initial test administration, ample time had been provided for examinees to attempt every question, it was considered reasonable to assume that deleting certain items would not appreciably affect examinee performance on a test consisting of the remaining items and, by the same token, that individual item data obtained in the initial administration could appropriately be used in estimating the reliabilities of the revised test sections. Thus, after the specific items to be included in the operational test had been fully determined, the SCALAR program was again run using as input data only the designated items.

Internal consistency (KR-20) reliability estimates for the items comprising each of the subscales of the Core and Literacy Skills sections of the operational test were uniformly very high (.93 to .98; see Table 1), with the single exception of the Writing scale of the Literacy Skills section, for which the obtained coefficient was .58. This may be due in part to the fact that items included in the Literacy Skills Writing scale involved two appreciably different types of writing activities: "rote" tasks in highly specified contexts (e.g., filling out a form, addressing an envelope); and considerably freer tasks (e.g., a 2-3 sentence composition on "What do you want to do in the United States?"). Separately calculated KR-20 reliabilities were .57 for the free composition exercises and .83 for the more highly contextualized tasks. Because items for the operational form were deliberately selected from among the available items with respect to reliability, validity, and relatively low overlap with other scales (as well as for content coverage), the reported reliability estimates may be slightly inflated by comparison with the results that would be obtained in test administration to a second examinee group. However, previous experience with use of the SCALAR program suggests that, with an examinee sample of the the size involved (217) and a large proportion (over 70 per cent) of the original items retained in the operational test, cross-validation reduction in reliability would be minimal.

TABLE 1 Internal Consistency Estimates for Individual Test Sections

Core Section

Listening Comprehension	.95
Communication	.95
Fluency	.98
Reading/Writing	.97

Literacy Skills Section

Reading	.93
Writing	.58

External Validity

The main demonstration of the validity of the B.E.S.T. is considered to be its high content similarity to the types of language-use tasks it is intended to represent. However, additional validity-related information was available in the correlations of the test's scale scores with the general English proficiency rating assigned to each examinee by the teaching program staff. On the six-point scale previously described, the mean proficiency rating for the 217 students was 3.07, representing a level very slightly higher than "lower-level intermediate" on the rating scale. Pearson product-moment validity coefficients for each test scale against this external criterion are shown in Table 2. The observed correlations show substantial relationships between teaching staff judgments of student language proficiency and corresponding scores on the B.E.S.T. On the assumption that the proficiency-rating criterion is probably somewhat unreliable in its own right, as well as based to some extent on factors not directly associated with language proficiency per se (for example, student personality, diligence in completing assignments, etc.) even higher validity coefficients might be shown using external criteria more directly and accurately reflecting language proficiency.

TABLE 2   Correlations with External Proficiency Ratings

Core Section	
Listening Comprehension	.52
Communication	.49
Fluency	.71
Reading/Writing	.61

$\underline{N}$ = 217

Literacy Skills Section	
Reading	.51
Writing	.54

$\underline{N}$ = 101

Scoring Reliability

During the initial test administration, scoring reliability for the Core section was investigated by having another rater (drawn on an iterative basis from the pool of regular raters) sit in on all Core section tests and independently score the students' performance while the test was being administrated. Based on the scoring of those (and only those) items included in the operational test, obtained inter-rater reliabilities were as shown in Table 3. Scoring reliability for both Communication and Fluency was extremely high, and reliability of the Core Section Reading/Writing scale, while somewhat lower, is quite respectable in view of the relatively few (9) items involved.

The obtained scoring reliability for Listening Comprehension may reflect to some extent a technical artifact of the administration conditions under which these raters were asked to operate. Specifically, they were asked to make themselves as unobtrusive as possible during the testing, which generally meant sitting at some distance from the examiner and examinee. Although this posed little or no problem in evaluating spoken responses, the raters found it difficult in several instances to determine whether the examinees' silent gestures in response to certain listening comprehension questions were or were not not correct (e.g., "Where's her [a pictured ill child's] stomach?", for which the appropriate response is to point to a relatively small portion of the photograph). An administration situation in which they would in fact have been able to "look over the shoulder" of the examinee would in all probability have resulted in a higher scoring reliability for the listening comprehension questions - as well as for the reading questions in the reading/writing scale, which also involve the examinee's pointing to certain portions of the photograph booklet. For psychological reasons, however, it was considered preferable to have them "keep some distance" during the test administration, even at the expense of not being absolutely sure of the examinee's response in some instances.

TABLE 3 Inter-rater Reliabilities

Core Section	
Listening/Comprehension	.81
Communication	.93
Fluency	.97
Reading/Writing	.80

$\underline{N}$ = 217

Literacy Skills Section	
Reading	.99
Writing	.93

$\underline{N}$ = 101

Answer sheets for the Literacy Skills section were also double-scored, yielding virtually perfect (.99) inter-rater reliability figures for the Reading scale (fully anticipated in view of the multiple-choice nature of this section) and the quite high value of .93 for Writing.

Interscale Correlations

Intercorrelations of the four Core section scoring scales are shown in Table 4. The interscale correlations are moderate, ranging from .61 to .74, and their individual magnitudes are in keeping with the anticipated relationships among these scales. For example, the highest correlation (.74) is between the two speaking-oriented scales, Communication and Fluency; correlations between Reading/Writing and any of the aural-oral scales (Listening Comprehension, Communication, and Fluency) are uniformly lower than are any of the latter among themselves.

TABLE 4 Interscale Correlations

	Listening Comprehension	Communication	Fluency
Communication	.69	1.00	.74
Fluency	.67	.74	1.00
Reading/Writing	.61	.65	.65

N = 217

Correlations of Listening Comprehension, Communication, and Fluency with examinee native language (.03, .03, and .02, respectively) were all very close to zero and statistically nonsignificant. There was a slight positive relationship (.14, just reaching significance at the .05 level) between native language background and Reading/Writing; this may reflect the relatively more urban background of the Vietnamese students in the sample who on the whole would be expected to have somewhat greater literacy opportunities than examinees from the other language groups.

FURTHER TEST DEVELOPMENT AND VALIDATION ACTIVITIES

Statistical and other information obtained thus far on the measurement characteristics of the B.E.S.T. is felt by the project staff to permit some optimism concerning the effectiveness of its use as a measure of functional language skills of Indochinese and other refugee populations in the U.S. With respect to further test development activities, authorization and funding has been received to begin the preparation of two additional forms of the test, which will be equated to the original test through common-item procedures. Further studies of the administrative and statistical performance of the initial form of the test are currently being planned, including correlation of B.E.S.T. scores with the global performance ratings on the Interagency Language Roundtable (ILR) speaking proficiency scale, as modified by the American Council on the Teaching of Foreign Languages and Educational Testing Service (ACTFL/ETS) for use with examinees whose performance is in the lower portion of the rating scale.[2]

In addition, it is anticipated that ORR/HHS will shortly fund the development of three to five demonstration projects for refugee training which will, along with their other activities, serve on an ongoing basis for ESL test administration and analysis. In collaboration with teaching staff in these demonstration projects, it is hoped to develop descriptive scales of English proficiency which are skill and situation specific for use by the instructors in evaluating their students' language performance as exemplified in the training program. Conceptually similar rating procedures, often referred to as can do scales, have previously been developed for use with U.S. college students studying modern foreign languages;[3] an analogous approach would appear useful in establishing further shing further external validity data through comparison of B.E.S.T. scores for Fluency, Listening Comprehension, and other factors (as well as examinee performance data on those test questions addressing a specified functional area, e.g., telling time, reading price labels) with the corresponding can do ratings of the student provided by the teacher.

Opportunities to obtain detailed predictive validity information are also expected to be provided in connection with activities being carried out by another agency (RMC Corporation, for the Bureau of Refugee Programs/Department of State) in a longitudinal study of refugee performance in actual employment settings and other non-academic situations involving English language use. The B.E.S.T. has been administered during the RMC study as a measure of refugee language proficiency on entry into the U.S. and after approximately six months of residence, and will constitute one of the major predictor variables in the study. In addition to carrying out the various activities described above, project staff would very much appreciate receiving information from other users or potential users of the B.E.S.T. concerning possible areas of collaboration in its further administration and validation.

NOTES

1. The present article deals only with the ESL test battery developed for use in training programs based in the United States. However, through other projects, CAL has developed additional ESL tests designed for administration at in-country training centers in Southeast Asia, as well as cultural orientations tests for in-country use. Further information on these testing projects may be obtained from the authors.

2. For background information on the ILR scale and its use, see Pardee Lowe, Jr. and Judith E. Liskin Gasparro, Testing Speaking Proficiency: The Oral Interview, ERIC Clearinghouse on languages and linguistics, 1983 and for the ACTFL scale, see ACTFL Provisional Proficiency Guidelines.

3. These scales are discussed in John L. D. Clark, Survey results: language, Chapter 9 in Thomas S. Barrows, College Students' Knowledge and Beliefs: A Survey of Global Understanding, New Rochelle, N.Y.: Change Magazine Press, 1981, pp. 87-100. Typical can do statements used in this project included, for example, "Ask for directions on the street" and "Introduce [oneself] in social situations, [using] appropriate greetings and leave-taking expressions." Examinee rating categories for each can do statement were, quite easily, with some difficulty, with great difficulty, and not at all.

APPENDIX 1

Reading/Writing

The Core Section questions addressed to basic literacy skills include a number of "sight vocabulary" items ("push", "no smoking", "don't walk", etc.), together with an elementary writing task (completion of a simple biographical data form).

For each of the "sight vocabulary" questions, identified by the symbol ⟁ , scoring is as follows:

>   1 = examinee indicates comprehension by pointing to the appropriate photograph
>   0 = examinee points to the wrong photograph or does not respond

For the Writing task, each of 5 different items on the biographical data form are scored separately: data, name, address, alien registration number, and age. For each, scoring is as follows:

>   2 = response is comprehensible and complete in form. (For example, the answer to question 45, "Date", should include some indication of month, day, and year, in a form comprehensible in the United States [e.g., July 14, 1982, 14 July 1982, 7/14/82, but not 14/7/82]. The answer to question 47, "Address," should contain street, city, and state information [ZIP not required].) Misspellings that do not affect comprehensibility are acceptable
>   1 = response is totally or partially incomprehensible and/or is not complete in form
>   0 = no response

Pronunciation

At the end of the test, a single global rating is given for pronunciation, taking into account the examinee's general performance throughout the test. In assigning a pronunciation rating, attention should be paid only to the overall comprehensibility of the response; these responses can be heavily accented and still receive the maximum score, provided that the words themselves are understandable. Rating is as follows:

> 3 = examinee's answers are readily understandable (from a pronunciation standpoint) throughout the test
> 2 = examinee's answers are generally understandable, but occasionally difficult or impossible to comprehend as a result of pronunciation problems
> 1 = examinee's answers are frequently not comprehensible

The score assigned should be marked on the front page of the Scoring Booklet.

APPENDIX 2

Part 10 - Composition

In this part, the examinee is asked to write 6-8 sentences on one of three topics: "your family", "your job", or "what you like or do not like about the place where you now live". Responses should be evaluated as a whole, on the following basis:

> 7 = an extensive amount of comprehensible information is conveyed (regardless of grammatical accuracy per se)
> 5 = a reasonable amount of comprehensible information is conveyed; examinee shows some attempt at elaboration
> 3 = "bare-bones" information (should be awarded if any amount of comprehensible writing is present)
> 0 = some writing, but not at all responsive to the question, or incomprehensible
> Blank = no response

Do not award any in-between scores (i.e., 1, 2, 4, or 6). If the examinee writes on more than one topic, score the topic most extensively treated and ignore the other topic(s).

7.
Issues in the Validation of the English Language Testing Service (ELTS) 1976-1983

Ian Seaton

I have selected two broad issues to discuss as I cannot review all the work that went into the development of the English Language Testing Service (ELTS) over the past seven or eight years; work that involved teams of sometimes over twenty and never less than four people. To try and give shape to the discussion, I will refer to Figure 1 appended to this article. It sets out three areas (Research, Production, Operation) and three categories of professional (Researcher, Constructor-Validator and Manager). I will try to look at the two issues I have chosen through the eyes of the people in each category, to show the different approaches and priorities and the tension that is produced as well as the way ELTS attempted to provide working solutions. Like many charts or diagrams in English language testing (ELT) it may have the appearance of giving stable and fixed divisions, of definite boundaries etc., but this is largely spurious.

First I must provide some background information on ELTS. I will be brief because there is a range of literature available that gives a better, fuller description (cf. Carroll 1981; Seaton 1981). The British Council administers, on behalf of the British Government and a number of international and other agencies, over 10,000 students annually coming to Britain - to universities, polytechnics, colleges, etc. - for study or training for periods of three months to three years. The students' English language adequacy is an important factor in all this and the Council has used language tests for over twenty years to inform the decisions it takes and the guidance it provides. The main test used in the 1960s and 1970s was the English Proficiency Test Battery which went through four versions. In the early 1970s various committees, working parties, and discussion groups inside and outside of the Council decided it was time for a completely new system of testing and the idea of a testing <u>service</u> took hold. And now, in the early 1980s, ELTS is the Council's sole system of language testing for overseas students coming to Britain. The whole Service was developed from 1975 to 1980, was introduced in 40 countries in 1980, in another 40 in 1981/82, and operates now in 110 test centres, all this in full partnership with the University of Cambridge Local Examinations Syndicate and using the statistical and development services of the University's Test Development and Research Unit. In its first year of operation it tested 3,876 students, in year two 7,018, and in 1983 it tested 10,000 students.

ELTS is made up of five sub-tests requiring a total testing time of 175 minutes. Two are general tests of reading and listening comprehension and three are (so-called) modular tests of language study-skills in the modes of reading, writing and listening-speaking. These modular sub-tests are in six versions using texts specific to the subject areas of Life Sciences, Physical Sciences, Technology, Medicine, Social Studies and General Academic. There are parallel versions of all sub-tests except the first modular sub-test. ELTS, then, is a secure, centrally monitored, on-demand, ESP (English for Specific Purposes) proficiency test which reports scores in terms of different levels or bands of ability which have performance descriptions and whose results can also be used diagnostically to recommend different periods of English language tuition to bring students up to predetermined levels or bands of ability.

That is probably too much or too little information on ELTS but I will move on to the issues I have chosen (see Figure 1). The first issue is in the area of construct and content validity. I am not going to discuss here current models showing the various notions of validity feeding mobius-like or deriving hierarchically into or from each other. Rather, as I mentioned above, I want to look at the issue through the eyes of the professionals I have somewhat arbitrarily put into these categories.

For the <u>Managers</u> what emerged from the discussion of the early seventies was that any new test should be transparent and friendly for its users.

FIGURE 1

Research ———	Production ———	Operation
researcher	constructor- validator	manager

ISSUE ONE
– construct validity
 	
– needs analysis models
 	
– notions of competence
 	
– sampling for content
  specifications
	– descriptive framework
	  and language use
	
	– requirements for
	  proficiency and
	  diagnostic testing
	
	– conversion of content
	  specifications to
	  tests
	
	– available item/task
	  types
	
	– levels and their mean-
	  ing
		– information system
		
		– user considerations
		
		– decisions on
		  adequacy or further
		  tuition
		
		– washback into learn-
		  ing programmes
		
		– system control and
		  resources

ISSUE TWO
– validation of con-
  struct
 	
– selection of appro-
  priate analysis
 	
– refinements of sample
  and data
 	
– interpretation
	– validation of predic-
	  tions
	
	– quality of samples and
	  data
	
	– procedures of data
	  gathering and storage
	
	– first level analysis
	  and feedback to oper-
	  ation
		– quality of informa-
		  tion
		
		– user-satisfaction
		
		– outcomes of
		  decisions
		
		– plans for revision
		  and rewrite

It should provide both proficiency and diagnostic information, appear to be "up-to-date" and have a benevolent washback into courses and classrooms. It should also be robust and controllable as well as being stable, secure, and so forth. In short, what was wanted was an attractive information system that was amenable to being refined and consolidated. Such considerations were important; tests and examination are where the ELT world and the much larger non-ELT world meet (or collide?) - particularly so with tests that have the role of an ELTS or a Test of English as a Foreign Language (**TOEFL**).

To the left on Figure 1, we come to the concerns of the Constructors: the organization of the content of the tests, the selection of item and task types, whether the test (both its overall format and its components) will be able to meet demands of validity and reliability and, a concern shared particularly with the managers, whether there are sufficient resources (staff, time, money ... energy) to sustain development and then maintain quality.

Clearly there is also close contact and interaction with Researchers into language testing and their concern to investigate the construct of language competence, how to define it and gather empirical evidence to support their definitions through a variety of measurement and statistical analysis procedures.

Without, I hope, raising the people in this category to the role of protagonists in the story, the Constructor-Validators had to reconcile the demands and the tensions that emanated from the concerns of Managers and Researchers. These included Managers' wanting information on how language was used communicatively in key English for Academic Purposes (EAP) settings, reported reliably in terms that had direct criterion meaning as well as providing diagnostic guidance on remedial language tuition. They also included the researchers' concerns with current research, or rather lack of research into these issues, the doubts about the various competence hypotheses, about the effect of different methods of analysis on data, the effect of item type on test performance and the lack of an agreed model, metalanguage or taxonomy of components of language. There is a rhyme which is used in playing a game of deciding when something will happen: "this year, next year, sometime, never". On this issue the Manager column wanted results "this year", the Constructor column promised "next year" and the Researcher column counselled "sometime" or "never" depending on who you asked and when!

However in 1976 ELTS faced the need to produce the kind of test that J.B. Carroll described thus:

An ideal English language proficiency test should make it possible to differentiate to the greatest possible extent, levels of performance in those dimensions of performance which are relevant to the kinds of situation in which the examinees will find themselves after being selected on the basis of the test (1961).

This, operationalized, meant a need to decide on what set of parameters to choose to describe language use. Those most immediately to hand were syllabus needs-analysis models derived from the approaches of people like Jacobson and Hymes. The model chosen by ELTS to organize a survey of the language demands made on overseas students studying or training in Britain and to control test content specification was that developed by a colleague in the Council, John Munby, first presented in his Ph.D. thesis and later published (Munby 1978).

To give an overall approach, Appendix A shows an evaluation framework adapted from the recent Ph.D. thesis of another Council colleague, Roger Hawkey (1982). The first column is adapted from parameters of Munby's (1978) Communicative Needs Processor that the six survey teams used to draw up specifications for ELTS. A personal account of this specification exercise was given by Brendan Carroll (1981) in his "Specifications for an ELTS". The constructors next needed a checklist of the dynamic characteristics of communication to attempt to build these characteristics into the test tasks and items that were emerging from the collation and editing of the specifications. The third part of this framework derives from Munby's (1978) original parameter 6, "Target Level". It was first used to describe the dimensions of particular activities for conversion into test tasks; a description that could use linguistic terms and be more "objectively" observable. It was then used to describe examinee performance on the test tasks using these criteria.

Clearly this "shorthand" framework raises a host of issues, issues I cannot discuss here. But for mainly operational reasons, ELTS chose not to define a range of test tasks via dimensions, and performances via criteria. It took both sets of features to define and describe nine levels, or in ELTS terms bands, of language ability, sets of bands to assess test performance directly in the written and spoken modular subtests and a set of bands to establish levels of proficiency for score reporting. Also the dynamic characteristics set out by Hawkey (1982) could not be systematically applied in 1978 by teams of test writers producing a test that had to be economically and stably administered in over a hundred countries. At this stage of a priori and qualitative construction and validation such listings did, however, provide a valuable checklist in test production.

To return to the issue of the specifications and the validity of such a broad multi-dimensional construct of communicative competence, the model had been chosen, the survey teams had produced their specifications for students in post-graduate studies in the six broadly defined subject areas; the issue

facing the Constructors was to derive test-content specifications from all this work and then to realize these in subtests,
tasks and items.

The first problem was that though the model does produce,
via a taxonomy of language micro-skills and functions, detailed
lists of these skills that can be fairly directly realized in
language, and though it can be argued that these skills are
generalizable (i.e., important for considerations of proficiency)
... no hierarchy or pattern of the relationship of the skills is
offered. Once Humpty Dumpty has been broken into little
pieces, there is no blueprint available to put him back together
again! This leads to the usual problem of selection and sampling for a 2-3 hour test from specifications that could generate
a 2-3 year syllabus and which in turn are selections from an
even larger whole. The researchers, having pointed out the
paucity of research, would, nevertheless, seek to validate the
construct by empirical experimentation. The Constructor-
Validator (and certainly the Manager) would raise practical
questions of the use of resources in, say, applying multi-
trait/multi-method procedures to a "good" sample of the target
population for the eventual tests as well as more theoretical
questions about the type of analysis to use, the interpretation
of results and inferences about the construct. In the production of an operational test like ELTS what happened was that
the specifications were edited down to a common core of tasks
and skills; as if the six sets were placed on top of each other
and someone looked down through them.

The second problem was more easily resolved if only
because considerations in the management column restricted the
room to manoeuvre. Although the framework pulled toward the
organization of the whole system in terms of multi-mode events,
activities, and tasks, this would have been too innovative and
too complex to maintain and renew and would have posed too
many reliability problems in a test that was to operate in over
a hundred countries. Only the last two modular sub-tests
could set up tasks to be directly assessed. An important
factor in allowing this was that the Council has offices all over
the world with an accessible and trainable staff). The other
three sub-tests would have to be, and still are, realized in
multiple-choice item-types although each item is labelled in
terms of the language micro-skill it predominantly tests.

The second issue is more in the area of predictive validity.
There is only a dotted line in Figure 1 because it goes without
saying that you need a full and precise description of what you
are validating before you start validating. It is to emphasize
this mutually informing link that I have called those in the
middle column, Constructor-Validators. ELTS was developed
from a consideration of specific purposes; it operates and

reports scores which are interpreted with a consideration for this specific purpose so it can only be appropriately validated against actual outcomes in the specific purpose. So how has ELTS set about predictive validation, the monitoring and follow-up of the students it tests?

I should mention first studies that ELTS has commissioned from two British universities. Alan Davies and the Institute for Applied Language Studies at Edinburgh University are in the third year of a study looking at the concurrent relationship of ELTS to other language proficiency tests as well as investigating the methodology of special studies into predictive validity. Charles Alderson at the Institute for English Language at Lancaster University is extending a study of the Institute to look at some constructs of ELTS, in particular the use of different subject-specific modular tests (Alderson and Urquhart 1983). ELTS seeks to set up or to participate in studies that will involve work across the three categories so that small-scale, highly controlled research studies inform and are informed by a large-scale and more robust validation programme. ELTS, in its own monitoring, wanted to follow up the real thing: the authentic, purposeful, motivated sequence of testing, tuition, placement and study. It did not wish abstract "guinea-pigs" from this sequence to apply extra and experimental procedures. The managers knew that the Council, administering so many students literally from their start to their finish, would be uniquely placed to do this; it has the access and the administrative machinery. So they were concerned to make a robust, manageable, welcomed (by British institutions in tertiary education) programme that would have a direct feedback to ELTS; in the short term, consolidating and/or adjusting the score reporting and the received "meaning" of the bands; in the long term, informing the planned (for 1984-1986) evaluation, revision and rewrite of ELTS.

The Constructor-Validators were concerned to get a "good" sample, a four-figure number at least (up to 5,000 students) and a representative one (regarding the proportions taking different modules, from different countries, etc). The design of the instruments for data collection would have to be efficient and economic - management requirements - and yet contain all the variables that the research side would want to process. And then there was the choice of a computer programme that would handle the information/data files and the analyses.

The Researchers had to set up what they wanted to investigate, the analyses to use - from straightforward correlations to the generation of more complex matrices - and consider the interpretation of possible results. Areas for investigation included: the relation of band scores between subtests and modules for the whole sample and any significant subsamples as defined by one or more variables; the effect of different periods of language tuition; the identification of any stereotype groups of students; the relationship of bands derived from the test and bands assessed by either English language teachers or subject supervisors; the relationship of ELTS bands to other commonly used criterion descriptions such as good, fair, weak or adequate, inadequate; and levels of adequacy in terms of ELTS bands across institutions or across modules. There was also an interest to make the data readily available to any special studies so that they could profit from "authentic" large-scale sampling and also add to the programme with finer-grained follow-up (using student questionnaires, listing and accounting for affective factors, re-testing of small samples), possibly relating results not just to bands but to scores in subsections or groups of items in the subtests.

So the validation programme appended to this article (Figure 2) divides the sequence into seven stages with two main routes. Route A is that of the candidate moving through the stages from his or her home country through to the second or third month of study/training at a British university, poly-technic or whatever. As the candidate moves along so does his or her ELTS documentation - route B. In particular, at stages 1, 5 and 7 data forms for each student are issued, completed, returned (samples of the forms are appended). The data on each form is stored on files in a Rapid Access Management Information System (RAMIS) programme on the IBM mainframe computer at the Cambridge Examinations Syndicate. There are standard and routine interrogations put through the RAMIS programme for management information and as the files build up so the analyses that interest the Constructor-Validators and Researchers can be run.

At stage 1 when the candidate/student is tested, a test report form (Appendix B and C) is issued, evaluated at stage 2 and sent to wherever the student is applying for entry. It is a fairly compact form, five sections and a key providing candidate details and Test details (referring to the six modules and different combinations of subtests called patterns). The scores are presented as a profile and overall; the bands have brief performance descriptions but the results can be interpreted further using sections of the Test Administrator's Manual. The recommended period of tuition is blocked off from the score for obvious reasons; it is an operational requirement but it is professionally at the crystal-ball end of testing and teaching. The form, unfortunately, has to come in sets of six copies but that gives an idea of how many users, individual and institutional, ELTS has to serve.

At stage 3 the successful candidate can take two sub-routes: direct placement in universities, polytechnics, etc., or not. If further English language tuition (four weeks to four or more months) is recommended then the student is placed in a language school or university language centre. When he or she has completed that period, he or she is assessed using test validation form 1 (Appendix D). The key sections for this are Standards and Bands, where two separate assessments are asked for, one described in general terms, one prescribed in ELTS terms. This approach derives from work undertaken by another Council colleague, Alan Moller, in his recent Ph.D. thesis (1982), in building checks and balances into subjective assessments to increase reliability. The Student details, of course, link it to the appropriate test report form file now on RAMIS. This form is also used by the English Tuition Co-ordinating Unit (ETCU), which is the central unit in the Council in London that recommends language tuition for more immediate monitoring of individual students.

For both types of students, the final ELTS stage is number 7, when their tutors/supervisors know them well enough to make an assessment of their English language proficiency but before too many "unknown" variables intervene. Test valida-tion form 2 (Appendix E) is then completed and the third file on RAMIS is build up. When this programme is running smoothly, both professionally and logistically, there is much more information about each candidate (currently built up on paper files) that could, lego-like, be added. As with the whole of ELTS, the validation programme will be evaluated, refined, revised and we hope, consolidated. I am conscious of having given a rather bland account of the issues chosen but anyone with experience of large-scale ELT projects and the problems they can run into will be able to set the account into context. I am conscious too of a major omission in Figure 1, a column for the category student, but it is understood that concern to improve the way we take account of language adequacy so as to ensure, in partnership with all the others involved, that each student gets the most out of both studying and living in Britain has been the prime mover in the development of ELTS.

120

FIGURE 2 Route of Candidate and Data Forms from Initial Testing to Successful Completion of Studies

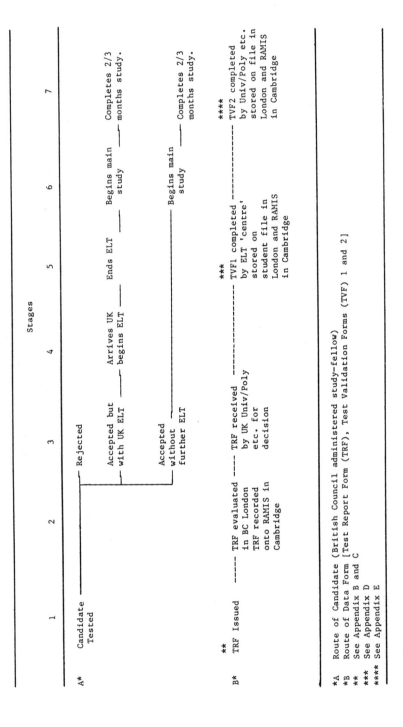

Stages

	1	2	3	4	5	6	7

A* Candidate Tested ─── Rejected

Accepted but with UK ELT ─── Arrives UK begins ELT ─── Ends ELT ─── Begins main study ─── Completes 2/3 months study.

Accepted without further ELT ─── Begins main study ─── Completes 2/3 months study.

**   ***   ****

B* TRF Issued ─── TRF evaluated in BC London TRF recorded onto RAMIS in Cambridge ─── TRF received by UK Univ/Poly etc. for decision ─── TVF1 completed by ELT 'centre' stored on student file in London and RAMIS in Cambridge ─── TVF2 completed by Univ/Poly etc. stored on file in London and RAMIS in Cambridge

*A   Route of Candidate (British Council administered study-fellow)
*B   Route of Data Form [Test Report Form (TRF), Test Validation Forms (TVF) 1 and 2]
**   See Appendix B and C
***   See Appendix D
**** See Appendix E

REFERENCES

Carroll, B. 1981. Specification for an English language testing service. In Alderson, J., and A. Hughes (eds.), ELT Documents III - Issues in Language Testing. London: The British Council.

Carroll, J. 1961. Fundamental considerations in testing for English Language proficiency of foreign students. In Center for Applied Linguistics, Testing the English Proficiency of Foreign Students. Washington, D.C.: Author. [Reprinted in Allen, H., and R. Campbell (eds.), Teaching English as a Second Language, 2nd edit. New York: McGraw-Hill, 1972.]

Hawkey, R. 1982. Unpublished Ph.D. Dissertion, University of London.

Moller, A. 1982. A study in the validation of proficiency tests in English as a foreign language. Ph.D. Dissertation, University of Edinburgh.

Munby, J. 1978. Communicative Syllabus Design. Cambridge: Cambridge University Press.

Seaton, I. 1981. Background to the specifications for an English language testing service and subsequent developments. In Alderson, J., and A. Hughes (eds.). ELT Documents III - Issues in Language Testing. London: The British Council.

APPENDIX A

EVALUATION FRAMEWORK

Parameters	Dynamics	Dimensions
Participant	Information gaps	Size
Purpose	Inter-subjectivity	Complexity
Activities	Authentic context	Functional range
Setting	Unpredictability	Referential range
Interaction	Creativity	
Instrumentality	Self-monitoring	
Dialect	Natural chunking	
Code	Real time	
Communicative operations		

Criteria

Formal accuracy
Referential
adequacy
Socio-cultural
appropriateness
Fluency
Flexibility
etc. (as needed)

DEFINITIONS OF EVALUATION FRAMEWORK COMPONENTS

Parameters

1. **Participant** (as subject and communicator in the test event)

2. **Purpose** (of the participant(s) in the communicative event and of the event itself)

3. **Activities** (sub-tasks involved in achieving the purpose)

4. **Setting** (physical and psycho-social context of the event)

5. **Interaction** (role set and social relationships of participants)

6.   **Instrumentality**   (medium, mode, channel of communication for the event)

7.   **Dialect**   (dialect and accent of participants in the event)

8.   **Code**   (forms and functions conveying the messages of the event)

9.   **Communicative operations**   (skills and strategies required to achieve the purposes of the event)

Dynamics

1.   **The existence of relevant information gaps** (i.e., a universe of discourse from which the participant has to process not-yet-known information of a kind relevant to his real-life situation and fill a similarly relevant gap for his interlocutor)

2.   **Inter-subjectivity** (i.e., that the speaker/writer should want to know that the hearer/reader knows that the former knows what the latter knows...)

3.   **Authenticity of setting** (i.e., that scene and setting are specified or inferable as appropriate to subject matter and participants)

4.   **Unpredictability** (i.e., that the task allows for the occurrence of activities that could not normally be foreseen from the initial given or shared knowledge)

5.   **Creativity** (i.e., that the task offers scope for participants to be "novel" to assert their communicative independence as they might in a naturalistic event)

6.   **Self-monitoring** (i.e., that the task allows participants to use their discourse processing strategies to evaluate communicative effectiveness and make adjustments during the course of the event)

7.   **Natural chunking** (i.e., that the size and scope of task activities are such that participants are processing the kind of input segments that they would normally expect to)

8.   **Real time** (i.e., that the tasks has to be accomplished under normal time constraints)

Dimensions

1. **Size**   (the amount of communication,
                            receptive and/or productive,
                            that is involved in the event)

2. **Complexity**   (the degree of grammatical
                            complexity, the range of
                            cohesion devices likely to be
                            required)

3. **Functional range**   (the degree of variety of
                            illocutionary acts involved in
                            the event)

4. **Referential range**   (the breadth and depth of lexical
                            knowledge required to handle
                            activities in the event)

Criteria

1. **Formal accuracy**   (covering range and control of
                            major and minor patterns; effect
                            on communication)

2. **Referential   (covering range and accuracy of
    adequacy**   usage; repair and avoidance
                            strategies; effect on
                            communication)

3. **Socio-cultural   (covering adaptation of
    appropriateness**   ulterances to the social
                            context; effect on
                            communication)

4. **Fluency**   (covering speed, evenness, ease
                            and intersentential connection)

5. **Flexibility**   (covering ability to adapt to and
                            initiate topic switches)

APPENDIX B Form Used for Initial Evaluation and
Sent to the Student's Institution

UNIVERSITY OF CAMBRIDGE
LOCAL EXAMINATIONS
SYNDICATE
THE BRITISH COUNCIL

English Language Testing Service
Test Report Form

Candidate Details

Centre Code   Year Quarter   Cand. No.   Nationality   Mother Tongue

Name/last or family/first/middle   Sex M/F   Date of Birth

Test Details (see key below)

Pattern taken   Module taken   Version taken   Scheme   ELTS taken before   Date of test

Result Details/Profile Bands (see key below)

G1 Reading   G2 Listening   M1 Study Skills   M2 Writing   M3 Inter   Overall Band

Interpretation

_____

_____

_____

_____

Distribution of forms (blu_____)   **Tuition Recommended** (Full time in the UK)

Home Division   Sponsor   _____ving Institution   Weeks   by   ETCU   or   Centre

Centre Details

Centre _____

Country _____

Centre Administrator _____

Post _____

Signature _____   Stamp

---

*Editor's Note: See Appendix C for the Key which appears at the
bottom of this form.

APPENDIX C   Key providing Candidate Details and Test Details

Band Description

9 Expert User: fully operational command of the language; appropriate, accurate and fluent with complete understanding.

8 Very Good User: fully operational command of the language; occasional minor inaccuracies, inappropriacies or misunderstandings possible in unfamiliar situations.

7 Good User: operational command of the language; occasional inaccuracies, inappropriacies and miusunderstandings in some situations.

6 Competent User: generally effective command of the language, although occasional misunderstanding and lack of fluency could interfere with communication.

5 Modest User: partial command of the language coping with overall meaning in most situations although some misunderstanding and lack of fluency could block communication.

4 Limited User: basic functional competence limited to familiar situations, but frequent problems in understanding and fluency can make communication a constant effort.

3 Extremely Limited User: below level of functional competence; although general meaning can be conveyed and understood in simple situations there are repeated breakdowns in communication.

2 Intermittent User: no real communication possible although single-word messages may be conveyed and understood.

1 Non-User: unable to use the language or does not provide relevant evidence of language competence for assessment.

Pattern Description

A All five subtests: for comprehensive information for making decisions about course placement and language tuition for academic courses.

B Modular subtests: An alternative to pattern A, for applicants who have used English to a major extent in their education and/or occupation.

C Non Academic Training Modular test: for applicants for occupational training courses or attachments. Sub-tests in this separate module are designated: M1 Listening, M2 Reading and Writing, M3 Interview. The highest achievable band in any of these tests is 6.

D Subtest G1: a preliminary screening procedure; no test report form issued.

E Subtests G1, M2, M3: for short stay (three months approximately) professional visitors who need to show some evidence of language ability.

Modular Descriptions
GA General Academic, LS Life Sciences, ME Medicine, PS
Physical Sciences, SS Social Studies, TE Technology, NA
NonAcademic

Scheme
OD Overseas Development Administration
BC British Council Scholarships, BU British Council Bursars,
EE EEC/EDF Awards, CF Country Financed, CB Confederation of
British Industry, UN UN Agencies, PR Private, OT Other

Interpretation
In addition to the band descriptions, overall performance can
be interpreted for placement on academic training courses.
This interpretation provided by the English Tuition
Coordinating Unit (ETCU) or by the Test Centre is in ideal
terms. The real outcome for individual candidates will be
varied by such factors as his/her age, mother tongue,
educational and cultural background, language learning
history, motivation, etc.

128

APPENDIX D   Form Used for Evaluation after Initial English Language Training

UNIVERSITY OF CAMBRIDGE
LOCAL EXAMINATIONS
SYNDICATE
THE BRITISH COUNCIL

English Language Testing Service
Test Validation Form 1

Candidate Details

Centre Code   Year Quarter   Cand. No.   Nationality   Mother Tongue

Name/last or family/first/middle   Sex M/F   Date of Birth

Foreword

This set of forms should be completed for the student named below at the end of his/her period of EL tuition. Both assessments should be made by the teacher/s most closely responsible for the progress of the student. The set (all 3 copies) should be returned to the **English Tuition Coordinating Unit (ETCU) in The British Council, London.**

Student Details

Name/last or family/first/middle   Centre Code   Year Quarter   Cand. No.

B C File Reference Number   Wks   Wks   Tuition Recom.   Tuition Rec'd.   Tuition began   Language school/centre

Standards

Please assess the student's performance in the four language 'skills' listed below by ticking one appropriate box for each skill

	Fluent	Good	Fair	Weak		Fluent	Good	Fair	Weak
Listening					Reading				
Speaking					Writing				

* Bands

Use the descriptions of levels of language ability set out below and assess the student's ability by ticking one appropriate box for each skill.

9 Expert User: fully operational command of the language; appropriate, accurate and fluent with complete understanding.
8 Very Good User: fully operational command of the language; occasional minor inaccuracies, inappropriacies or misunderstandings possible in unfamiliar situations.
7 Good User: operational command of the language; occasional inaccuracies, inappropriacies and misunderstandings in some situations.
6 Competent User: generally effective command of the language, although occasional misunderstanding and lack of fluency could interfere with communication.
5 Modest User: partial command of the language coping with overall meaning in most situations although some misunderstanding and lack of fluency could block communication.

4 Limited User: basic functional competence limited to familiar situations, but frequent problems in understanding and fluency can make communication a constant effort.
3 Extremely Limited User: below level of functional competence; although general meaning can be conveyed and understood in simple situations there are repeated breakdowns in communication.
2 Intermittent User: no real communication possible although single-word messages may be conveyed and understood.
1 Non-User: unable to use the language or does not provide relevant evidence of language competence for assessment.

	9	8	7	6	5	4	3	2	1
Listening									
Speaking									
Reading									
Writing									

Additional Comment (if applicable)

Teacher Details

Name   Position   Signature   Date

British Council use (ETCU)

*Editor's Note: See Appendix C for Band descriptions.

APPENDIX E Form Used for Evaluation before Beginning Course of Studies

UNIVERSITY OF CAMBRIDGE
LOCAL EXAMINATIONS
SYNDICATE
THE BRITISH COUNCIL

English Language Testing Service
Test Validation Form 2

Supervisor and Receiving Institution Address

Foreword

This set of forms is an important part of a programme to improve the English language testing and teaching of overseas students administered by the British Council before they study/train in the UK. The Testing Service would be grateful, therefore, if the member of staff who has most teaching contact with the student named below could fill in each section beginning with Student/Trainee Details. The assessments made will be stored on computer but without recording the names of either the assessed or the assessor. Please return the completed set of forms within one month of receipt to ELTS Liaison in the British Council in London using the enclosed pre-paid envelope. Thankyou.

Student/Trainee Details

Name/last or family/first /middle — Centre Code — Year Quarter — Cand. No.

BC File Reference Number — Subject of study/training — Date study/training began — Final Qualification

Activities
Assess the 'student's' English language performance in the activities listed below by ticking one appropriate box for each activity.

A = More than adequate B = Adequate C = Inadequate D = Not Applicable

	A	B	C		A	B	C	D
Lectures				Tutorials				
Seminars				Practicals/lab work				
Essays				Classwork				
Project Work				Training Attachment/field work				

* Bands
Use the descriptions of levels of English language ability set out below and assess the student's ability by ticking one appropriate box for each 'skill'.

9 Expert User: fully operational command of the language; appropriate, accurate and fluent with complete understanding.
8 Very Good User: fully operational command of the language; occasional minor inaccuracies, inappropriacies or misunderstandings possible in unfamiliar situations.
7 Good User: operational command of the language; occasional inaccuracies, inappropriacies and misunderstandings in some situations.
6 Competent User: generally effective command of the language, although occasional misunderstanding and lack of fluency could interfere with communication.
5 Modest User: partial command of the language coping with overall meaning in most situations although some misunderstanding and lack of fluency could block communication.

4 Limited User: basic functional competence limited to familiar situations, but frequent problems in understanding and fluency can make communication a constant effort.
3 Extremely Limited User: below level of functional competence; although general meaning can be conveyed and understood in simple situations there are repeated breakdowns in communication.
2 Intermittent User: no real communication possible although single-word messages may be conveyed and understood.
1 Non-User: unable to use the language or does not provide relevant evidence of language competence for assessment.

	9	8	7	6	5	4	3	2	1
Listening									
Speaking									
Reading									
Writing									

General Comment (if applicable)

Tutor/Teacher/Training Officer making the assessments

Name — Position — Signature — Date

*Editor's Note: See Appendix C for Band descriptions.

8.
The Associated Examining Board's Test in English for Educational Purposes (TEEP)

Allan Emmett

INTRODUCTION

In Pursuit of the Communicative Paradigm

In the wake of a greater emphasis on communication in language teaching, a similar paradigm shift is apparent in recent approaches to language testing, which take, as their starting point, language in use as against language usage. These approaches are influenced by a sociolinguistic model of communication where the concern is with the abilities and processes at work as speakers - in this case second language learners - attempt to handle the formal and functional dimensions of speech acts relevant to their needs in given situations.

In order to evaluate samples of performance, in certain specific contexts of use, created under particular test constraints, for what they can tell us about a candidate's underlying competence, it would first seem necessary to develop a framework of categories which would help us to identify the activities our target group are involved in. Only then can we construct realistic and representative test tasks corresponding to these activities. By applying these categories at the a priority test task validation stage we would hope to avoid some of the problems which have arisen in some earlier efforts at communicative testing where no attempt was made to produce explicit specifications of the candidates' projected language needs in the target situation before test task construction took place. Though we would be cautious in claims for the directness of fit possible between test realization and specification, we would argue that this approach enables us to come closer to matching test tasks with appropriate activities in the target behaviour than would be possible using nonempirical approaches.

This article presents a brief description of how we at the Associated Examining Board[1] (AEB) have attempted to ensure the content validity of our tests of English as a foreign language for overseas students. The three initial research and development stages reported below have been carried out in the context of a project which has been under way since 1978 to develop a Test in English for Educational Purposes (TEEP) which would have particular application for such students as wish to enter institutions for higher education in the United Kingdom. The aim of the test is to provide a profile of a candidate's proficiency in listening, reading, writing and speaking which will reflect how well or badly he or she might be expected to cope with the English language demands of an educational environment, and to provide diagnostic information to ESL programs for such students.

STAGE I: Who to test?

In Stage I of the TEEP project we established the levels, the discipline areas and the institutions where overseas students were enrolling in the further and higher education sectors. On the basis of the information gathered during this stage, we focused our research on students following courses in the general subject areas of science, engineering, and social, business and administrative studies.

STAGE II: What to test?

In Stage II, we sought to ascertain the communicative demands that are made on students following courses in these general discipline areas. Two methods of enquiry were employed to determine the language tasks facing students in a number of different academic contexts.

During 1980, we carried out a series of visits to educational institutions in different sectors of tertiary education. Observations of science, engineering, and social science courses were made at the Universities of Exeter, London and Reading and also at colleges in Farnborough, Bradford, Newbury and Padworth. During these visits, the general language tasks facing students taking part in lectures, seminars and practical classes were recorded using an observation schedule derived from A Science Teaching Observation Schedule (Egglestone 1975) and from John Munby's Communicative Syllabus Design (Munby 1978). The data generated by these exercises provided us with the framework for our second method of enquiry: the questionnaire (See Weir 1983a and b for a more detailed discussion of this stage).

During 1981 we contacted all the university and polytechnic science, engineering, and social science departments and colleges offering General Certificate of Education (GCE) Advanced Level science, where we knew from earlier research that there were large numbers of overseas students, and asked them to assist us in our project. We then asked those who were willing to co-operate to let us have details of the numbers of overseas students enrolled in specific courses within their departments, for whom English was not the first language in the country of origin together with numbers of the staff who taught them. Questionnaires were then sent to staff and through them to both British and overseas students. Completed questionnaires were received from 940 overseas students, 530 British students and 559 staff in respect of 43 post-graduate courses, 61 undergraduate courses and 39 "A" level centres.

In the questionnaire we asked the students to estimate the frequency with which certain events and activities occurred in respect of the total programme of study they were enrolled on. They also provided us with a general estimate of the amount of difficulty various activities and constraints caused them. The staff were asked to give an overall impression of the frequency of occurrence of various activities on the programme we had specified, with particular reference to the courses they taught. They were also asked to estimate the proportion of overseas and British students in these courses who had encountered difficulty with particular activities or under particular constraints.

In terms of the type of question that we were able to ask in the questionnaire, reading and writing differed from listening and speaking in that it was easier to ask a more complete set of frequency questions about the former because they are relatively free of the performance constraints that affect the latter. Although we were able to collect data in respect of the level of difficulty these activities and constraints caused in listening and speaking, for various reasons it was often not possible to collect data on the frequency with which they occurred (Tables 1 and 4).

Questionnaire results

Tables 1-4a summarize the questionnaire returns concerning the frequency with which students had to carry out various communicative activities in the academic context and the relative levels of difficulty encountered by overseas students as compared with their British counterparts in coping with these tasks and attendant performance constraints.
Difficulty Each table summarizes the data collected for one skill (listening, reading, writing, speaking). The activities and performance constraints related to that skill are listed in the table according to the percentage of overseas students who reported having "some" or "a lot of" difficulty in each area. The second column provides a modified rank order of difficulty for these students calculated by deducting the percentage of British students reporting similar difficulty.

Tables 1, 3 and 4 also present data from university staff members on their perception of the relative difficulty of the various activities and performance constraints which they felt would apply to overseas students. The results are based on the percentage of staff reporting "some" or "a lot of" difficulty. As before, there is also a modified rank order representing the difference between the estimates of overseas and British students experiencing difficulty. Table 3 (writing) also presents an estimate of the relative importance of the specified criteria according to the percentage of staff who marked each one as being of "high" or "medium" importance.
Frequency Frequency data are reported in Tables 1a, 2a, 3a and 4a for subsets of the items listed in Tables 1-4. These data summarize responses from overseas students studying in various disciplines with respect to the frequency with which they were required to use English in the specified areas. Within each discipline group, the percentage of students reporting either that they "never" had to do the task or were "often" required to do it is indicated in these tables.

Taking this frequency data separately or, where possible, in conjunction with the difficulty data, we have tried to establish what might be considered as "key" activities and constraints across levels and disciplines. As most tests can only sample a limited part of the possible domain it seemed prudent to ensure that we included in the battery those tasks which were common and frequent across disciplines and levels and/or

TABLE 1 *Rank Order of Difficulty Experienced in Listening Tasks as Estimated by Students and Staff

Task	OS	OS–BR	Staff OS	Staff OS–BR
Teachers and other students talk very fast	1 (55.0)	2 (35.7)	–	–
Accents or pronunciation differ from the accustomed	2 (52.7)	3 (27.6)	–	–
Writing down quickly and clearly all the desired notes	3 (41.5)	10 (8.9)	–	–
More than one person is speaking (e.g., group discussion)	4 (41.1)	4 (26.4)	–	–
Understanding informal language	5 (38.6)	1 (36.9)	3 (52.5)	1 (47.5)
Thinking of and using suitable abbreviations	6 (33.9)	7 (21.7)	–	–
Understanding spoken description or narrative	7 (31.0)	6 (26.3)	2 (53.2)	2 (41.9)
Recognizing individual words in what is being said	8 (30.8)	6 (26.3)	–	–
People speak quietly	9 (29.3)	13 (2.3)	–	–
Recognizing what is important and worth noting	10 (28.0)	12 (5.8)	–	–
Understanding completely what was said and linking it to what was said earlier	11 (23.6)	9 (12.9)	–	–
Understanding spoken instructions	12 (21.1)	8 (19.0)	4 (44.1)	3 (35.3)
Organizing notes so they are comprehensible later	13 (18.2)	15 (–0.8)	–	–
Understanding the subject matter of the talk	14 (18.1)	14 (0.6)	1 (66.2)	5 (11.4)
Recognizing where sentences end and begin	15 (9.9)	11 (7.8)	–	–

*Rank based on percentage of those reporting "some" or "a lot of" difficulty. Actual percentage reported in brackets.

OS =	Overseas students
OS–BR =	Difference between overseas students and British students having difficulty
Staff OS =	Staff estimate of overseas students having difficulty
Staff OS–BR =	Staff estimate of difference between overseas and British students having difficulty

TABLE 1a *Estimated Frequency of Performing Specific Listening Tasks Based on the Highest Returns (Never and Often)

Task	Engineering U Never	Engineering U Often	Engineering P Never	Engineering P Often	Science P Never	Science P Often	Science A Never	Science A Often	Social Sciences U Never	Social Sciences U Often	Social Sciences P Never	Social Sciences P Often
Understanding Spoken Instructions	20-39	60-79	20-39	20-39		40-59		40-59		40-59		60-79
Making Notes		40-59				20-39				20-39		

*Range of Frequencies expressed as a percentage   U = Undergraduate   P = Post-graduate   A = Advanced level GCE

TABLE 3a *Estimated Frequency of Performing Specific Writing Tasks Based on the Highest Returns (Never and Often)

Task	Engineering U Never	Engineering U Often	Engineering P Never	Engineering P Often	Science P Never	Science P Often	Science A Never	Science A Often	Social Sciences U Never	Social Sciences U Often	Social Sciences P Never	Social Sciences P Often
More than a paragraph in:												
coursework		40-59		40-59		20-39		40-59		20-39		20-39
examinations		40-59		40-59		20-39		40-59				20-39
About a paragraph in:												
coursework		20-39		20-39		20-39		20-39		20-39		40-59
examinations	20-39	20-39		20-39	20-39	20-39		20-39		20-39		20-39
Less than a paragraph in:												
coursework		20-39		20-39		20-39		20-39		40-59		20-39
examinations		20-39		40-59	20-39	20-39		20-39		20-39		60-79

*Range of frequencies expressed as a percentage   U = Undergraduate   P = Post-graduate   A = Advanced level GCE

TABLE 2 *Rank Order of Difficulty Experienced in Reading Tasks as Estimated by Students

Task	OS	OS-BR
Reading texts where the subject matter is very complicated	1 (67.9)	7 (8.4)
Critical reading to establish and evaluate the author's position on a particular topic	2 (55.3)	2 (21.8)
Reading quickly to find out how useful it would be to study a particular text more intensively	3 (49.7)	1 (26.2)
Search reading to get information specifically required for assignments	4 (39.6)	3 (18.3)
Reading carefully to understand all the information in a text	5 (35.0)	6 (8.5)
Making notes from textbooks	6 (25.9)	5 (12.7)
Reading to get the main information from a text	7 (25.8)	4 (14.3)

* Rank based on percentage of those reporting "some" or "a lot of" difficulty. Actual percentage reported in brackets.

OS = Overseas students
OS-BR = Difference between overseas students and British students having difficulty

TABLE 2a *Estimated Frequency of Performing Specific Reading Tasks Based on the Highest Returns (Never and Often)

Task	Engineering U Never	U Often	P Never	P Often	Science U Never	U Often	P Never	P Often	A Never	A Often	Social Sciences U Never	U Often	P Never	P Often
Critical reading to evaluate author's position on particular topic	40-59		20-39		40-59		20-39		40-59			20-39		40-59
Scanning to establish utility of more intensive text reading	20-39	20-39		20-39	20-39	20-39		20-39	20-39			20-39		40-59
Search reading to fulfill an assignment		40-59		60-79		40-59		60-79		20-39		80		60-79
Reading carefully to understand all information in:														
– duplicated notes		40-59		60-79		40-59		60-79		20-39		40-59		40-59
– questions done in class or for homework		40-59		40-59		40-59		40-59		40-59		40-59		20-39
– laboratory worksheets	60-79	40-59	20-39	40-59		20-39		20-39	20-39	20-39				
– examination questions		40-59		40-59		20-39		20-39	20-39	40-59	40-59	20-39		20-39
– textbooks whole or part		20-39		40-59		40-59		60-79		20-39		60-79		60-79
Making notes from texts	20-39			20-39				20-39		20-39		60-79		60-79
Reading to get the main information from a text		20-39		20-39		20-39		40-59		20-39		40-59		60-79

*Range of frequencies expressed as a percentage   U = Undergraduate   P = Post-graduate   A = Advanced level GCE

TABLE 3 *Rank Order of Difficulty Experienced in Writing
Tasks as Estimated by Students and Staff

Task	OS	OS–BR	STAFF OS	STAFF OS–BR	STAFF IMPT.
Using a wide and varied range of vocabulary	1 (61.9)	1 (41.2)	5 (66.9)	3 (30.1)	10 (41.3)
Using a variety of grammatical structures	2 (47.2)	3 (30.7)	4 (70.0)	5 (17.7)	12 (22.2)
Using appropriate vocabulary	3 (46.4)	2 (34.2)	7 (63.8)	1 (33.2)	4 (69.6)
Expressing what you want to say clearly	4 (40.8)	7 (14.5)	3 (70.2)	4 (21.5)	2 (90.9)
Using appropriate grammatical structures	5 (40.4)	4 (24.8)	2 (71.4)	2 (30.6)	8 (43.3)
Arranging and developing written work	6 (35.8)	8 (13.7)	6 (65.5)	9 (10.3)	3 (82.1)
Writing grammatically correct sentences	7 (33.5)	5 (20.7)	1 (75.3)	6 (16.3)	6 (46.9)
The subject matter	8 (29.9)	6 (18.8)	9 (60.6)	10 (10.2)	1 (91.8)
Spelling	9 (24.3)	10 (2.0)	8 (62.1)	8 (11.3)	9 (42.3)
Punctuation	10 (21.4)	9 (8.9)	10 (59.6)	7 (12.9)	11 (39.3)
Tidiness	11 (16.8)	12 (−5.3)	12 (47.1)	12 (−4.3)	5 (62.8)
Handwriting	12 (14.2)	11 (−4.1)	11 (49.4)	11 (−2.3)	7 (44.6)

* Rank based on percentage of those reporting "some" or "a lot of" difficulty.
Actual percentage reported in brackets.

OS =	Overseas students
OS–BR =	Difference between overseas students and British students having difficulty
Staff OS =	Staff estimate of overseas students having difficulty
Staff OS–BR =	Staff estimate of difference between overseas and British students having difficulty
Staff Impt.	Staff estimate of importance of criterion based on "high" and "medium" ratings

TABLE 4 *Rank Order of Difficulty Experienced in Speaking Tasks as Estimated by Students and Staff

Task	OS	OS–BR	Staff OS	Staff OS–BR
Giving oral reports or short talks	1 (50.3)	1 (38.4)	** 7 (39.9)	**10 (12.3)
Expressing counter-arguments to points raised by teachers in discussions	2 (48.1)	4 (26.6)	3 (54.4)	6 (17.9)
Explaining your opinions when they are not immediately understood in discussions	3 (45.9)	3 (27.7)	2 (55.3)	3 (23.8)
Expressing counter-arguments to points raised by other students in discussions	4 (45.0)	2 (29.8)	** 5 (47.8)	** 7 (17.2)
Expressing your own opinions in discussions	5 (37.2)	4 (26.7)	4 (50.6)	1 (25.2)
Answering questions asked by teachers	6 (31.6)	6 (20.9)	1 (63.2)	5 (19.6)
Asking teachers questions	7 (22.0)	7 (17.5)	6 (46.8)	4 (23.3)
Answering questions asked by other students	8 (19.3)	9 (12.7)	** 8 (31.0)	** 8 (12.8)
Working with other students using English to communicate	9 (18.7)	8 (16.4)	9 (30.8)	2 (24.0)
Asking other students questions	10 (14.5)	10 (11.8)	**10 (23.3)	** 9 (12.4)

* Rank based on percentage of those reporting "some" or "a lot of" difficulty. Actual percentage reported in brackets.

```
OS =              Overseas students
OS–BR =           Difference between overseas students and British students
                  having difficulty
Staff OS =        Staff estimate of overseas students having difficulty
Staff OS–BR =     Staff estimate of difference between overseas and
                  British students having difficulty
```

**High proportion of "don't know".

TABLE 4a *Estimated Frequency of Performing Specific Speaking Tasks Based on the Highest Returns (Never and Often)

Task	Engineering U		Engineering P		Science U		Science P		Science A		Social Sciences U		Social Sciences P	
	Never	Often	Never	Often	Never	Often	Never	Often	Never	Often	Never	Often	Never	Often
Giving oral reports or short talks	40-59		20-39		40-59		40-59		40-59					20-39
Answering questions asked by teachers	20-39	40-59		40-59		40-59		20-39		40-59		60-79		40-59
Asking teachers questions		40-59		20-39		40-59		20-39		40-59		20-39		20-39
Working with other students using English to communicate	80-			40-59		40-59		40-59		40-59		60-79		60-79
Actively participating in discussions	20-39			20-39		20-39		20-39		20-39		40-59		40-59

*Range of Frequencies expressed as a percentage

U = Undergraduate
P = Post-graduate
A = Advanced level GCE

seemed, from the available evidence, more likely to cause problems for the overseas as against the British students.

For example, if we take Tables 2 and 2a, where the major focus is on reading activities, the most frequent activity students have to perform is "search reading to get information specifically required for assignments". Compare this with "reading critically to establish and evaluate the author's position on a particular topic", which is marginally more important in terms of the relative amount of difficulty it occasions overseas as against British students. In fact, however, it is only the social science student who really has to cope with this task to any great extent. It would seem prudent, in taking decisions about what reading tasks to include in a time constrained, communicative, proficiency test, to have this kind of information available.

STAGE III: How to test

During the third stage of the project, we were concerned with designing and validating a variety of test formats to establish the best methods for assessing a student's performance level on those tasks and under those constraints that the research to date has indicated to be important to overseas students following academic courses through the medium of English.

The pilot version of the test battery contained two components. The first, Session I, was designed to be taken by all students. The texts, considered to be accessible to candidates from all disciplines, were selected from the area of "general science". The second component, Session II, had two versions. Session IIA was intended for students in the fields of arts, social sciences, business and administrative studies. Session IIB was intended for students in the fields of science and engineering. The texts in both versions were selected from written and spoken sources in the appropriate discipline area, and test tasks in both Sessions IIA and IIB were parallel.

In Session I and both versions of Session II, candidates are required to demonstrate their proficiency in reading, listening and writing. A variety of test formats are used in Session I and Session II to test a candidate's proficiency in the range of enabling skills required to operate successfully in the various study modes. In addition to testing specifically the constituent enabling skills underlying abilities in reading, listening and writing, we also included a more integrated task in each of the Sessions, in which reading and/or listening activities lead into a writing task.

Pre-tests of Session I and both versions of Session II were carried out on groups of GCE Advanced Level, first year undergraduate and one year post-graduate native and non-native students in the academic disciplines mentioned above.

A third Session testing ability in spoken English was prepared in collaboration with the Association of Recognised English Language Schools with whom the test will be jointly administered. This Session was pre-tested with a number of overseas students in various educational establishments most of them ARELS schools. The assessment criteria developed for use with Session III are listed in Appendix 1.

The pre-tests of all sessions and a number of other checks enabled the Board to carry out a great deal of internal and external validation of the tests. This in turn enabled the determination of the final format of the examination which can be seen in Appendix 2.

By following the stages of test development outlined in this article and incorporating the results as much as possible into the test format, we have tried to ensure that the final form of this examination will provide an accurate profile of the candidate's ability to cope with the language demands of an academic environment.

NOTES

1. The AEB is one of the largest of the General Certificate of Education (GCE) boards operating in England, Wales and Northern Ireland. Its first examinations were given in 1955. By 1982 it had grown to the extent that over 160 external examinations were offered in 4,174 centres in the United Kingdom and 198 centres overseas. The total number of candidates entering these and other special examinations was 471,717 (17,116 of them overseas) and the total number of subject entries was 916,013 (37,250 of them overseas).

144

REFERENCES

Egglestone, J. 1975. <u>A Science Teaching Observation Sched</u>-<u>ule</u>. London: Macmillan Educational.
Munby, J. 1978. <u>Communicative Syllabus Design</u>. Cambridge: Cambridge University Press.
Weir, C. 1983a. Identifying the language problems of overseas students in tertiary education in the United Kingdom. Ph.D. Dissertation, University of London, Institute of Education.
Weir, C. 1983b. The Associated Examining Board's test in English for academic purposes: an exercise in content validity. In Hughes, A., and D. Porter (eds.), <u>Develop</u>-<u>ments in Language Testing</u>. London: Academic Press.

APPENDIX 1

ASSESSMENT CRITERIA

A. LISTENING COMPREHENSION

1. Understands too little for the intended communication to take place. Interlocutor has to search constantly for individual words or phrases that interviewee does understand.

2. Understands intended communication only if half-speed speech is used and this only if interlocutor frequently repeats and/or rephrases.

3. Understands intended communication if slightly slowed speech is used and occasional repetitions and/or rephrasings are given.

4. Understands intended communication at normal speed given the need for occasional repetitions and/or rephrasings.

5. Understands intended communication at normal speed. Seems only to be very occasionally thrown by colloquialisms, low-frequency items or "noise".

6. Understands intended communication with native speaker competence.

B. "ACCENT"

1. Severe and constant pronunciation, stress and intonation problems cause almost complete unintelligibility.

2. Frequent and severe pronunciation, stress and intonation problems make understanding very difficult and require frequent repetition from interviewee.

3. Pronunciation, stress and intonation errors require concentrated listening but only occasional misunderstanding is caused or repetition required.

4. Marked "foreign accent" but no misunderstanding caused or repetition required.

5. No conspicuous pronunciation/stress/intonation errors. Full intelligibility with normal listening though would not be taken for a native speaker.

6. Native speaker pronunciation/stress/intonation.

C. FORMAL ACCURACY

1. Almost all grammatical patterns inaccurate except in a few stock phrases. Inaccuracies cause very frequent breakdowns in communication.

2. Frequent grammatical inaccuracies show control of few major patterns and often cause breakdowns in the intended communi cation.

3. Quite frequent grammatical inaccuracies show ome major patterns not under control. Occasional breakdowns in communication caused.

4. Occasional grammatical inaccuracies showing imperfect control of a few patterns. No breakdowns in the intended communication caused by them.

5. Only infrequent and minor grammatical inaccuracies. Intended communication not even hampered by them.

6. Native speaker grammatical accuracy.

D. REFERENTIAL ADEQUACY

1. Vocabulary inadequate even for the most basic parts of the intended communication.

2. Vocabulary inadequacies restrict participant to communication on only a few topics and even then with frequent lexical inaccuracies.

3. Vocabulary inadequacies hamper a significant part of the intended communication. Fairly frequent lexical inaccuracies.

4. Vocabulary adequate for most of the intended communication. Occasional lexical inaccuracies and/or circumlocutions.

5. Vocabulary adequate all round for the intended communication. Only very occasional lexical inaccuracies and/or circumlocutions.

6. Vocabulary as broad and accurate as a native speaker.

Note: Assessors should if possible add any evidence of a difference of adequacy between participant's vocabulary in non-specialist communication and his vocabulary in communication about his specialist subject.

E. SOCIOCULTURAL APPROPRIATENESS

1. Communicative competence level so low that participant has no possibility of adapting his language use appropriately to the social situation.

2. Only stock phrases seem socially appropriate. Otherwise no real sign of participant adapting utterances to the social situation.

3. Frequent errors in the rules of social language use result in communication that is often inappropriate to the setting, role-set or in tone. Errors significant enough to cause occasional social misunderstanding.

4. Occasional errors in the rules of social language use result in communication that is sometimes inappropriate to the setting or role-set, or in tone. Errors not significant enough to be likely to cause social misunderstanding.

5. Rare, insignificant errors in the rules of social language use do not result in communication that is inappropriate to the setting, role-set or in tone, thus do not cause social misunderstanding.

6. Native speaker control of the rules of social language use.

F. FLUENCY

1. Utterances so halting and fragmentary that communication is virtually impossible. No helpful intersentential connections.

2. Utterances very slow, uneven and often incomplete except in a few stock remarks and responses. Only a narrow and repetitive range of inter-sentential connectors.

3. Utterances fairly slow, hesitant and uneven. Some utterances incomplete but some are suitably inter-connected.

4. Utterances produced at a reasonable speed though with occasional hesitancies. Most unevenness caused by groping, rephrasing and repair. A reasonable range of suitable inter-sentential connectors used.

5. Utterances quite fast, fairly effortless and well-connected inter-sententially.

6. Utterances produced with a native-speaker's speed, effortlessness and inter-sentential connections.

APPENDIX 2

SESSION I

Part One

is a test of candidates' ability to read in English and to
write in English about what they have read. They have
<u>2 tasks</u> to do in 75 minutes.

> <u>Task One</u> — they have to write a summary of parts of a
> passage. To help them to do this, they
> should make brief notes while reading the
> passage.

> <u>Task Two</u> — they have to write short answers to a
> number of questions on the same passage.

Part Two

is a test of candidates' ability to understand spoken
English. They have one task to do in approximately 10
minutes.

They hear a short tape recording once only. During pauses
in the recording, they have to write down, in the space
provided in the answer booklet, what the speaker has said.

Part Three

is another test of candidates' ability to understand
spoken English. They have to make notes and use them to
answer a number of questions. They have <u>2 tasks</u> to do in
approximately 50 minutes.

> <u>Task One</u> — they hear a tape recording of a short lecture
> once only. A written outline of the main
> points of the lecture is printed in the answer
> booklet to help them to follow what the
> speaker is saying. This lecture outline
> consists of three important statements from
> the passage, each followed by questions.
> While listening to the lecture they have to
> make notes in the spaces provided as, after
> the lecture, they have time to go through
> these notes and use them to write answers.

> <u>Task Two</u> — they have to write a summary of parts of the
> lecture, using the lecture outline and their
> notes and answers.

150

SESSION II
(A and B)

Part One

is a test of candidates' ability to read in English. There are 2 different reading passages. They have <u>2 tasks</u> to do in 50 minutes.

Task One - establishing where words are missing from a passage and writing these words in spaces provided.

Task Two - writing short answers to a number of questions on a second passage.

Part Two

is a test of candidates' ability to understand spoken English by making notes and using them to answer questions. They have <u>one task</u> to do in 30 minutes.

They hear a short tape recording of a short interview once only. A written outline of the interview is printed in the answer booklet to help them to follow what the speakers are saying. The outline consists of a number of questions. They have to make notes in the spaces provided while they are listening to the interview. After this interview, they have time to go through the notes they have made and use them to write answers.

Part Three

is a test of the candidates' ability to write in English, in complete sentences, and organize their work so that what they write is clear and answers the questions they are asked. They have <u>2 tasks</u> to do in 65 minutes.

Task One - writing a summary using:

    a) notes made on the second reading passage in Part One;
    b) relevant information from Part Two.

Task Two - rewriting a short passage which contains a number of errors, making all the necessary corrections.

SESSION III

This is a test of candidates' ability to speak in English.
The test is in five parts.

Part One

Candidates have to speak about themselves for one minute.

Part Two

Candidates have to respond to a number of remarks that might
be made to them, or to situations they might find themselves
in when they are in Britain.

Part Three

Candidates have to imagine they are in a small discussion
group. They listen to a discussion and at certain points
they have to answer questions or give their opinions.

Part Four

Candidates have a specific task to complete, which involves
asking questions relating to non-verbal information, e.g.,
charts, diagrams, graphs, etc.

Part Five

Candidates are given a printed passage to study. They have
five minutes in which to prepare an answer to a question set
on this material. They then have two minutes to present
their answer to the question.

9.
If I Had Known Then What I Know Now: Performance Testing of Foreign Teaching Assistants

Kathleen M. Bailey

INTRODUCTION

As the title suggests, this article is written from the comfortable vantage point of hindsight.[1] My purpose in writing it is to look critically at a second language performance test which I helped develop and to suggest some possible improvements to that test. In my title, "then" refers to the initial design and development phases of test construction (Carroll 1980:13), which took place in 1978-79, while "now" refers to a period of time some five years later. During the intervening period, I have witnessed a great deal more of the real-life behavior this test was intended to capture. It is hoped that the conclusions drawn from my learning process will be helpful to other designers of performance tests.[2]

The non-native speaking (NNS) population whose oral English proficiency was assessed by this performance test consisted of foreign graduate students employed as teaching assistants at UCLA. In U.S. universities, teaching assistants, or "TAs", assume one of three important roles within the instructional ranks: (1) they conduct follow-up discussion sections in support of professors' lectures (e.g., in history, physics, mathematics, and linguistics), (2) they supervise students conducting laboratory experiments in conjunction with science courses; or (3) they have primary responsibility for self-contained lower-division classes, particularly in English composition, remedial mathematics, and foreign languages. Regardless of their main function, almost all TAs respond to individual students' questions during office hours or in tutoring centers. Some assist professors in grading tests and preparing course materials.

CONTEXT OF THE PROBLEM

The 1970s witnessed an increase in the proportion of foreign graduate students attending U.S. universities. Many factors contributed to this trend, but one of the results was that the proportion of teaching assistantships awarded to NNSs increased at many colleges. Survey research utilizing self-report data indicates that at UCLA the "typical" NNS TA is a male working towards a doctorate in either mathematics, engineering, or the sciences. It is likely that he has studied English for seven years or more, and that he feels his spoken English can be characterized as "good" to "fluent". He would probably describe his teaching as "good" or "very good". There is about a one-in-three chance that he is Asian (Bailey 1982a:81). Anecdotal evidence suggests that the NNS TAs, like many teaching assistants in the sciences, probably view their assistantships as a means of supporting themselves in graduate school, rather than as an entry into the college teaching profession (Lnenicka 1972:97; Stockdale and Wochok 1974:345).

As more NNS TAs entered the instructional ranks, undergraduate students complained that their TAs' English speaking ability (or lack thereof) was negatively influencing their education (Bailey 1982a; Berdie, Anderson, Wenberg and Price 1976; Kelley 1982; Lurie 1981; Mestenhauser et al. 1980; Shaw 1982; Swanbeck 1981; Timmerman 1981). Parents wrote angry letters to administrators, who then turned to TESOL specialists and TA trainers for help. As a result, English second language (ESL) based training programs for NNS TAs were implemented at many colleges. (See Bailey 1982a:18-20 for references to these programs.)

Where programs spring up, testing is seldom far behind. In 1979, Jones called for a performance test to assess the English speaking proficiency of NNS TAs. Hinofotis, Bailey and Stern (1981) responded to Jones' statement of need and to complaints about NNS TAs at UCLA by developing such a performance test. It was used in an advanced oral communications course that was designed for prospective NNS TAs

(Hinofotis and Bailey 1978). The test consisted of a task and a rating instrument which functioned as the entry and exit mechanism for the course. Raters who used the instrument in various phases of the research connected with that course included ESL teachers, TA trainers, and undergraduate students (Hinofotis and Bailey 1981). The instrument was pilot tested and revised, based on the results of statistical analyses and raters' reactions. (See Hinofotis et al. 1981 for a description of this process.) However, this performance test was not used on a campus-wide basis to screen applicants at the departmental level. Instead, it was used only with those NNSs who sought out help or were sent to the ESL courses by their graduate advisors.[3]

THE PERFORMANCE TEST

The tangible portion of this performance test is a rating instrument (see Appendix A) based on the Likert scale model. Raters viewing a videotape of a prospective TA first took notes on the examinee's performance. Then they indicated their Initial Overall Impression by circling a number from 1 (poor) to 9 (excellent).

Because we wanted the instrument to provide specific diagnostic information as well as global scores, raters were also asked to mark nine-point Likert scales for twelve performance subcategories grouped under three main categories. For each performance subcategory, the raters were given a brief explanation (see Appendix B).

These categories and their descriptions had in fact been developed during the pilot study (Hinofotis et al. 1981) in which ESL teachers viewed videotapes of NNSs performing a task (described below) and rated them holistically on a nine-point Likert scale. The raters' open-ended comments about the language samples and the factors that had influenced their ratings were tabulated and then organized - the results being the three main categories of Language Proficiency, Delivery, and Communication of Information, along with the twelve subcategories and their descriptors. These main categories in some ways parallel the three components of communicative competence (linguistic, strategic and sociolinguistic competence, respectively) proposed by Canale and Swain (1980) in their original model. (See Hinofotis and Bailey 1981:123 for further discussion of this point.)

After marking the performance categories, the raters circled a Final Overall Impression score. Then they indicated whether or not the examinee's English proficiency was sufficient for him to assume the role of a TA (a) lecturing in

English, (b) leading a discussion section, or (c) conducting a lab section.

But a test is more than an instrument by which performance is rated. In discussing communicative language testing, Wesche (1983:43) notes that language tests usually consist of stimulus material, a related task which demands a response from the examinee, and criteria for scoring the examinee's performance. The existing performance test for NNS TAs is discussed below in terms of Wesche's framework.

Stimulus Material

In the performance test devised by Hinofotis et al. (1981), the stimulus material consisted of five subject-specific vocabulary items or concepts (printed on individual index cards) along with the following statement:

> Here are five terms related to your academic field. Choose one that you would feel comfortable explaining.
> Imagine that you are the teaching assistant for an introductory _____ course and that I am a student in the class. I missed a lecture and I have come to you for help before an examination. I don't know this term, which I came across in my reading, and I think it will be on the test. You have five minutes to explain this term to me in any way you can without writing or drawing anything. You can take some time to think about what you'll say. Do you have any questions?

The terms had been chosen from the glossaries of introductory texts in the various disciplines of the examinees. Each person was allowed to reject all five terms and choose from among five others if they wished. This process continued until the examinees found a vocabulary item with which they were comfortable since the intent here was to assess the subjects' abilities to explain familiar material rather than to test their knowledge of the subject matter. This decision reflects a central concern in second language performance testing: "the aim is to assess communicative proficiency in the subject concerned, not to test specific knowledge of it" (Carroll 1980:38).

Task and Response

In designing a performance test that could be used with TAs from a variety of disciplines, we decided on the situation described above - that of helping an individual student during office hours - because it would be common to all TAs, regardless of their departments or their functions. The task of the examination would be to explain the chosen term to the "student" who asked questions and expressed uncertainty in order to keep the prospective TA interacting for five minutes. The examinees' response consisted of their initial explanation and their reactions to the "student's" questions. The role-play was videotaped.

This procedure provided language samples of equal length and roughly comparable content which were restricted to speech and gestures. Videotaping of the performance permitted delayed and repeated ratings of the speech samples. Furthermore, "by putting the assessor in the background and bringing in a non-assessing native speaker as a role player" (Carroll 1980:54-55), we allowed the various raters to concentrate on the evaluation process with no responsibility for eliciting speech samples. Finally, videotaping permitted a later detailed analysis of the native speaker's behavior in the role-play (Pike 1979).

Criteria

The term criteria has at least two meanings in the language testing literature. One is the use of criteria to designate the categories or topics on which the examinees are to be rated. This definition applies to the performance categories on the present rating instrument.

The second meaning of criteria in language testing refers to the guidelines for assigning scores to the examinees' performance on the specified categories. Carroll has called these types of guidelines performance scales (1980:30-31). The use of performance scales is familiar in the research on evaluating students' writing. (See, for example, Brown and Bailey 1980; Mullen 1977.) In fact, while compiling a status report on writing assessment, Stiggins identified the use of such scoring grids as one of the key features of analytic scoring, in which "raters rely on written guidelines... to assist them in assigning scores" (1982:149). In oral proficiency testing, the familiar level descriptions of the **Foreign Service Institute (FSI)** Oral Interview provide an example of scoring guidelines.

Although the performance categories had been systematically developed and then investigated through regression analysis (Hinofotis et al. 1981) and factor analysis (Hinofotis 1980), the present performance test for NNS TAs did not include explicit scoring guidelines (the second meaning of

criteria). Instead, the various raters who had judged examinees' performance with this instrument developed a sense of
intersubjective agreement by viewing, rating and discussing
sample videotapes during a training period. This process
parallels the use of range finders (model papers that typify
given rating levels) in holistic scoring of compositions
(Stiggins 1982:147).

A cursory glance at the performance category descriptors
reveals that the rating instrument was intended to focus the
raters primarily on the prospective TAs' language - not their
teaching skills per se, though the line between the two is fuzzy
at best. This decision to try to test language proficiency
(albeit in a teaching situation) was motivated by several
factors. First, it would have been impossible for the ESL
specialists to assess the prospective TAs' subject-matter
knowledge. How well they knew chemistry, engineering,
physics, etc., was clearly a matter to be left to the individual
departments which were responsible for ensuring the instructional effectiveness of their teaching assistants. Second, it
was the students' and parents' complaints about the NNS TAs'
English, not their teaching, that was being addressed through
the advanced oral communications course and the testing
research. Thus, with some trepidation about not being able to
clearly define where language usage left off and language use
began (see Widdowson 1978 and Carroll 1980:7), we set out to
examine the performance of potential NNS TAs in a teaching
situation.

RESEARCH RESULTS

Several studies were undertaken using data generated by
this performance test. A pilot study was conducted to assess
the instrument's intra- and inter-rater reliability. Videotapes
of prospective NNS TAs (made before and after they had taken
the advanced oral communications course) were randomized and
viewed by ESL teachers, TA trainers and undergraduate
students who rated the examinees' performance. A generalizability study was also conducted to estimate the various
sources of error in the ratings of prospective NNS TAs' oral
English proficiency. Some results of these studies are
summarized below.

Experimental Research

The performance test generated intra-rater reliability
coefficients for nine raters ranging from .66 to .96 in the pilot

study, with an average intra-rater reliability coefficient of .87 (Hinofotis et al. 1981:111). Inter-rater reliability coefficients on the Overall Impression scores ranged from .78 to .95 ($\underline{n}$ = 9) in the pilot study (1981:112), from .78 to .92 for ESL teachers and TA trainers ($\underline{n}$ = 6), and from .80 to .93 for the undergraduate raters ($\overline{\underline{n}}$ = 10) (Hinofotis and Bailey 1981:131). These figures range from acceptable to good as measures of the instrument's reliability.

In the research which used pre- and post-treatment videotapes of prospective NNS TAs performing the task, the group means reflected statistically significant improvement in performance, whether the raters were ESL teachers and TA trainers or undergraduate students (1981:129). However, no control group was available, so we were unable to attribute the observed improvement unambiguously to the advanced oral communications course.

In comparing the undergraduate raters' reactions to the videotaped speech samples with those of the TA trainers and ESL teachers, one difference emerged which foreshadowed later findings. Although both the undergraduates and the older raters rank ordered Pronunciation as the most important factor among the twelve performance categories, the TA trainers and ESL teachers ranked Ability to Relate to Student eighth, after all four Language Proficiency variables, Development of Explanation, Presence, and Clarity of Expression.

In contrast, the undergraduates ranked it second (1981:125). In a later study (Bailey 1982a), affective factors associated with TA-student relationships again emerged as important variables in students' ratings of TAs' overall teaching effectiveness.

The pilot study data were also subjected to a generalizability theory analysis (Bolus, Hinofotis, and Bailey 1982). This research yielded low (i.e., desirable) variance component estimates for raters and rating occasions (the generalizability study facets analogous to inter- and intra-rater reliability, respectively). Variance component estimates for the subject-by-occasion and rater-by-occasion facets were also low. However, there was a large variance component estimate for the subject-by-rater facet, indicating that various raters reacted differently to the videotaped performances of NNS subjects. This result is worrisome since it may be a source of uncontrolled error in many types of language testing in which raters judge NNSs' performance (Ray Moy, personal communication, March 1983). In a later study using this performance test (Hinofotis and Bailey 1981), the number of raters was increased in order to minimize this source of error.

The foregoing discussion has introduced the context of the "foreign TA problem", described the development of a second language performance test by a team of researchers, and summarized some of the results obtained with that test. But what do I know now that we didn't know then?

In developing the performance test described above, Hinofotis et al. (1981) drew on several sources of information. These included our own experience as teachers and classroom observers, students' and parents' complaints about NNS TAs, the communicative skills and shortcomings of the prospective TAs enrolled in the advanced oral communications course, discussions with experienced and inexperienced TAs (both native and non-native speakers of English), and a needs assessment of chemistry and economics TAs conducted by Chaudron (personal communication). We also considered information from other ESL-based TA training programs at several universities.

What we did not do at that stage was to conduct our own needs assessment based on observations of NS and NNS TAs in actual classrooms. This step was taken later (Bailey 1982a) during the test development phases which Carroll calls trial application and validation and test analysis (1980:13).

Classroom Research

As part of a larger study (Bailey 1982a) twelve NS TAs and twelve NNS Asian TAs were observed teaching lower-division physics and mathematics classes at UCLA. The data consisted of approximately sixty-nine hours of observational field notes. The main purpose of these observations was to specify the communicative problems of the Asian TAs in comparison with their NS counterparts. (See Bailey 1982b for further discussion of this topic.) Students' evaluations of these twenty-four TAs were also available. They consisted of mean ratings on two variables: the TAs' overall teaching effectiveness and their willingness and accessibility in helping students outside of class.

A two-way analysis of variance of the students' ratings showed that the native speaking TAs had been rated significantly higher than the non-native speakers on both variables. There were no main effects for discipline (physics vs. mathematics) and no interaction effects (Bailey 1982a:140-142). Although the sample size is very small, the trend is clear: students perceived NS TAs as being better teachers than the NNS TAs.

An ethnographic analysis of the teaching styles of the twenty-four physics and mathematics TAs revealed that students' ratings of the TAs' teaching effectiveness were systematically related to independently defined types of TAs.

The five types identified are summarized below, with the mean ratings of overall teaching effectiveness awarded each group given in parentheses.

Type I: The Active Unintelligible TAs attempted to actually teach their students. However, the gaps in their linguistic competence - especially their common pronunciation problems - were so serious as to impede communication ($\overline{X}$ = 36.8, Group consisted of 3 NNSs).

Type II: The Mechanical Problem-Solvers did not seem to engage in active teaching behaviors or to establish affective bonds with the students. Instead, they were rather passive and spoke somewhat quietly. Their "barebones" teaching style primarily involved demonstrations of laboratory equipment and non-interactive solutions to homework problems ($\overline{X}$ = 42.7, Group consisted of 5 NNSs and 1 NS).

Type III: The Knowledgeable Helpers/Casual Friends seemed to typify the basic acceptance level of TA performance for the students. These TAs could all be understood, they all engaged in purposeful on-task teaching activities, and they demonstrated some affective bonding behaviors ($\overline{X}$ = 55.0, Group consisted of 2 NNSs and 6 NSs).

Type IV: The Entertaining Allies were two native-speaking TAs. Their teaching style, while purposeful, was characterized by a consistent and active use of humor and a "one-of-the-group" attitude. While the students were actively taught, they were also entertained by these TAs ($\overline{X}$ = 59.0).

Type V: The Inspiring Cheerleaders, consisted of two TAs (one NS and one NNS), who generated infectious enthusiasm for the subject matter and high regard among the students. In addition to using well-organized and purposeful teaching behaviors, these two TAs communicated a sense of personal interest in the students as individuals and a sense of high expectations for the students' success ($\underline{X}$ = 62.7) (Bailey 1982a: 136-137, 140).

A one-way analysis of variance revealed statistically significant differences among the mean scores listed above (F = 5.63, df = 4, $p \leq$ .01), but Scheffe's test for a posteriori comparisons failed to pinpoint the specific locations of the differences. It is apparent, however, that those TAs who exhibited more positive affect for their students (types III, IV, and V above) were rated increasingly higher than were the others (types I and II above).

As part of the study in which these observations were conducted, 392 UCLA students enrolled in regularly scheduled classes responded to a questionnaire[4] about the extent to which the oral English proficiency of their NNS TAs (n = 29) interfered with their understanding of the subject matter. One-way analyses of variance were computed using the students' assessments of their TAs' English as the dependent variable. The criterion levels for the ANOVAs were based on the NNS TAs' **FSI** Oral Interview scores, which were awarded by a team of trained testers. Scheffe's test for a posteriori comparisons did not identify many significant differences among the students' ratings of TAs in the **FSI** 2 to 5 range. However, those NNS TAs rated as 1+ or lower on the **FSI** Oral Interview were judged to be significantly different (i.e., worse) by the students. This finding suggests that a NNS wishing to be a TA should have a minimum **FSI** Oral Interview rating of at least 2. (See Bailey 1982a:97-102 for a more detailed discussion of these issues.)

When the questionnaire results were analyzed further, it was found that approximately one third of the student respondents shared a common major with their TAs. These students had rated the NNS TAs significantly less harshly than the non-majors had. Among other things, this finding indicates that students who share a common professional lexicon and perhaps common life goals with their NNS TAs are less critical than students from other disciplines, who may, in fact, resent having to take required courses outside their majors. Unfortunately, this finding is similar to a conclusion reached by Orth (1983) who showed at the University of Texas (Austin) that a measure of students' dissatisfaction with their grades was a better predictor of their NNS TAs' teaching evaluations than was a measure of the TAs' speaking ability.

The results of the classroom research are discussed in much greater detail elsewhere (Bailey 1982a and b). My point here is simply to show that although the complaints had hinged on NNS TAs' language problems, the students were apparently reacting to more than purely linguistic variables. Given this background, let us turn to a reconsideration of the existing performance test.

PROBLEMS WITH THE PERFORMANCE TEST

In an informal effort to determine how well the performance test captured the communicative processes of classrooms, the rating instrument was filled out following one observation of each TA in the classroom setting. This trial application revealed several problems with our initial assumptions in designing the rating instrument and the task used in the performance test.

Unequal Power Discourse

The problems to which I refer center primarily on the differences between the discourse task of the performance test and the reality of the college classroom. The performance test described above consisted of a dyad in which the NNS TA's interlocutor was polite, even supportive. Both parties knew it was a role-play in which the power in the unequal power discourse context of a test had temporarily changed hands by mutual agreement: the tester became the student and the examinee became the teacher.

In their actual classrooms, however, the TAs had to perform in one-to-many discourse situations, in which the number of students ranged from three to over fifty. There was also a wide range of behaviors exhibited by these interlocutors: friendly support, interest, boredom, confusion, passive indifference, sarcasm, and even open hostility. (Such attitudes are part of what Hymes [1974] has called the key or tone of a speech event.) In contrast, the tone of the performance test remained fairly constant. The examinees were not challenged to deal with different attitudes from a variety of participants.

Indeed, participants was another variable identified by Hymes as important in describing a speech event. Hymes specified four possible participant roles: addressor, addressee, speaker, and audience. The performance test we used included only an addressor and an addressee whose roles switched, just as they do in real life, when questions were posed and answered. In actual classrooms, however, the presence of an audience is a very real factor - certainly for the teacher as he performs his role and also for the student who takes a verbal turn in classroom discourse. Regular instances of one-upmanship, whether humorous or hostile, occurred in my observations of TAs. In dialogues between the teacher and a single student the silent students become the audience. The presence of (temporarily) non-interacting students as an audience is one factor which distinguishes classroom lessons from tutorials. The presence of an audience and the teacher's response to it may be just as important in teaching as is the audience in the often cited speech event of ritual insults called sounding (Abrahams 1974; Coulthard 1977; Kochman 1972).

The dyad of the performance test was also different from typical classroom discourse in that turn distribution played only a minor role. Except for occasional overlaps or interruptions, turn-taking in the performance test was governed by the (American English) conversational rules that "at least and not more than one party talks at a time" and that "speaker change recurs" (Coulthard 1977:53 citing Sacks, in manuscript).

Turn-taking in classrooms is far more complicated, as several recent studies have shown (e.g., Allwright 1980; Moss and Corneli 1983; Sato 1982). In a discussion of unequal power discourse in classrooms, Hatch and Long point out that "potentially, at least, teachers have great power and students much less" in that teachers usually control "who speaks, when, and to whom" (1980:17) as well as what is talked about.[5] None of these potential problems in the management of classroom discourse were tapped during the dyadic role-play of an office hour meeting. Thus in some ways the test activity was easier than the language use situations faced by TAs in classrooms.

Setting Variables

Hymes (1974) has also identified setting as one of the key variables in defining any speech event. In the role-played performance test, the examinee and the student were seated at a table in a quiet classroom with only the videotape camera present. Although this setting approximates that of an office-hour consultation, in classroom lessons TAs are seldom seated. In fact, while teaching, many NS TAs and some of the NNS TAs observed used frequent hand and arm gestures and sometimes entire body movements to communicate their intended meaning. In so doing, they added the nonverbal channel to the oral and graphic information they conveyed (Bailey 1982a).

The setting we used in administering the performance test did not take into account the tremendously varied physical surroundings in which TAs teach. For example, the presence of concrete referents in describing procedures for using laboratory equipment generates different language forms (more imperatives and deictics accompanied by gestures) than occur in "chalk-and-talk" explanations of mathematics problems.

Setting also influences paralinguistic variables in language use and performance testing. Coping with noise while teaching (that is, noise from laboratory machinery, conversations among students, traffic and construction equipment outside, chairs scraping the floor, people talking and whistling in the halls, etc.) is an ongoing fact of life for many TAs. However, some NNSs come from cultures with norms different from ours for conversational loudness (Larsen-Freeman 1982). For these

TAs, making sure the students can hear them over such distractions can be the key to ensuring that the students understand them. In this sense, our performance test did not tap the NNS TAs' paralinguistic repertoire.

Classroom seating arrangements are another setting variable that TAs must respond to. Lecture halls with amphitheatre floorplans and theatre seats may demand different behaviors in the main category of Delivery (including eye contact with students at the back of the hall) than do mathematics or economics classrooms with traditional rows of desks and blackboards on three walls. Still other communication problems are inherent in physics or chemistry laboratories, with raised platforms and machinery on laboratory tables impeding the students' view of the TA. These environmental factors all interact with the NNS TAs' strategic competence (Canale and Swain 1980) which was not greatly challenged in our performance test.

Even within one setting, TAs may have to perform many speech acts in varied speech events. At the level of the speech event, NNS TAs must understand the concept of a lesson or discussion section, how to begin and bring about closure, as well as how to use English during the event. Physics laboratory TAs often give mini-lectures explaining concepts or laboratory procedures to groups of eight to twenty students. They then must circulate and help pairs or small groups of students to execute the experiment. But regardless of the setting or specific speech event, teaching apparently consists of a great variety of speech acts. These include those that are overtly teaching-related, such as defining, illustrating, analogizing and restating, as well as other "off-task" speech acts (e.g., greeting, leave-taking, encouraging, cajoling, personalizing,[6] etc.). Our performance test did not assess prospective TAs' versatility in this respect.

The decision to limit the examinees' responses in the performance test to the oral mode was also problematic. While we wanted to keep the examinees from relying on drawings or written formulae instead of speaking during the test, we did not consider the possibility that in classrooms TAs must be able to speak and write at the same time.[7] All the native speakers and some of the NNS TAs in these observations were able to write and speak simultaneously as they explained homework problems or laboratory procedures. This combined use of writing and speaking "may be unique to the discourse of teaching or lecturing situations where one interlocutor makes use of both channels to convey information to his listener(s)" (Bailey 1982b:25). Since the persistent combined use of both productive modes was so prevalent in the classes of the more successful TAs observed, any performance test of NNS TAs' communicative competence should include this option.

Characteristics of the Performance Test

Carroll (1980:13-16) lists four characteristics which a performance test should possess:

Relevance: How relevant is the behavior being tested to the meeting of communicative needs?

Acceptability: Will the users of the test accept its content and format?

Comparability: Can test scores obtained at different times and from different groups be compared?

Economy: Do tests provide as much information as is required with the minimum expenditure of time, effort and resources?

The classroom research discussed above and the specification of communicative needs it provided (Munby 1978) revealed a mismatch between the original performance test and the most critical target language use situations faced by many NNS TAs. By choosing the dyadic role play described above, we had ensured comparability across examinees, but at some expense to relevance.

In terms of economy, this performance test yielded sufficient information with a minimum of time and effort, provided that what we sought to measure was situated linguistic competence. Canale and Swain define linguistic (or grammatical) competence as "knowledge of lexical items, rules of morphology, syntax, sentence-grammar semantics, and phonology" (1980:29).[8] On our instrument these variables were measured by the four performance categories (Vocabulary, Grammar, Pronunciation, and Flow of Speech) under the main heading of Language Proficiency. The performance categories listed under the main headings of Delivery and Communication of Information were intended to capture the other variables identified in the pilot study as important to the speech event of an explanation. But the entire issue of economy rests on determining what exactly constitutes sufficient information. The classroom research results summarized above suggest that more emphasis should be given to sociolinguistic competence in a performance test for NNS TAs.

The acceptability of this performance test has not been investigated thoroughly. The users who must judge its acceptability include not only the user agencies, the university administration, the departments, and ultimately the students, but also the NNS examinees themselves. In a survey of NNS TAs at UCLA ($n = 81$) nearly half (49.4 per cent) thought that foreign graduate students should not have to pass an oral English language exam before becoming TAs. Over a third of the respondents (37 per cent) thought they should be required to pass such a test, while 8.6 per cent of the respondents said this requirement should depend on the TAs' disciplines (Bailey 1982a:77).

At this juncture another problem arises. As a screening test for foreign TAs focuses less on purely linguistic competence and more on the specific functional skills involved in teaching, it will become, paradoxically, less fair and, presumably, less acceptable. At what point do we stop testing contextualized oral English proficiency and start testing teaching ability instead? This question, which hinges on the use/usage distinction discussed above raises issues about the (as yet unassessed) baseline performance of comparable native English speaking TA candidates prior to their classroom assignments. For a second language performance test to be both fair and acceptable, NNSs should not be asked to do anything that NSs in the same role are not expected to do.

Unfortunately, in second language performance testing, it is not enough to measure linguistic competence per se. The whole point of performance testing is to have the second language learners use the target language in performing the function for which they are learning the language. Indeed, in the case of NNS TAs, these measures of language proficiency do not correlate particularly well with external student assessments of the NNS TAs' teaching or their English. Only moderate correlations were obtained between NNS TAs' ratings on five categories of the **FSI** Oral Interview and the students' ratings of the NNS TAs' oral English proficiency (r = .49, $p \leq$ .005 to .66, $p \leq$ .001, n = 29). Similar moderate correlations were found between the NNS TAs' global self-ratings of their oral English proficiency and the **FSI** subscale ratings (r = .58 to .64, $p \leq$ .005, n = 45). Only very low correlations were obtained between the students' ratings of NNS TAs' teaching and the **FSI** subscales of vocabulary (r = .28, $p \leq$ .05, n = 40) and fluency (r = .30, $p \leq$ .05, n = 40). These low to moderate correlations should not be surprising. If linguistic competence were the only factor influencing teaching success, then every native speaker would be a successful teacher (Bailey 1982a:84-90).

POSSIBLE REVISONS OF THE PERFORMANCE TEST

The experimental studies and classroom research on NNS TAs suggest several possible revisions in the performance test designed by Hinofotis et al. (1981). These changes would affect the stimulus material, the task, and the criteria by which responses are judged.

Task, Response, and Stimulus Material

In revising the existing performance test to better fit the realities of classroom discourse, the basic task should be redefined as follows. The prospective TA would still have to explain a subject-specific term or concept of his choosing, but rather than in an office-hour dyad, the explanation would occur in a classroom setting which includes an accessible blackboard. There would be at least six students present. Unknown to the examinee, the students would be assigned specified roles. For instance, undergraduate students working in USC's international TA training program are given roles to play as collaborative, competitive, participant, avoidant, dependent or independent learners during the NNS TAs' practice lessons (Cheney-Rice, Garate, and Shaw 1980). Other possible students types include the joker, the space case, the grade grubber and the eccentric genius (Sadow and Maxwell 1983:255).

Within this context the examinee's response could include beginning the lesson appropriately, explaining the term, entertaining questions from the students, dealing with a side conversation developing between two students, keeping or regaining control of the discourse, checking or confirming students' understanding of the concept, dealing with an interruption at the doorway from a student who is in the wrong part of the building, and ending the lesson appropriately. This procedure would take approximately ten minutes if the terms to be explained were chosen carefully and the examinees were given a brief preparation period to organize their lessons.

While the particular concept to be explained would be specific to the examinee's own field, the rest of the role play would be very similar across prospective TAs. One final element, that of a homework assignment, could be introduced to guarantee further comparability of the examinees' responses to the task. That is, each examinee would receive the following additional stimulus material in the form of a note from his professor: "Homework - read chapter 4, do problems 5, 6, 12 and 14, prepare for the test next week." He would then have to communicate this information to the students successfully.

Criteria

But what does it mean to assert that a candidate has responded "successfully" to the task presented in the stimulus material? It is one thing to say that a potential NNS TA's English is rated "2+" on the **FSI** Oral Interview scale and therefore will probably be acceptable to his undergraduate students. But it is altogether a different matter to claim that he has successfully defined a term, or provided an informative analogy, or effectively brought about closure in a lesson. To date relatively little work has been done to quantify successful performance of these and other teaching-related speech acts.

In the absence of easily quantifiable data, testers typically utilize panel members' ratings on specified categories (the first meaning of criteria). A candidate's rating is the mean score awarded by the raters; it is an index which represents a collective judgement.

One possible improvement in the existing performance test would be to provide judges with clearly defined scoring guidelines (the second meaning of criteria) by which to rate the performance of the prospective NNS TAs. However, the development of specific scoring criteria is a long and involved process, and there is a danger in performance testing that the grid statements developed by the "experts" may not capture the key variables to which the consumers (in this case, the undergraduate students of the NNS TAs) are reacting. In fact, this mismatch of consumers' and specialists' perceptions may be a problem in the existing performance categories, since they were based on the pilot study data generated by ESL teachers rating speech samples. Unfortunately, Orth (1983) recently found little correspondence between students' ratings and ESL teachers' ratings of NNS TAs.

An alternative to developing a detailed scoring grid would be to borrow the concept of range finders from holistic composition scoring. Sample videotapes of NNS TAs performing the above task could be prepared which typify desirable, acceptable and unacceptable levels of communicative competence for the role.[9] But designating one NNS TA's model performance as acceptable and another's as unacceptable is a decisiion which should include input from representatives of the end users, here, the undergraduate students, as well as the language testing specialists, TA trainers and faculty members from the potential TA's department.

Furthermore, such standard setting would have to be a situation-specific process. Performance that is acceptable at one school might be deemed desirable or unacceptable at another, depending on local need, size of the applicant pool, and the tolerance or linguistic and cultural sophistication of the undergraduate students affected by decisions regarding TAs. And even though the process of standard setting is systematic, in the long run, the agreed upon standards reflect a basically subjective question: how good is good enough? Any scoring criteria established or range finders chosen must reflect the attitudes of the test consumers, a fact which complicates matters considerably, since the research shows that the undergraduate students are not attending strictly to linguistic factors alone (Bailey 1982a; Hinofotis and Bailey 1981; Orth 1983).

Alternatives to a Performance Test

It will certainly be argued that, even with fully developed scoring guidelines, the number of people involved in the role-play (not to mention the raters who would subsequently view the videotapes) would make this performance test unfeasible for use on a wide scale. In situations where large numbers of applicants for teaching assistantships make labor-intensive direct performance testing impossible, indirect but situationally-based pencil and paper tests might serve as initial screening devices to narrow the test population. Items for such a test could be derived from the observed classroom performance of both native speaking and non-native speaking TAs. For example, faulty utterances recorded in NNS TAs' classrooms (Bailey 1982a:23) provide the distractors in the following multiple choice item:

Following an explanation in a lesson, if the students are silent, the TA should ask:

    A. There is any question?
    B. Are there any question?
    C. There are any questions?
    D. Are there any questions?

However, while such an item is situationally based, it does not tap the NNS TAs' sociolinguistic competence, which the class-room research has shown to be an important variable.

More desirable as an indirect measure of the NNS TAs' communicative competence would be a multiple choice test based on Farhady's (1980) model of a functional test, in which the correct option is both linguistically correct and sociolinguistically appropriate. Of the three distractors, one is linguistically accurate but inappropriate, one is sociolinguistically appropriate but ungrammatical, and the third is both ungrammatical and inappropriate. However, as Wesche notes (1983:50), development of a functional test is time consuming and the finished product may tap only sentence-level recognition, not discourse-level competence. The development of such a test for preliminary screening of NNS TAs would probably only be justified in situations where the longer direct performance test is not possible.

But the use of paper and pencil tests, even if they do assess NNS TAs' sociolinguistic competence, sidesteps (or postpones) the question of requisite oral English proficiency.

As Jones (1979) noted in his early call for a performance test of NNS TAs, speaking is the most critical skill in teaching. Furthermore, most written exams cannot measure a NNS's degree of accentedness. This gap is important because students' perceptions of NNS TAs' pronunciation achieved moderate correlations (r = .50, n = 27, $p \leq$ = .005) with students' ratings of those TAs' overall effectiveness as teachers (Bailey 1982a:92).

The alternative, of course, is to utilize a direct oral English proficiency test (e.g., the **Test of Spoken English** or the **FSI** Oral Interview) which is not, strictly speaking, a performance test, and to confine ourselves to measuring linguistic competence without worrying about all the sociolinguistic issues raised above. In fact, at most large schools, initial teaching assistantship awards are made even before the graduate students arrive on campus. In such cases an internationally administered direct oral proficiency exam, such as the **Test of Spoken English,** may prove to be a very useful preliminary indicator of NNS candidates' potential success or problems as TAs.[10]

CONCLUDING REMARKS

In deciding whether and how to screen potential NNS TAs, the time, expense and manpower involved in developing and administering a performance test must be weighed against the seriousness of making a wrong decision in the absence of performance-based data. In research on the use of the **Test of Spoken English** in the health professions, Stansfield and Powers (1983), borrowing a metaphor from statistics, note that there are two types of errors which can be made when trying to determine cutoff scores. Testers can err either by passing someone who is not proficient or by failing someone who is proficient. The seriousness of these two types of errors depends to a large extent on the profession which the examinees seek to enter and the role of the target language in that profession.

In performance testing of NNS applicants for teaching assistant-ships, either type of error is serious. Barring a potentially effective teacher from the classroom because his English is judged inadequate can have negative consequences on his financial status and his future in graduate school. This decision would also deprive the university of a functioning member of the instructional staff. In addition, such an error would indirectly hurt the students, the very people whom the testing process was intended to protect.

On the other hand, putting a NNS TA in the classroom whose English is not sufficient can be harmful to both the undergraduate students and the educational system, as well as to the TA himself. Anecdotal evidence suggests that this type of error has been made when general indirect language proficiency tests alone (e.g., **TOEFL** scores or university placement exam results) have been used to screen NNS TA applicants (Bailey 1982a:21-22). In my observations of NNS TAs in regularly scheduled classes, some students teased the TAs verbally, argued with them, drew caricatures of them, hissed, booed, left class early, did not attend class at all, corrected both the TAs' English utterances and their misunderstandings of the students' questions, and talked, ate, and read newspapers during the TAs' explanations (Bailey 1982a and b). These behaviors occurred primarily in the classes of the less proficient NNS TAs who were unable to maintain control of the discourse.[11]

It is now clear that linguistic competence, at least at the 2 level on the **FSI** Oral Interview scale, is a necessary but not sufficient condition for successful performance by NNS TAs. Their strategic and sociolinguistic competence are potentially even more important variables. Linguistic differentness - especially accentedness - is certainly a highly salient feature influencing students' reactions to NNS TAs. However, other factors, including role management and TA-student relationships, also enter into the so-called foreign TA problem. Moreover, research by Orth (1983) shows that students' attitudes toward NNS TAs and college professors are influenced by nonlinguistic factors, such as ethnicity and nationality. For these reasons, trying to predict NNS TAs' teaching success on the basis of linguistic competence alone is a bit like using a butterfly net to chase an elephant. We ought to be developing means to pursue the broader construct of communicative competence instead.

It should now be possible to implement a second language performance test for NNS TAs that would be relevant, acceptable, and relatively economical, and would yield comparable test results. But more work is needed on the development of specific scoring criteria for the functional uses of language in teaching-related speech acts, for which the norms of native speaker behavior are not yet clearly understood.

NOTES

1. This article is an expanded version of a presentation given at the Conference on Second Language Performance Testing, University of Ottawa, March 12, 1983. The research reported in this paper was funded in part by the Office of Instructional Development at the University of California, Los Angeles (UCLA).

2. I am indebted to my colleague, Susan L. Stern, and to my dissertation advisor, Frances B. Hinofotis, for valuable input on this topic. The test revisions I suggest and the issues raised here are not to be construed as criticisms of them or of their work on the original performance test. Like most test designers, we used our best judgement based on our knowledge at the time.

3. This observation suggests that we were probably working with a non-random sample of the target population: those TAs who actively wished to improve their English or those whose communication difficulties were serious enough that their graduate advisors channelled them to us for help.

4. This questionnaire was based on the Supplemental Questions from the Student Instructional Report, which was developed by Educational Testing Service (ETS). I adapted the survey instrument for use with TAs by permission of ETS.

5. See Bailey 1982c for further discussion of classroom power struggles as they relate to the problems of NNS TAs.

6. See Candlin, Bruton, Leather and Woods (1981) for a discussion of the importance of these and other speech acts or functions in doctor-patient communication, and Omaggio (1982) on the importance of personalized speech in the foreign language classroom.

7. In discussing the four skills traditionally associated with second language learning, Carroll (1980:27) has noted the combined uses of reading and writing in note-making, listening and speaking while conversing, and listening and writing while taking lecture notes in an academic setting. However, he does not discuss the combined uses of speaking and writing, the two productive modes.

8. In addition to this particular performance test, NNS TAs have also been tested on these components of linguistic competence in the oral mode with the **Test of Spoken English** (Clark and Swinton 1980) and **FSI** Oral Interview (Bailey 1982a), using the subscales of grammar, pronunciation, fluency and vocabulary. According to Clifford (1978:194), these subscales represent the four factors most commonly identified as contributing to oral language proficiency.

9. Data from one set of raters who used the existing performance test indicate that TAs who scored 4 or lower on the nine-point Likert scale were perceived as not being fluent enough to be TAs. The raters basically agreed that those subjects who scored 7 or better were thought to be acceptable as TAs (Hinofotis et al. 1981:117). But what constitutes a 4 as opposed to a 7 (or, worse yet, a 6 as opposed to a 7) is an open question. Given the large rater-by-person variance component estimates obtained with these data (Bolus et al. 1982), this judgement in practice may be a matter of personal choice.

10. See Clark and Swinton (1980) for a report of a validation study on the **Test of Spoken English** which involved international teaching assistants at several schools. Hinofotis, Erickson and Hudson (in progress) are now conducting research with this test on NNS TAs at UCLA.

11. To the best of my knowledge, the effects of such negative reactions from native speakers have not been systematically investigated. But these behaviors may conceivably be harmful to the NNSs' self-esteem, their impressions of Americans, and even their desire to improve their English.

REFERENCES

Abrahams, R. 1974. Black talking on the streets. In Bauman, R., and J. Sherzer (eds.), Explorations in the Ethnography of Speaking. London: Cambridge University Press.

Allwright, R. 1980. Turns, topics and tasks: patterns of participation in language learning and teaching. In Larsen-Freeman, D. (ed.), Discourse Analysis in Second Language Research. Rowley, Mass.: Newbury House, Inc.

Bailey, K. 1982a. Teaching in a second language: the communicative competence of non-native speaking teaching assistants. Ph.D. Dissertation. Ann Arbor: University Microfilms.

Bailey, K. 1982b. The classroom communication problems of Asian teaching assistants. In Ward, C., and D. Wren (eds.), Selected Papers in TESOL. Monterey: Monterey Institute of International Studies.

Bailey, K. 1982c. Power of language, language of power: the teaching behavior of native and non-native speakers. Paper presented at the Classroom Research Colloquium, 1982 TESOL Convention, Honolulu, Hawaii.

Berdie, D., J. Anderson, M. Wenberg, and C. Price. 1976. Improving effectiveness of teaching assistants - undergraduates speak out. Improving College Teaching 24(3): pp. 169-171.

Bolus, R., F. Hinofotis, and K. Bailey. 1982. An introduction to generalizability theory in second language research. Language Learning 32(2).

Brown, J., and K. Bailey. 1980. An analysis of a categorical instrument for scoring second language writing skills. Paper presented at the CATESOL State Conference, San Diego, Calif., April 18-20.

Canale, M., and M. Swain. 1980. Theoretical bases of communicative approaches to second language teaching and testing. Applied Linguistics 1(1): pp. 1-47.

Candlin, C., C. Bruton, J. Leather, and E. Woods. 1981. Designing modular materials for communicative language learning; an example: doctor-patient communication skills. In Selinker, L., E. Tarone, and V. Hanzeli (eds.), English for Academic and Technical Purposes. Rowley, Mass.: Newbury House.

Carroll, B. 1980. Testing Communicative Performance: an Interim Study. Oxford: Pergamon Press.

Cheney-Rice, S., E. Garate, and P. Shaw. 1980. Pedagogy as E.S.P. Paper presented at the Eleventh Annual CATESOL State Conference, San Diego, April 18-20.

Clark, J., and S. Swinton. 1980. The test of spoken English as a measure of communicative ability in English-medium instructional settings. TOEFL Research Report No. 7. Princeton, N.J.: Educational Testing Service.

Clifford, R. 1978. Reliability and validity of language aspects contributing to oral proficiency of prospective teachers of German. In Clark, J. (ed.), Direct Tests of Speaking Proficiency. Princeton, N.J.: Educational Testing Service.

Coulthard, M. 1977. An Introduction to Discourse Analysis. London: Longman Group Ltd.

Farhady, H. 1980. Justification, development and validation of functional language testing. Ph.D. Dissertation, University of California, Los Angeles.

Hatch, E., and M. Long. 1980. Discourse analysis - what's that? In Larsen-Freeman, D. (ed.), Discourse Analysis in Second Language Research. Rowley, Mass.: Newbury House.

Hinofotis, F., and K. Bailey. 1978. Course development: oral communication for advanced university ESL students. In Povey, J. (ed.), Workpapers in Teaching English as a Second Language, 12, pp. 7-19. Los Angeles: University of California.

Hinofotis, F., and K. Bailey. 1981. American under graduates' reactions to the communication skills of foreign teaching assistants. In Fisher, J., M. Clarke, and J. Schachter (eds.), On TESOL '80 - Building Bridges: Research and Practice in Teaching English as a Second Language. Washington, D.C.: TESOL.

Hinofotis, F., K. Bailey, and S. Stern. 1981. Assessing the oral proficiency of prospective foreign teaching assistants: instrument development. In Palmer, A., P. Groot, and G. Trosper (eds.), Selected Papers from the Colloquium for the Validation of Oral Proficiency Testing at the 1979 TESOL Convention. Washington, D.C.: TESOL.

Hinofotis, F., M. Erickson, and T. Hudson. In progress. In-house report on the Test of Spoken English and foreign TAs (working title). Office of Instructional Development, UCLA.

Hymes, D. 1974. Foundations in Sociolinguistics: an Ethnographic Approach. Philadelphia: University of Pennsylvania Press.

Jones, R. 1979. Performance testing of second language proficiency. In Briere, E., and F. Hinofotis (eds.), Concepts in Language Testing: Some Recent Studies. Washington, D.C.: TESOL.

Kelley, J. 1982. Foreign teachers bring language problems to U.S. campuses. Los Angeles Times, Part I-C, June 18, 1982, p. 12.

Kochman, T. 1972. Black American speech events and a language program for the classroom. In Cazden, C., V. John, and D. Hymes (eds.), Functions of Language in the Classroom. New York: Teachers College Press.

Larsen-Freeman, D. 1982. The WHAT of second language acquisition. In Hines, M., and W. Rutherford (eds.), On TESOL '81. Washington, D.C.: TESOL.

Lnenicka, W. 1972. Are teaching assistants teachers? Improving College and University Teaching 20(2): p. 97.

Lurie, L. 1981. Personalizing the university: an under graduate's view of TAs. The TA at UCLA Newsletter, 7, p. 4.

Mestenhauser, J., W. Perry, M. Paige, M. Landa, S. Brutsch, D. Dege, K. Doyle, S. Gilette, G. Hughes, R. Judy, Z. Keye, K. Murphy, J. Smith, K. Vandersluis, and J. Wendt. 1980. Report of a Special Course for Foreign Teaching Assistants to Improve Their Classroom Effectiveness. Minneapolis: University of Minnesota International Students Adviser's Office and Program in English as a Second Language.

Moss, W., and M. Corneli. 1983. Turntaking and ethnicity in the ESL classroom. Paper presented at the CATESOL State Conference, Los Angeles, April 15-17.

Mullen, K. 1977. Using rater judgements in the evaluation of writing proficiency for non-native speakers of English. In Brown, H., C. Yorio, and R. Crymes (eds.), On TESOL '77: Teaching and Learning ESL, Trends in Research and Practice. Washington, D.C.: TESOL.

Munby, J. 1978. Communicative Syllabus Design. London: Cambridge University Press.

Omaggio, A. 1982. The relationship between personalized classroom talk and teacher effectiveness ratings: some research results. Foreign Language Annals 14(4): pp. 255-259.

Orth, J. 1983. Language attitudes and naive listeners' evaluations of speaking proficiency. Paper presented at the Seventeenth Annual TESOL Convention, Toronto, March 15-20.

Pike, M. 1979. An investigation of the interview's role in oral proficiency testing. Unpublished Master's thesis, University of California, Los Angeles.

Sadow, S., and M. Maxwell. 1983. The foreign teaching assistant and the culture of the American university classroom. In Clarke, M., and J. Handscombe (eds.), On TESOL '82: Pacific Perspectives on Language Learning and Teaching. Washington, D.C.: TESOL.

Sato, C. 1982. Ethnic styles in classroom discourse. In Hines, M., and W. Rutherford (eds.), On TESOL '81. Washington, D.C.: TESOL.

Shaw, E. 1982. No comprende! Foreign TAs try to cope with English. The Daily Pennsylvanian, February 15, 1982, p. 3.

Stansfield, C., and D. Powers. 1983. Towards standards of English language proficiency for the health professions: a preliminary study. Paper presented at the Fifth Annual Language Testing Research Colloquium, University of Ottawa, March 13.

Stiggins, R. 1982. A status report on writing assessment. In Cronnell, B., and J. Michael (eds.), Writing: Policies, Problems and Possibilities. Los Alamitos, Calif.: SWRL Educational Research and Development.

Stockdale, D., and Z. Wochok. 1974. Training TA's to teach. Journal of College Science Teaching 3(5): pp. 345-349.

Swanbeck, H. 1981. Foreign TAs experience communication gap in classroom. The UCLA Daily Bruin, October 26, 1982, pp. 1, 9 and 10.

Timmerman, M. 1981. Foreign profs' language barrier irritates students. The UCLA Daily Bruin, May 4, 1981.

Wesche, M. 1983. Communicative testing in a second language. The Modern Language Journal 67(1): 41-55.

Widdowson, H. 1978. Teaching Language as Communication. Oxford: Oxford University Press.

APPENDIX A ORAL COMMUNICATION RATING INSTRUMENT

Subject: _____ Class: _____ Date: _____ Observer: _____

  I. INITIAL OVERALL IMPRESSION   1 2 3 4 5 6 7 8 9

 II. PERFORMANCE CATEGORIES

      Directions: Rate this subject on each of the following fifteen
                 categories. Please circle only one number for each
                 category.

                              (Poor)   (Excellent)

A. Language Proficiency	1 2 3 4 5 6 7 8 9	
1. Vocabulary	1 2 3 4 5 6 7 8 9	
2. Grammar	1 2 3 4 5 6 7 8 9	
3. Pronunciation	1 2 3 4 5 6 7 8 9	
4. Flow of Speech	1 2 3 4 5 6 7 8 9	
B. Delivery	1 2 3 4 5 6 7 8 9	
5. Eye Contact	1 2 3 4 5 6 7 8 9	
6. Other Non-verbal Aspects	1 2 3 4 5 6 7 8 9	
7. Confidence in Manner	1 2 3 4 5 6 7 8 9	
8. Presence	1 2 3 4 5 6 7 8 9	
C. Communication of Information	1 2 3 4 5 6 7 8 9	
9. Development of Explanation	1 2 3 4 5 6 7 8 9	
0. Use of Supporting Evidence	1 2 3 4 5 6 7 8 9	
1. Clarity of Expression	1 2 3 4 5 6 7 8 9	
2. Ability To Relate to Student	1 2 3 4 5 6 7 8 9	

III. FINAL OVERALL IMPRESSION   1 2 3 4 5 6 7 8 9

      Is this subject's English good enough for him to be a teaching
      assistant in his major department at UCLA in the following
      capacities? (Please circle yes or no).

            A. Lecturing in English   Yes   No
            B. Leading a discussion section   Yes   No
            C. Conducting a lab section   Yes   No

Optional Comments:

APPENDIX B

Descriptors of the Performance Categories on the Oral
Communication Rating Instrument

In viewing the videotapes, you will be asked to rate the
subjects in three general categories and twelve specific
subcategories. These topics and the areas they cover are
listed below. You may refer to this sheet during the rating
process if you wish.

A. LANGUAGE PROFICIENCY

1. Vocabulary: including semantically appropriate word
   choice, control of idiomatic English and subject-
   specific vocabulary.
2. Grammar: including the morphology and syntax of
   English.
3. Pronunciation: including vowel and consonant sounds,
   syllable stress and intonation patterns.
4. Flow of Speech: smoothness of expression, including
   rate and ease of speech.

B. DELIVERY

5. Eye Contact: looking at the "student" during the
   explanation.
6. Other Non-verbal Aspects: including gestures, facial
   expressions, posture, freedom from distracting
   behaviors, etc.
7. Confidence in Manner: apparent degree of comfort or
   nervousness in conveying information.
8. Presence: apparent degree of animation and enthusiasm, as reflected in part by voice quality; may
   include humor.

C. COMMUNICATION OF INFORMATION

9. Development of Explanation: degree to which ideas
   are coherent, logically ordered and complete.
10. Use of Supporting Evidence: including spontaneous
    use of example, detail, illustration, analogy and/or
    definition.
11. Clarity of Expression: including use of synonyms,
    paraphrasing and appropriate transitions to explain
    the term; general style;
12. Ability to Relate to "Student": including apparent
    willingness to share information, flexibility in
    responding to questions, and monitoring of
    "student's" understanding.

10.
Évaluation de la performance linguistique de professeurs d'université

Laure Krupka

Comme son titre l'indique, cette présentation porte sur un test de langue seconde assez spécial. Il s'agit en effet d'un test destiné à évaluer le niveau de performance linguistique de professeurs réguliers de l'Université d'Ottawa, afin d'établir son adéquation vis-à-vis des exigences langagières de l'institution.

L'Université d'Ottawa est, de par sa charte, une institution bilingue (français et anglais); de ce fait, elle a dû se doter d'un règlement régissant le niveau de bilinguisme exigé des membres de son personnel enseignant. On peut y lire, par exemple, qu'à court terme

> l'Université doit faire en sorte que [...] tous les membres de son personnel enseignant soient partiellement bilingues, c'est-à-dire qu'ils maîtrisent toutes les fonctions de l'une des deux langues officielles et les fonctions passives de l'autre.

À plus long terme, "[...] l'Université doit s'efforcer d'augmenter graduellement le nombre des membres du personnel enseignant intégralement bilingues." À la suite de la publication du règlement sur le bilinguisme, il devint nécessaire, pour fins de promotion ou de permanence, d'évaluer le niveau de performance de professeurs que l'assemblée des pairs de la faculté d'attache n'arrivait pas facilement à établir. C'est à la faculté des Sciences sociales que les premiers cas se présentèrent.

Comme on l'imaginera sans peine, on trouve une grande variété de disciplines dans une telle faculté, de la psychologie à la sociologie en passant par la récréologie, la criminologie, les sciences politiques, l'économie, etc. Pour en arriver à produire un instrument de mesure qui puisse rendre justice aux candidats tout en respectant la diversité des disciplines en présence, il a fallu que les membres de l'équipe chargée de l'élaboration du test se penchent minutieusement sur la question avec les autorités de la faculté des Sciences sociales afin de déterminer un ensemble d'exigences fondamentales, valables pour toutes les disciplines. C'est ainsi qu'on en vint à une forme de compromis entre les objectifs à court terme, qui ne portaient que sur les fonctions réceptives en langue seconde, et l'objectif à long terme : le bilinguisme intégral. Il fut décidé, par exemple, que les membres du personnel enseignant devraient, à l'écrit, pouvoir lire et comprendre des articles de journaux et de périodiques, des travaux d'étudiants, des textes d'ordre administratif, etc., mais que le niveau de production serait limité à la production de courtes notes ayant trait à la vie professionnelle courante. Même répartition à l'oral, _mutatis mutandis_, où l'expression se limiterait à répondre succinctement à des questions d'étudiants et à de brefs commentaires concernant la sphère d'activité du candidat. L'instrument de mesure devait donc examiner plus en profondeur les savoirs réceptifs sans, pour autant, négliger complètement la capacité de parler et d'écrire.

Suite à ces précisions préliminaires, un instrument de mesure fut préparé. Il comprend huit parties qui peuvent schématiquement être décrites comme suit :

1. une conversation entre l'examinateur et le candidat, portant principalement sur la vie estudiantine ou professionnelle;
2. des textes oraux tirés d'émissions radiophoniques, que le candidat doit résumer à grands traits dans la langue de son choix;
3. un extrait d'une réunion régulière du conseil de la faculté des Sciences sociales, suivi de questions posées en français auxquelles le candidat peut répondre dans la langue de son choix;
4. une sélection de textes écrits touchant au domaine de spécialisation de chaque candidat, dans lesquels une

section encadrée doit faire l'objet d'un résumé ou d'une traduction libre;

5. des textes d'étudiants, dont le candidat doit évaluer la qualité du contenu, relever les principales erreurs de forme et donner une appréciation globale;

6. une note administrative à résumer dans la langue de son choix, en en faisant ressortir les points saillants;

7. une courte note de service à rédiger, par exemple pour annoncer une absence, donner des directives, etc.;

8. un test de closure (texte à trous) portant sur un texte d'intérêt particulier pour le candidat examiné.

Il va sans dire que la préparation d'un tel instrument n'allait pas se faire sans un apport très important des professeurs de la faculté des Sciences sociales; il n'est pas inutile de le signaler, leur coopération n'a jamais fait défaut. Par exemple, ils ont fourni de nombreux textes spécialisés à l'équipe d'élaboration du test; lorsque nos propres recherches nous ont permis de découvrir des textes à première vue intéressants, ce sont eux encore qui ont pu nous renseigner sur la pertinence de ces écrits face à l'état actuel des sciences sociales; c'est aussi de ces collègues que nous avons obtenu des travaux d'étudiants, des thèses, bref tous les écrits qui devaient permettre de construire cette partie de l'instrument en la basant sur des documents authentiques.

Il y a également lieu de souligner le fait que nous, membres d'une autre faculté, ayons eu accès à des enregistrements intégraux de séances du conseil de la faculté des Sciences sociales. Il est amusant de noter que l'extrait de discussion qui a été retenu porte sur le cas d'une étudiante étrangère qui n'a pas réussi à obtenir une note de passage à son test de langue (les étudiants de l'Université d'Ottawa doivent satisfaire à des exigences en langue seconde). C'est tout ce qui lui manque pour obtenir son diplôme; son avion part dans les jours qui suivent et elle est attendue dans son pays par son gouvernement. Le sujet ne manque pas d'intérêt en soi; à plus forte raison pour les candidats qui doivent en traiter, vu leur propre situation.

Pour ce qui est des divers textes utilisés dans le cadre du sous-test de closure et adaptés au domaine de spécialisation de chacun, ce sont également des documents authentiques qui en constituent la base. Ces quelques exemples devraient suffire à illustrer l'effort qui a été fait en vue de permettre au candidat de faire la démonstration de son niveau de performance dans des contextes qui devraient lui être familiers et où il est appelé à oeuvrer.

Le test dure environ quatre-ving-dix minutes. Les épreuves sont présentées dans l'ordre indiqué plus haut, ce qui donne le sous-test d'expression orale en premier lieu, puis deux sous-tests de compréhension de la langue parlée, trois sous-tests de compréhension de la langue écrite, un sous-test d'expression écrite et le sous-test de closure. Le sous-test de conversation ne peut s'administrer qu'individuellement. Il est enregistré en vue d'une correction éventuelle par d'autres juges que l'administrateur. Quand aux autres sous-tests, ils pourraient se prêter à l'administration en groupe dans la mesure où l'examinateur prendra soin, le cas échéant, de distribuer les textes spécialisés aux bons candidats.

L'évaluation du niveau de réussite se fait sur deux plans, celui de la communication et celui de l'emploi du code. Etant donné que l'objectif premier de tout l'exercice est de déterminer dans quel mesure le candidat répond à certaines des exigences communicatives de son poste, il est normal que l'on porte attention à des critères comme l'intelligibilité du message, sa pertinence dans le contexte où il est transmis et, d'une façon plus générale et subjective, l'impression globale qui subsiste à la suite de l'accomplissement de l'une ou l'autre des tâches imposées par le test. Il était cependant ressorti clairement des consultations avec des membres de la faculté d'attache que le poste impliquait également des exigences quant à la capacité d'utiliser le code selon des normes acceptables. D'où, dans le processus d'évaluation, une double dimension, communicative et grammaticale.

Dans un autre temps, l'évaluation porte non seulement sur la qualité de la langue utilisée en situation de communication, mais aussi sur la pertinence de ce qui est produit face au domaine. La partie essentiellement linguistique de l'évaluation est donc faite par une équipe de deux spécialistes du domaine de la didactique des langues secondes auxquels peut s'ajouter une troisième personne au besoin. C'est à ce moment de l'évaluation que sont jugées l'habileté à communiquer et celle à employer correctement l'instrument de communication.

Pour ce qui est de la pertinence de la production, il est évident que cette dimension dépasse les connaissances normales d'un professeur de langue. C'est alors qu'entre à nouveau en jeu la collaboration entre l'équipe de testing et les membres de la faculté d'attache du candidat. Ce sont ces derniers, en effet, qui possèdent la compétence nécessaire pour porter des jugements valables, que ce soit au niveau du contenu, à celui des rapports habituels entre les professeurs et les étudiants de leur faculté, ou à d'autres niveaux. Cette évaluation par les pairs fait l'objet d'un rapport qui devient partie intégrante du rapport global d'évaluation.

Il faut noter enfin que la décision finale quant à la capacité actuelle (ou éventuelle) du candidat de fonctionner efficacement dans son environnement professionel n'appartient pas à l'équipe des examinateurs. Tout ce que ceux-ci veulent faire est de fournir à la faculté d'attache des données aussi précises, détaillées et objectives que possible pour permettre à cette dernière de les intégrer dans l'ensemble des facteurs qui conduiront à une recommandation bien éclairée et documentée à l'administration centrale.

On peut penser, à juste titre d'ailleurs, qu'il doit être coûteux de préparer ainsi des tests faits sur mesure pour chacun des candidats. Mais il faut bien considérer également l'importance de l'enjeu : obtention de la permanence ou d'une promotion, ou bien obligation péremptoire de corriger les lacunes à très brève échéance ou, pis encore, renvoi pur et simple. Dans ces conditions, la solution économique risque fort de ne pas être satisfaisante.

La formule d'évaluation qui vient d'être décrite est employée selon les besoins de l'institution. Dans la pratique, cela équivaut à quelques rares fois par année. Les traitements statistiques applicables aux tests de masse sont donc exclus et c'est au niveau du fonctionnement ultérieur du candidat dans son milieu qu'il devient possible de porter un jugement sur la valeur de l'instrument. Les résultats obtenus jusqu'à maintenant tendent à montrer que les évaluations qui ont été faites correspondaient assez bien aux savoirs des candidats. Ainsi, on ne saurait vraiment s'étonner qu'au niveau universitaire l'écrit soit plus développé que l'oral et que ce soit sur ce dernier plan que des interventions correctives s'avèrent le plus souvent nécessaires. La formule du test est connue, ce qui permet au candidat éventuel de travailler sur ses points faibles. Enfin, dans la mesure où, selon la formule retenue par les organisateurs du présent symposium, "le test évalue l'habileté de quelqu'un à manipuler une langue seconde pour exécuter une fonction précise dans un contexte donné", l'instrument que nous venons de décrire présente, selon nous, plusieurs des caractéristiques d'un test de performance.

11.
Assessing the Readiness of ESL Students to move into Regular Academic Programs

Beryl Tonkin

Any ESL teacher who has taught the "top" class of a regular ESL program knows that there is always a fair number of students in that class who think because it is the "top" class that they have "finished" ESL and are ready to go on to other, better things in English. These students are frequently good students: highly motivated, hard-working, ambitious, with a good educational background in their native language. But the fact remains that most often they are not ready. Nevertheless, they apply for admission to the institute or program of their choice, and are disappointed when they are rejected on the grounds that their English is not good enough. Some are indeed accepted by the program or institution, only to encounter problems later on.

Because of this situation, the ESL Department at Camosun College, a community college in Victoria on Vancouver Island in British Columbia, decided to try to establish a procedure which would help these students to move into regular programming more smoothly, if not necessarily more easily. Since any such procedure has to be based upon the academic and administrative requirements of the particular situation, an attempt was made in 1981 to define these needs and work out a way to meet them. The circumstances may be summarized as follows:

1. The Admissions and Advising sections of colleges and universities are not always able to place ESL students in appropriate academic courses (in English or other subjects) even when they have the results of the **TOEFL** or other similar test because a test score is not always an indication of a student's ability to function at a post-secondary level in a program given entirely in English;

2. ESL students themselves are often unaware that they have been misplaced in academic programs. Because they "passed the English test" and because their qualifications in other subjects met the required standard, they assumed they are correctly placed;

3. ESL students may indeed perform satisfactorily in academic courses, not realizing that they are being assessed on their knowledge of a particular subject even when their English language skills may leave a lot to be desired;

4. If there is an English course in the academic program they have chosen, this will almost certainly be the most difficult course for an ESL student to pass; but when students are given passing grades in other subject areas, they tend to assume that they will "pass English" as well and do not therefore seek special help;

5. ESL students may ask their ESL teacher for advice on what courses they should take next, but ESL instructors cannot always correctly judge student readiness to proceed to regular programming because the standard of English required of native English-speaking students is so variable;

6. Instructors in regular college-level programs may refer students to the ESL department (if there is one) for assessment, or suggest to students who are having problems that they should seek help with their English, but such a step is often regarded by the students as a backward step (and usually involves an extra course in their workload), and the advice is frequently ignored. Even if it is taken, student disappointment and low motivation impede progress and the drop-out rate of these students is high. It is therefore much better to catch such students before they find themselves in this invidious position.

In January 1982 a net was put in place at Camosun College to catch these students. It is in the form of an assessment procedure which attempts to determine whether students are ready to take Advanced Written Composition (ELT 039 and ELT 049). These are advanced ESL courses emphasizing writing skills, but also including listening comprehension, speaking practice, grammar review, reading and study skills. (This is, unfortunately, sometimes the third or fourth time the students have been tested at the same college.) The advanced writing courses are described to students as a means of gaining admission to the English course or regular academic program of their choice by demonstrated ability rather than by a one-shot examination. Students are encouraged to regard the ESL writing classes as the last English courses in which they should expect to receive special help as non-native speakers of English. These classes are therefore presented as a way of bridging the gap between ESL courses and regular college courses.

All applicants - including those already in the ESL program, referrals from other departments and "walk-in" students from outside the college - are asked to take the test for admission to the Advanced Written Composition classes. The test consists of a 30-minute, 50-item multiple choice grammar test and a 30-minute one-page written assignment on "My Plans for the Future" The grammar test used is the upper level of the ESL Placement Test by Donna Ilyin and her colleagues at Alemany College in San Francisco. There it is used to place students in the upper three levels of a six-level ESL program. We look for a score in the high thirties or forties (out of 50) to indicate a fairly sound grammar knowledge. The written assignment gives a general idea of the student's educational and career goals, as well as a sample of the student's ability to write on a personal theme. There is an interview during which the writing sample is corrected by the student and interviewer together. The student is asked about his/her educational background and the information given in the writing sample is discussed. In this way a profile of each individual applicant can be obtained. The interview also provides an opportunity for the interviewer to assess the student's ability to understand spoken English, and the subjective evaluations of the writing sample and interview are considered together in determining the starting point for each student, but the writing sample is the major factor.

Advanced Written Composition classes are offered five hours a week (two evenings of 2½ hours) for 16 weeks in the fall term, 16 weeks in the winter term and 8 weeks in the spring. There are two levels, and progress from the lower to the upper level is by demonstrated ability. Students always want to know how long the course is, and it has to be made clear that the length of time any student stays in the program depends upon individual progress.

Exit procedures from the writing courses are designed to meet the entrance requirements of the program or course which the students want to take next. After discussions with the Adult Basic Education Department and the English Department at the college, it was decided that we would make use of existing procedures in the educational system. In British Columbia a Post-Secondary English Placement Test prepared by the Educational Research Institute of B.C. (ERIBC) is used by post-secondary institutions in the province to assess the writing skills of English-speaking students who apply for admission to their programs. The existence of this test gave us a ready-made and accepted standard against which to measure the writing ability of ESL students in the Advanced Written Composition courses. It was agreed that the final assignment of the upper level of the two writing classes would be a 2-hour, 300/500-word essay of the type required by the B.C. Post-Secondary English Placement Test. The essay would be written in class, under examination conditions but in a non-threatening environment. During the course, students are made familiar with the test instructions, the format required, and the criteria for marking. In the upper level writing class, students are given practice in how to follow instructions care-fully, how to choose the topic on which they are best able to write, how to plan an essay and do rough work, as well as actual practice in writing paragraphs on selected topics, gradually working towards an essay of the required length. The criteria for scoring essays are explained so that students understand what is required and can concentrate on specific areas of improvement. Essays are marked under three main headings: (1) Content, Development and Organization; (2) Sentences - structure, grammar, punctuation; and (3) Words - precision, vocabulary, level of usage, spelling. There are three ranking levels under each heading: high, middle and low, each of which has three possible marks. Students write an essay along these lines and under these conditions in the middle of the term and at the end. The ESL instructor submits good essays to an evaluation committee consisting of the co-ordinators of the ESL Department, the Adult Basic Education Department and the English Department. This team assesses student readiness to move into other programs within the college. At the end of each term there are usually from three to six essays from a class of twenty plus considered suitable for consideration by the evaluation team.

Students who feel that they should be studying for, and attempting to pass, the **TOEFL** test are given sample test materials to work with; using the tests in class provides grammar review at an appropriate level for all students. When either the **TOEFL** or the B.C. Post-Secondary English Placement Test is offered locally, students are encouraged to take them, if they wish. By incorporating the external tests into the program in this way, it is hoped that the apprehension about the enormous hurdle of the all-important English Test will be reduced. It is also hoped that encouraging students to stay with the writing program, to keep practising and to see their own improvement, they will help them to recognize the fact that it is more advantageous for them to gain admission to regular courses by taking the composition class and by writing the final assignment rather than by attempting to pass a one-shot examination. It is pointed out to them that passing the **TOEFL** test (or any test) is not passing English. Indeed, passing such a test is not the end of English, but only the beginning. Once an ESL student has been admitted to regular courses, he/she will need to demonstrate sufficient ability in all English language skills to be able to work alongside English-speaking peers. The philosophy of the ESL Department is therefore to offer an assessment process rather than a measurement tool; to provide an opportunity for constant practice and progress along the path of transition from ESL to regular academic programming.

Just over one hundred students have taken the Advanced Written Composition courses in the fifteen months since their inception. Some students have repeated the same level more than once or have moved from the l lower leve to the upper level, making a total of 137 registrations in the seven courses held since January 1982. The original exceptation was that ESLd students woul make the transition into regular English classes at the Grade 10 equivalent level offered by the Adult Basic Education Department. In fact, no one has made the transition at that level. So far, half a dozen have been accepted into Grade 12 equivalent English classes in the College Preparation program and three have moved directly into the first-year college level English courses offered at Camosun. Others have been admitted to courses in other subject areas at the college. We do not know how many students have gone on to programs elsewhere. There are 38 students in the Advanced Written Composition courses which end in April 1983 and no predictions are made for them. In any case, it is too early to report statistics of any substantial significance.

It has been encouraging, however, to have the reactions of students and instructors, both ESL teachers and teachers in the regular English classes or other courses to which ESL students have progressed. More than two hundred students have enquired about the advanced writing courses and have taken the entrance test to see how they rate. It has shown us how important it is to have established a realistic starting point for these students. ESL instructors teaching the classes have seen enthusiasm and hard work in class, and have been told by students that the program meets their needs; students have said that they prefer the "course route" to the "test route" and recognize the value of continued practice. Instructors in the other courses to which students from the advanced writing classes have been admitted have found that the non-active speakers of English fit into their groups very well, and often perform at a standard which is higher than average.

12.
The Standardized Testing of Oral Proficiency in the Netherlands

José Noijons

INTRODUCTION

One of the main tasks of the Dutch National Institute for Educational Measurement (CITO) in the domain of secondary education is the development of tests for the Dutch central examinations, on the one hand, and tests to be used in school examinations, on the other. When in 1978 we started our work on foreign language oral proficiency tests we aimed at school examinations in which such skills as writing proficiency, listening comprehension and oral proficiency are tested.

TOWARDS A NEW TYPE OF ORAL PROFICIENCY TEST

Objectives

We formulated the general objective of oral proficiency tests as follows:

to assess a pupil's ability to use a foreign language in such a way that he can cope in everyday life-like settings.

A large majority of a sample of teachers who had seen some of our tentative tests approved of this objective, although it was felt that pupils at higher levels of education should be expected to have a greater command of the language. For the secondary school level, however, this objective seemed quite acceptable. Further study showed that our objective was in keeping with what language learning in general should aim at. When we look at the exact phrasing of our objective, a few elements need some clarification. It says: "in such a way that he can cope in everyday life-like settings". Now "cope" should be taken to mean "function properly, linguistically speaking". It is, of course, quite possible to function more or less properly without saying a word. Imagine one is in a non-smoking train compartment with people whose language one does not know. If someone lights a cigarette it is possible to shake one's head and point at the "no-smoking" sign. One has then shown one can cope without saying a word. What we mean, then, is that one must be able to show one's feelings and intentions in the sort of language that would be intelligible and more or less in accordance with social rules.

Another aspect of our objective is "everyday life-like settings." As in the study carried out for the Council of Europe, in which Van Ek (1976) listed many situations for which pupils should have a minimum (threshold level) knowledge of notions and functions to be able to communicate in another language, we made lists of all those situations and functions which pupils can be expected to recognize and perform after three or four years of training in a foreign language.

Validity

Finding a valid way of testing oral proficiency is not easy: we cannot put each examinee in a real situation and see how he copes (if reliable rating procedures can be developed for such situations at all). On the other hand we can imagine what he should be able to say in such situations. We must consider those speech-acts as the criteria for our tests.

Oral proficiency might also be assessed by testing the hypothetical subskills that contribute to it. The difficulty here is that there is little empirical evidence on the nature and the hierarchy of these subskills. If tests could be developed that correlated well with what were thought to be the most important subskills in oral proficiency such tests might be valid.

What we are left with, we believe, is the simulation of the situation with the examinee performing in it. Our tests should contain stimuli that call up speech acts that will resemble the speech acts in real life.

Format

Let us have a look at the tests as we have developed them. (For an example, see Appendix 1.) Basic to all tests is that they ask the pupil to engage in a conversation with a native speaker of the language concerned. The teacher has two functions here: he plays the role of the native speaker and he instructs the pupil in what to do. In general the tests consist of an introduction in which a pupil is told what situation he is going to find himself in and what role he is to play, followed by some ten items which may consist of one or more of the following elements:

1) a further development in the situation
2) an utterance by a native speaker
3) a stimulus
4) an instruction

It should be clear that the pupil is told what he is supposed to do; he is not given a written version of the instructions.

As the test is monolingual, a pupil's listening comprehension will be tested as well. We believe that this cannot and should not be avoided as it is part of what happens in a real situation: without understanding the other person one cannot engage in conversation. One might argue that the instructions need not be in the foreign language. We believe that instructions in the mother tongue would interfere with a simulation of a foreign language setting. Another objection is that pupils look for translations, rather than speaking out freely. It has also been found that pupils instructed in their first language tend to explain how they would behave, rather than show the behaviour required. From a methodological point of view there is hardly any objection. It was found in a study on listening comprehension that the use of the mother tongue in the formulation of the questions resulted in a less difficult test, but the pupils were assigned to the same ability groups as in the monolingual test: the hierarchy of pupils remained the same (Groot 1975).

THE DEVELOPMENT OF RATING SCALES

Having established the format of the tests on the basis of the objective we had in mind, we turned to the development of rating scales. The difficulty here was that on the one hand they should be reliable, and on the other hand they should be easy to handle, keeping in mind that the teacher has two functions: playing the part of the native speaker and being the assessor of the pupils' performances. We felt that rating scales that could only be used with taped performances or with an extra assessor would complicate matters so much that teachers would object. One should also realize that the rating scales themselves meant a deviation from everyday school practice: most teachers are accustomed to giving an "impressionistic" assessment at the end of a brief performance.

Format

We believed that such an impressionistic or global assessment would not be reliable enough, as assessors might base their judgements on the parts of the performance they remembered, rather than on the whole performance as it was given. Thus the last part of a performance might be given too much weight. Also, a rater might be struck by certain idiosyncracies in a pupil and listen for them in the first place.

We therefore decided that we should have a repeated judgement of the pupil's performance. As we had opted for the dialogue format this did not cause any problems. We decided on a minimum of 20 assessments which meant that two tests of 10 items each should be used in the assessment of each pupil's oral proficiency.

On the basis of the main objectives formulated for these tests, specific criteria were distinguished:

1) Responses should be effective or functional in the given context.
2) Responses should conform to the linguistic and other conventions of the language in question.

The first criterion implies that:

1) Responses should correspond to the stimulus given by the teacher.
2) Responses should be intelligible to native speakers.

The second criterion implies that:

3) Responses should contain no idiomatic or grammatical errors.
4) Responses should be reasonably fluent.
5) Pronunciation and accent should not interfere with intelligibility.

First Efforts

We then developed tentative rating scales for German on the basis of these criteria. The agreement we found among raters who assessed pupils' performances with the help of these scales was R (Intraclass) = 0.47. A global impression of these performances by the same raters yielded R = 0.64, which meant that we had still a long way to go before our rating scales could replace traditional methods of assessment.

It must be added, though, that the global impressions were given after the raters had used our rating scales in the assessment of the same pupils, so one might argue that assessors had been trained by our rating scales and knew what to expect of the pupils. Nevertheless, we decided that $\underline{R} = 0.64$ would be a good target for our type of rating scales to aim at.

Further Research

Further research led to the formulation of the following criteria to be used in our rating scales (see Table 1).

TABLE 1 Rating Scale Criteria

		Point Deducted
A	Response is perfect or nearly perfect	0
B	Response is quite intelligible and appropriate, even if some (minor) mistakes are made	1
C	Response is quite intelligible and appropriate, but takes some effort to understand	3
D	Response is not forthcoming/is not intelligible/is not appropriate in the given context	5
E	Pronunciation is a) good b) sufficient c) bad	
F	Fluency is a) good b) sufficient c) bad	

As can be seen, A, B, C and D are actually derived from the general criterion of intelligibility, or in an even more general sense, from the criterion that communication must take place. Each response had to be judged on these criteria. There were two criteria that were only applied at the end of a pupil's performance when raters had to assess the pupil's pronunciation and fluency. We opted for the use of a point deduction system. It seemed the most practical as it indicated the distance to an ideal performance.

Rating Sessions

We then arranged sessions for three languages (German, French and English) at which ten to thirteen raters were asked to assess the taped performances of fifty pupils. These were untrained raters who had never seen a test like this before. The German test contained 17 items and the French and English tests contained 20 items. The results are reported in Table 2.

TABLE 2 Rater Assessment of Second Language Performance

	Criterion	German	French	English
Intraclass $\underline{R}$		.69	.68	.42
$\alpha 2$		.77	.63	.50
Fleiss' Kappa	A	.43	.51	.31
median value	B	.28	.35	.18
each criterion	C	.21	.18	.14
	D	.33	.42	.26
	E	.18	.19	.22
	F	.20	.27	.27

a) Intraclass $\underline{R}$ = correlation coefficient between raters total scores
b) $\alpha 2$ = homogeneity coefficient of the tests
c) Fleiss' Kappa = correlation coefficient between raters per criterion, per item
d) 0.51 with the first 25 pupils.

The following remarks can be made:

1) Intraclass $\underline{R}$ for German and French was now higher than the correlation we found when we asked raters for their global assessment with the earlier rating scale ($\underline{R}$ = 0.64). This was quite a stimulating improvement on the earlier rating scale.
2) $\alpha 2$ expresses the degree to which a test consists of items that measure more or less the same thing. For tests consisting of 17-20 items this was quite a good result. English showed less satisfactory results.

3) Fleiss' Kappa for the criteria of intelligibility and appropriateness showed that agreement among raters was highest in the two extremes A (response is nearly perfect) and D (response is unintelligible). This is what we often find in situations where there is a choice of four. But as many of the responses were placed (and will be placed) in category B, we were not yet satisfied.

4) Fleiss' Kappa for pronunciation and fluency had improved a little over earlier experiments, but we felt that we could not maintain these criteria as they now stood on the basis of these figures.

5) As can be seen from these figures the results in the case of English were not very satisfactory. When we had a closer look at the item difficulties we found that the tests were rather easy for the group of pupils that we had selected. In such cases raters tend to distinguish between pupils' performances where such distinctions cannot really be made, at least with our rating scales, thus causing the figures for homogeneity and reliability to become rather low.

Conclusions

On the basis of the observations mentioned above we concluded that:

a) Attempts should be made to improve the inter-rater reliability on the criteria B and C (response is intelligible, minor mistakes are made; response is intelligible, but takes some effort to understand).

b) The criteria of fluency and pronunciation should have less weight. As the assessments based on them are made only once (per pupil) they should not have too much influence on the total score of a pupil, bearing in mind that for the other criteria an assessor gives twenty distinct assessments. We therefore opted for a bonus/penalty system in which the assessor can add or subtract points for particularly good or bad performances as far as fluency and pronunciation are concerned.

c) It might be well worth trying to develop a training programme that would help raters to assign responses to their proper categories. It stood to reason to do this for English as the effects of such a programme might be clearest there.

THE TRAINING OF TEACHER RATERS

When we developed our training programme we kept in mind that such a training programme, if successful with our raters of English, should be suitable for more general purposes. Future users of our tests might find it helpful in becoming familiar with the tests, and certain general problems in the assessment of oral proficiency might also be dealt with.

As it is not possible to force teachers to attend training courses, we decided that the training programme should be on tape so that it could be sent to the teachers. Teachers would then have to play the tape and after being given a number of instructions, assess some recorded performances. They would then have to compare their assessment with what we thought to be the correct assessment and after they had repeated this procedure a number of times we hoped that they would have become familiar with our tests and turned into reliable raters as well.

In order to find out what caused raters to disagree with each other, we had a close look at the scores assigned in the English tests. We measured the disagreement among raters with the help of Intraclass R for each assignment (see Table 3). We also had a look at the difficulty index of each item (i.e., 0 to 5 deduction points given for each response).

We then selected those items which showed rather low agreement among raters combined with very high or very low difficulty indices. Our reasoning was that raters tend to agree with each other on extremes, so where there is disagreement in such cases there must have been serious problems in the assessment.

Hypotheses

We then drew up hypotheses explaining the disagreement among raters for each of the nine items that we selected for this purpose. Take for example Item 17 (see Appendix 1). As can be seen this task is rather complex. A pupil will have some difficulty in finding the correct idiomatic and grammatical forms to express his opinion. But we doubted that intelligibility would be reduced so much that the responses deserved being placed in the two lowest categories. When we then listened to the pupils' performances we found that in spite of many grammatical and idiomatic errors intelligibility was not often impaired so much that categories C or D applied. Yet this was exactly where quite a few raters had placed the

TABLE 3   Rater Disagreement

Item	Difficulty[a]	Intraclass $\underline{R}$[b]
1	1.11	.39
2	.90	.28
3	.95	.46
4	1.39	.23
5	.78	.24
6	.75	.18
7	.73	.18
8	1.38	.31
9	.94	.25
10	1.03	.15
11	.36	.36
12	.20	.34
13	.52	.37
14	1.51	.37
15	.69	.20
16	.51	.27
17	1.57	.21
18	.69	.22
19	.51	.33
20	.99	.40

a   Equal to the mean of the number of
points deducted per response
b   Before training
($\underline{N}$ of pupils = 50)

responses. We also found that some pupils gave rather short answers. Again, they did not deserve such low ratings: assessors should be told that a short response could be quite adequate.

Another item, Number 10, shows extremely low agreement among raters together with a rather high item difficulty index. When we looked at the task we supposed that "Explain why you hesitate" was quite difficult for pupils, which explained its difficulty index. We also supposed that some raters had not made sure whether hesitation had indeed been expressed. When we then listened to the taped performances we found that 75 per cent of the pupils had not hesitated. The majority of raters must have put these responses in category D (not appropriate in context), but some raters, judging from the low correlation coefficient, must have put them in categories A or B, as can be explained by the fact that many of the inappropriate responses contained no grammatical or idiomatic errors. We therefore concluded that our training programme should contain instructions on what to do when a response was not in accordance with the stimulus.

Conclusions

On the basis of this research programme we drew up a list of conclusions and suggestions bearing not only on the training of raters, but also on the definitions of the various categories to which responses could be assigned and on the construction of future tests. Thus we concluded that tasks asking for the expression of feelings (such as hesitation and anger) should be clearer than they had been so far. We also concluded that where too short a response to a stimulus can be expected an extra stimulus should be provided in the text. We also decided that category B should include those responses that were less acceptable from a social point of view. The following conclusions were included in the instructions of the training programme:

1) If a response displays a pupil's faulty knowledge of notions it is not therefore categorically unintelligible. It could be assigned to category C, or even category B.
2) If a response is not in accordance with accepted social conventions, it should be placed in category B.
3) If a response contains a large number of grammatical or idiomatic errors, raters should remember that if intelligibility is not really impaired, category B rather than category C or D will apply.
4) A response that is correct from a grammatical and/or idiomatic point of view but that is not in accordance with the stimulus should be placed in category D.
5) A response should not be judged on its length or density of information. If it is intelligible and appropriate, categories A and B apply.

Format

Our next step was to compile a training programme that was based on these conclusions and suggestions. We made use of some earlier recordings of pupils' performances that seemed typical of the sort of responses that created problems with raters. We carefully analyzed these problems and explained which category should be chosen for each response. We also included two trial runs of complete tests to familiarize raters with the procedures and to enable them to compare their ratings with ours.

As was pointed out before we thus hoped to improve agreement between raters on categories B and C. Another problem that we hoped to solve was the lack of agreement between raters on the criteria E and F, pronunciation and fluency. As will be remembered we had opted for a bonus/penalty system, so we included instructions on how to use this system. If a performance was remarkably good or bad as far as pronunciation and/or fluency was concerned, raters could add or subtract extra points. Having adopted the bonus/penalty system, we decided to use it for a new criterion, length of the response, as well. Although we had postulated that length (or rather shortness) need not interfere with intelligibility we felt that those pupils who took the risk of giving longer answers and making more mistakes should be eligible for extra points. Pupils who consistently gave minimal answers could have points deducted.

Rating Session

We then invited the same group of raters that had assessed the fifty performances on the earlier occasion. This time we asked them to assess only twenty-five performances to avoid the session becoming too long (the instruction tape having a length of 30 minutes). As the Intraclass R with the second 25 pupils had been considerably lower that that with the first 25 pupils due to low variance among the second group, it was clear that raters had not learned from their assessments. This implied that there were no methodological objections to restricting the rating session to the first 25 pupils.

Results

This session yielded the following results:

   a) the homogeneity (reliability) of the test increased from $\alpha 2 = .51$ to $.56$. Allowing for the fact that this figure is based on only half the observations of the original sessions, this is quite a good result, comparable now with the figures found for French and German.
   b) Intraclass R increased from $.51$ to $.59$. Taking into account that these figures are based on the performances of only 25 pupils, this is quite a satisfactory result.

c) When we have a look at the agreement per item (Table 4) we see a considerable increase in the majority of cases, the only exception being item 11, the first item in the "Holland" test. This was a rather easy task for the pupils, as can be seen from its difficulty index (.36). The task did not pose many problems for the raters, either, its Intraclass R being among the best. It is therefore no surprise that training did not help raters very much in this case.

TABLE 4 Rater Agreement Before and After Training

Item	Intraclass $\underline{R}$ [a]	Intraclass $\underline{R}$ [b]
1	.39	.52
2	.28	.43
3	.46	.57
4	.23	.40
5	.24	.45
6	.18	.31
7	.18	.38
8	.31	.52
9	.25	.55
10	.15	.31
11	.36	.33
12	.34	.48
13	.37	.55
14	.37	.40
15	.20	.42
16	.27	.45
17	.21	.48
18	.22	.38
19	.33	.50
20	.40	.59

a Before training, $\underline{N}$ of pupils = 50
b After training, $\underline{N}$ of pupils = 25

d) The bonus/penalty system for length, fluency and pronunciation yielded rather disappointing results. Some raters never used it, others used it in nearly fifty per cent of the cases. There was some agreement among raters with two pupils who were particularly good and bad as far as their fluency was concerned, but in only nine cases did we find that four (out of eleven) raters agreed with each other on the three categories.

We therefore decided that the categories of length, fluency and pronunciation could not be maintained in our rating scales as reliable rating did not seem possible. We are presently working on a separate pronunciation test for which teachers have shown a marked interest.

Judging from the relatively positive results for the homogeneity of the test and the reliability of the rating we believe that providing a standard training programme for future raters is justified, bearing in mind that most teachers in Holland have never assessed oral proficiency in this way. As we had taken these considerations into account when developing our research training programme, it was not difficult to develop a training programme for more general purposes.

SCORING

Now that we had developed reasonably reliable rating scales, one further task had to be fulfilled: the development of a scoring system together with a norm. On the basis of the criteria in our rating scales, eight different ratings per response could be distinguished. These and the corresponding system of deduction points are presented in Table 5.

Our rating scales have been designed in such a way that teachers, after some training, have found them easy to handle. For each response the teacher puts a slant in one of the five boxes corresponding to the five criteria at the top of the page. (See Appendix 2.) At the end of the pupil's performance (twenty or thirty responses) the teacher adds up the deduction points and subtracts them from the maximum of 180 or 120 (depending on the length of the test: 20 or 30 items). This is a rough score. To translate this score into a mark on the 10 point scale we have made the following distinctions:

A-norm A pupil's responses should generally be intelligible, that is in eighty per cent of the cases. In twenty per cent of the cases a native speaker may have some difficulty in understanding the pupil. Twenty per cent of the stimuli may have to be repeated.

For a sufficient mark (6 on a 10 point scale) a pupil would then need a rough score of about 135 for the longer test and about 90 for the shorter test.

TABLE 5 Possible Ratings for Each Response with Corresponding Deduction Points

1. Response is (nearly) perfect	0
2. Response is (nearly) perfect after repetition of stimulus	1
3. Response is intelligible; some minor mistakes	1
4. Response is intelligible; some minor mistakes after repetition of stimulus	2
5. Response takes some effort to understand	3
6. Response takes some effort to understand after repetition of stimulus	4
7. Response is unintelligible	5
8. Response is unintelligible after repetition of stimulus	6

0-norm This lower norm, devised for pupils of lower levels of education, requires responses to be intelligible in at least half of the cases; the other 50 per cent may cause some trouble in understanding; again twenty per cent of the stimuli may have to be repeated.

A similar conversion table to that of the A-norm has been developed for the 0-norm.

FURTHER DEVELOPMENTS

A survey among teachers revealed that the tests that CITO has developed so far best meet with the requirements of the lower levels of education. It was felt that students at the higher levels could be expected to be able to do more than just cope in everyday situations. As many of them continue their studies after secondary school, they will be confronted with situations in which they have to discuss matters with native speakers. It is clear that both on the notional and on the functional level these discussions require a greater command of the language.

CITO has now developed a set of oral tests that more or less meet these requirements. When developing these tests we had the following considerations:

a) The subject of a discussion should not be too specialized. Each pupil should be able to identify with the subject or topic;

b) Background knowledge of pupils should not interfere with the assessment of their linguistic skills;

Because of a and b it was decided to opt for a system in which a student is asked to study a text before engaging in a (structured) discussion with his assessor.

c) Memory should play as small a part as possible. The introduction of texts meant that pupils might try to learn the text by heart, so a relatively short time for preparation should be given;

d) Reading comprehension should not interfere. Texts should therefore be short and concise with no difficult vocabulary. Clear headings summarizing the paragraphs should be provided;

e) A number of characteristics of the oral tests for the lower levels could be used:

1) the new tests would be based on situations in which student and rater would each play a role;

2) the conversation would consist of a number of preconceived tasks leaving the student some freedom of opinion, of course.

One example of such a test can be found in Appendix 3. We do not yet have any further information, as we have only recently sent these tests to a number of teachers asking for their opinions. We do not really know what their reactions will be, but we believe they will be positive as these tests resemble the sort of conversations teachers usually have with their pupils when testing oral proficiency.

CONCLUSION

CITO oral proficiency tests have now been published.[1] They have met with wide acclaim, and teachers have said they will use the tests in school examinations. A large number of teachers have also ordered the instruction tape so that we have some confidence in the way our tests will be used.

NOTES

1. If further information is required, or if one wishes to order samples of the CITO oral proficiency tests, please write to:

CITO
t.a.v. J. Noijons
P.O. Box 1034
6801 MG ARNHEM
The Netherlands

REFERENCES

Groot, P. 1975. Testing communicative competence in listening comprehension. In Jones, R., and B. Spolsky (eds.), Testing Language Proficiency, pp. 52-53. Arlington, Va.: Center for Applied Linguistics.

Van Ek, J. 1976. The Threshold Level for Modern Language Learning in Schools. London: Longman Group Ltd.

APPENDIX 1

> You are hitchhiking through Britain. Late one
> afternoon you are walking along a country lane   CAMPING
> when you spot a nice place to pitch your tent.

1   You decide to ask for permission at the farm near-by.
    In the yard you see a woman. What do you say to her?

2   There is an official camp site a few miles down the
    road. Tell her why you think this is not very
    attractive.

3   Well, I don't know if my husband will approve. You
    think it's a matter of money. What do you suggest?

4   You can't stay there after all, so you go to the offi-
    cial camp site. You ask someone camping there one or
    two things about the accommodation.

5   You find the proprietor and he says: What can I do for
    you?

6   You want information about the charges. What do you ask
    the warden?

7   You are fond of fishing. What do you ask the
    proprietor?

8   You've planned a walking-tour the next day. You want to
    find out about the weather. What do you ask the
    proprietor?

9   You make tea, but you discover that you've run out of
    sugar. You go to the tent next to yours. What do you
    ask?

10 You watch some people playing cricket. One of them
    asks: Would you like to join in? Explain why you
    hesitate.

You are at a camp site. You have put up your
tent. You are asked by your neighbour to join
him for a cup of tea.

HOLLAND

11   I was wondering ... you're not English, are you? What
      do you tell him?

12   Isn't Rotterdam the capital of Holland? Correct him.

13   In which part of Holland do you live?

14   Is there much to see in your neighbourhood?
      (picture 1)

15   Is there much to do for young people like you? What do
      you do on Saturday nights?

16   What's the weather like in summer?

17   We have many foreigners living in Britain. What's the
      situation like in Holland?

18   How have you come to speak such good English?

19   Have you learnt any other languages? Tell him in
      detail.

20   Would you like to join me for a drink in a pub? Decline
      the offer politely.

APPENDIX 2* Judging Page with 2 Divisions

Pupil: _____ Class: _____ Date: _____

Answer (almost) perfect	Repetition of question (or instruction) necessary	Correct answer under-standable/incidental mistake(s)	Answer difficult to understand	No answer/absolutely incomprehensible in given context	
1					1
2					2
3					3
4					4
5					5
6					6
7					7
8					8
9					9
10					10
1					1
2					2
3					3
4					4
5					5
6					6
7					7
8					8
9					9
10					10

Total: _____ +_____ ×1 +_____ ×1 +_____ ×3 +_____ ×5 120

Points (marks) to be deducted: _____ + _____ + _____ + _____ = _____ Total marks deducted

_____ Rough score

_____ Mark required B

_____ Mark required A

* This is a translation of the original scoring sheet

212

APPENDIX 3

WERBUNG

TABAK, ALKOHOL

Werbung ist insofern vom rechten Wege abge-
kommen, als sie versucht, schädliche
Produkte an den Mann zu bringen, wie z.B.
Tabak oder Alkohol.

WIRTSCHAFT

Die Tatsache jedoch, daß hin und wieder für
unerwünschte Sachen geworben wird, ist kein
Grund dafür, die ganze Werbung abzuschaffen,
es sei denn, man möchte zugleich unser Wirt-
schaftssystem abschaffen. Unser Wirt-
schaftssystem beruht auf Wettbewerb. Ein
wichtiges, ja entscheidendes Mittel, den
Wettbewerb zu fördern, ist die Werbung.

WERBUNG UND
WETTBEWERB

Werbung informiert den Verbraucher über neue
und verbesserte Produkte und zwingt dadurch
die Konkurrenz, ihrerseits Produktverbesse-
rungen vorzunehmen. So entstehen bessere
Produkte. Und bessere Produkte kommen uns
allen zugute.

BEISPIEL

Wer trauert schon dem alten Grammophon nach,
wenn er heute seine Musik in Stereo hören
kann?

VERHALTEN DER
KÄUFER

Mittlerweile zeichnet sich eine günstige
Entwicklung im Verhalten der Käufer ab:
Immer mehr Konsumenten lassen sich von
objektiven Produktinformationen leiten,
insbesondere bei größeren Anschaffungen.

POSITIVES

Durchaus als positiv zu bewerten ist auch,
daß Werbung zur Zeit in Bereichen wie
Umweltschutz und Gesundheit angewandt wird.
Zu denken wäre an folgende Anzeigen:

APPENDIX 3
(Translation)

ADVERTISING

TOBACCO, ALCOHOL

Advertising has strayed from the proper path in the sense that it seeks to bring to the public damaging products such as tobacco or alcohol.

ECONOMY

The fact, however, that from time to time undesirable things are advertised, is not a reason to abolish all advertising, unless one wishes to eliminate at the same time our economic system. Our economic system is based on competition, and an important, even decisive means to promote competition is advertising.

ADVERTISING AND COMPETITION

Advertising informs the consumer about new and improved products and thus forces competitors to also undertake product improvements. And better products benefit all of us.

EXAMPLE

Who, after all, mourns the old grammophone when today he can hear his music in stereo?

CONSUMER BEHAVIOR

Meanwhile a favorable development is becoming apparent in consumer behavior: an increasing number of consumers are using objective product information, expecially for major purchases.

POSITIVE TRENDS

Another clearly positive trend is that advertising is currently being applied to the fields of environmental protection and health. One might think of the following advertisements:

13.
Developing Measures of Communicative Proficiency: A Test for French Immersion Students in Grades 9 and 10

Daina Z. Green

Although French immersion programs have been in existence for close to twenty years in Canada, there is still a tendency to consider them as experiments in bilingual education. The tentative status of such programs has meant a relatively long period during which little work was done to develop materials specifically designed to evaluate the French language skills of the immersion program students, especially as concerns tests of productive proficiency. As the programs progressed, however, researchers became more aware of the need for appropriate measures to assess the level of interpersonal communicative skills in French attained by these students. During the same period, work flourished in the field of applied linguistics in the development of theoretical frameworks (e.g., Canale and Swain 1980a and b) describing the domains of communicative proficiency.

The current paper is a brief account of one instance of the development of innovative, communicatively-based assessment instruments designed for measuring the French-language writing and speaking abilities of secondary school immersion students (Grades 9 and 10).[1] The focus is on the process of developing appropriate materials rather than on the specifics of the test instruments themselves.

To give some background on the form immersion programs commonly take in the Canadian context, students in early immersion programs typically learn the content of the school curriculum in French for a large part of the school day starting in kindergarten. French continues to be the medium of instruction for about half the school subjects well into the high school years. Variants of the program have also evolved, such as late immersion, which offer intensive study through French beginning at the Grade 6, 7 or 8 level.

The increased exposure to French and its use as a medium of instruction have been shown repeatedly to have a positive effect on the growth of students' receptive skills (Stern, Swain et al. 1976; Swain and Lapkin 1981) as well as on their ability to write and speak in French. And, by all accounts, this impressive development of second language proficiency is achieved at no long-term cost to the growth of the students' English skills.

Researchers at the Modern Language Centre of the Ontario Institute for Studies in Education have been involved in monitoring the success of French programs since 1970. The annual evaluations of the early lead classes and of subsequent groups indicate that the students successfully acquire native-like receptive skills in French by about Grade 6 (Swain and Lapkin 1981). In recent years, interest has increasingly been focused on the measurement of the productive skills, as well as more generally on the development of a measurement reflecting the students' ability to understand and produce French in communicative contexts. Two related projects currently under way in the Modern Language Centre are addressing these concerns through the development of an evaluation package with units intended for use at several grade levels, including one for Grade 9.

The Grade 9 unit consists of a student booklet, a set of written and oral tasks, and a guide to administration of the materials, including scoring procedures. The central component of the unit is a 12-page student booklet, entitled À vous la parole (roughly translated as "have your say"). The booklet offers information about two fictional summer-work projects for students 15 or 16 years old. The descriptions of these projects include information about the requirements for application, the nature of each job, the locations, leisure time activities and living conditions. The booklet also includes a partial list of government offices offering summer employment programs for youth, and it encourages students to write for further information.

The six tasks include four written and two oral exercises. They were designed to resemble activities that might commonly be carried out by native speakers. The writing tasks involved answering a letter, writing a note for a bulletin board, a composition and technical exercise. For oral production, students participate in a discussion with a group of peers and then in a simulated job interview with an adult.

The teacher's guide is a step-by-step explanation of the administrative procedures for giving the test to groups of students and scoring the responses. The scoring procedures include extensive examples of student production (taken from the pilot-test phase of the materials development) to permit teachers to make reliable and guided judgments in scoring the open-ended tasks carried out by their students.

The development of this testing unit has been complex, involving several full-time staff members, much consultation with other researchers, a thorough examination of the related literature, and much trial and error. We hope that the experience gained through this process can be shared with other researchers involved with similar projects. Swain (1983) has set out four principles guiding the development of evalua-tion materials, cited here to facilitate the discussion of the process involved in creating our tests:

1. Start from somewhere
2. Concentrate on content
3. Bias for best
4. Work for washback

Start from Somewhere

The first principle is a reminder that previous work related to test development, as well as work focusing on the theoreti-cal aspects of what it means to be proficient in a language, provided starting points for these projects. Concretely, we relied heavily on the framework of communicative competence developed by Canale and Swain (1980a), with its four compo-nents: grammatical, sociolinguistic, discourse and strategic competences. Using this framework as a basis allowed the research team to examine the spectrum of communicative func-tions in order to determine those on which the materials should focus. Another starting point for the project was the English writing assessment package developed for the British Columbia Ministry of Education (1978). This package served as a useful illustration of theme-related materials and contained clearly expressed scoring procedures with many examples which later became a model for our own.

Aside from the obvious expediency and credibility gained by basing new materials on existing theoretical and practical work there is another important advance achieved by "starting from somewhere". Simply put, future research and materials development work will not have to start from the beginning again. Just as we began with some of the ideas and techniques already refined by the British Columbia workers, we feel that the unit we have developed represents a practical advance from that point in the development of the scoring scales and criteria. Cooperation among researchers is the only way that the theoretical framework itself can be honed and adapted to its ultimate capacity for explanation and prediction.

Concentrate on Content

This was the most operationally complex of the four principles. In some ways, it is also the most innovative. Communication among people must always be about something, a fact many language textbook writers have often overlooked. Language occurs in context, and the real world is dependent on the motivation of interlocutors to exchange impressions and information about real things and ideas. Since our goal in developing these assessment instruments was to approximate real communication, a prerequisite to developing tasks for our students was to provide something for them to talk and think about. In this way, our testing unit has more in common with teaching modules than it does with most tests.

The content referred to here refers to the content of the stimulus materials as well as that of the tasks. Creating the stimulus materials was the first major task of the project staff. After sketching out the communicative tasks we planned to include in our test, we began to develop the student booklet which was to serve as the basis for tasks. In order to be able to create tasks addressing performance in the areas of sociolinguistics, discourse, grammatical and strategic competence, it was necessary to create stimulus materials which were, as Swain (1983) notes, motivating, substantive, integrated and interactive in nature.

Creating motivating materials for fifteen-year-olds required some investigation of what students of this age actually found motivating. We felt that this had to come from the students themselves and undertook a process of informal consultation with groups of francophone and immersion program youths. A strategy which proved successful was to make contact with a group of students in the same class and invite them to a restaurant for lunch on a day when school was not in session. Over lunch, we talked to them seriously about their interests. Excluding those topics of primary interest to one sex alone, the recurrent themes in these discussions included travel, animals, summer employment, music, and bicycle riding. Other topics that we had thought might be interesting, such as summer exchange programs and roller skating, simply were not.

After this process of consultation, the staff began work on a draft of a booklet which would incorporate as many of these themes of interest as possible. Two possible summer employment opportunities were described: one to take place in a francophone community in northern Ontario, organized around the theme of a series of rock concerts, and the other involving the tending of vegetable gardens and farm animals in the historic francophone national park at Louisbourg, Nova Scotia. Between the two projects, most of the students' ideas were incorporated. The early drafts of the booklet and tasks were pretested in classes containing some of the same students who had provided input in the design stages. Most students were thrilled to see their opinions in print. Further pilot testing has provided us with highly positive feedback on the materials. While we cannot claim to have hit on two topics of interest to all young people of this age, it is clear that the themes are interesting and relevant to the majority of students we have tested.

In order to increase the motivational potential of the materials, the booklet was designed to be colourful and attractive, with cartoon-like illustrations appropriate for the age level, as well as maps, a comic strip, and photographs. Another criterion for the content was that it be substantive, that is, it should provide students with new concepts or ideas. Put another way, it should give the students something to talk and write about. We felt that it was asking a lot to require students to spend several days working on the tasks without offering something real in return. We needed to create an informational gap; by providing something new, we would provide incentive for students to consider the materials carefully and sustain interest over the several days of testing. This is one of the primary reasons for including descriptions of the communities, some historical background, and pictures of the two locations. Much of this information becomes the basis for the tasks which the students must carry out. Other facts in the text are included for reasons of their inherent interest. The context focuses the students' attention and provides a backdrop for the tasks, while providing useful information of potential interest to the students.

A third goal of the materials was to integrate the content. The central theme of the unit was employment for youth, and all the activities and tasks related to the theme. Theme integration is still relatively rare in tests. The notion of creating contexts in testing has been pursued before, but usually at the level of a single task rather than at the level of the entire battery or unit. That is, every item may create its own context, but the items are not all related to each other. An exception to this, as mentioned above, is the British Columbia evaluation package for writing skills in English, which makes use of a series of themes to provide contexts for an extremely wide range of exercises. Not surprisingly, tests of this type also lend themselves to use as teaching materials, which is ultimately desirable, as we will see in our discussion of the fourth principle, work for washback.

The integration of the content in the student booklet can be seen to fulfill another goal of testing: the approximation of bona fide communicative situations. A test which is about something real is more likely to elicit language performance similar to that which the testee would produce in a true communicative interchange than a test constructed along the lines of grammatical structure. This latter type of test has recently come under fire for its potential to measure test-taking ability and metalinguistic awareness rather than proficiency in the language.

A final feature of the content is that it should promote linguistic interaction. By fostering an exchange of information, through the introduction of new concepts, and the elicitation of the students' own opinions on topics about which the students are likely to form a strong opinion, the evaluation process is made more communicative. The presentation and content of a reading passage might be motivating and attractive, the topic cohesive. However, if the questions that follow are multiple-choice reading comprehension items, then the criterion of interaction has not been reached.

To illustrate the interactive nature of this testing unit, we will describe one of the writing tasks, the letter. The student booklet includes an actual letter written by a fifteen-year-old boy, voicing his opinion on the way young people are treated. A translation of the letter reads as follows:

Dear friends,

I would like to share my point of view on the subject of the life of teenagers today. I am 15 years old and I can't believe the ignorance and lack of respect that adults show us. For them, we are inferior beings of little importance. For example, in stores and restaurants, adults get served before us even if we were there long before them.

What I find the most annoying is that adults also have priority over us in the work world. It's always been difficult for students between the ages of 15 and 17 to find a summer job, or a full-time job after graduation, and it will be even worse this year. Contrary to what most adults think, adolescents are more conscientious and open-minded than the teenagers of the 60s and 70s. We have a lot to offer in the working world.

The concerns of teenagers in the 80s are not just the threat of nuclear war, disappearing energy resources and political divisions in our country. There is also a problem we don't hear much about at school: unemployment. It turns out that we're just not prepared for the reality of the job market. It's a shame to waste so much money and time.

Adults judge our situation and make decisions for us without asking our opinion. Then, when their decisions don't meet our needs, they wonder why! Since they don't want to listen to us, it's time for us to have our say - à nous la parole!

Eric Martin

In the task associated with this letter, the students must write a reply to Eric giving their opinions and explaining whether they agree or disagree with him and why. This is a task which has elicited many strong opinions from students, with examples from their own experience.

The oral tasks were also "engaging" in a communicative sense. In one of the tasks, students in a group of four take part in a discussion on the topic of sharing responsibilities in group living as described in the booklet. The other involves a simulated job interview. The student's job is to persuade the interviewer (often the classroom teacher) to hire him or her for the summer project. The project, of course, is fictitious, and the teacher may not be as imposing a figure as an unknown interviewer. In comparing these tasks, we note that the discussion task does not require the students to assume roles and for that reason may be the more direct measure of communicative proficiency.

Bias for Best

A fundamental distinction can be made in testing theory between timed tests and power tests. In our opinion, there is good reason to believe that when adults outside the classroom environment are faced with writing tasks (e.g., letter writing, composing notes) they are generally under no pressure to complete them within a certain number of minutes. Within reasonable limits, people work at their own speed. We felt that this principle should apply to our tasks, since they are intended to create realistic situations and tasks for our teen-aged student testees. Our tests are not timed tests, and it is intended that students will work through the written tasks at their own pace. This is achieved in several ways.

The test unit is administered to a class or to a group of students over a period of at least three days. Students' accumulated work is stored in individual envelopes and returned to them at the beginning of every testing session. Each session contains a ten-minute period for students to complete or revise work undertaken in previous sessions. In addition to allowing time for students who work more slowly to complete the task, it allows for reflection on the part of the students arising from further experience with the stimulus materials as well as the sort of changes that writers make after thinking longer about something or rereading their work.

Much of our thinking on this topic has been influenced by Odell (1977), who asserts that some students cannot give their best performance on a timed test and that high-school level students are capable of making significant revisions of their written work. Odell also suggests that the testing situation, if it is to elicit the student's best work, should give testees the benefit of support materials such as dictionaries. We have embraced this notion gratefully, happy to eliminate from our materials some of the traditional arbitrariness and anxiety load of testing.

In carrying out the written tasks in this testing unit, students are encouraged to make full use of the student booklet and any dictionary which they find useful. The teacher-administrator, however, does not walk around the room and "give answers", and students do not consult with each other on their written tasks. The materials remain in the classroom at all times.

This balance of flexibility and order allows students to have fair access to the resource materials without disrupting the sessions or biasing the results. The reader should bear in mind that this testing unit explicitly addresses productive skills only, and that therefore it is the intention to ensure that all students understand the materials and what they are to do. The test administrator verifies that the students understand all directions and that they are carrying out the tasks appropriately. There is little value in evaluating a piece of work which does not conform to the objectives of the task.

Another way of helping the students to produce optimal work is to specify in the directions for each task exactly what is being tested. The directions include explicit statements about the target audience, the level of formality to adopt, and what to concentrate on in carrying out the task. For example, in the technical writing exercise, which requires students to transform information in point form into running prose, students are directed to match the style of the surrounding prose on the page where the information appears in the student booklet. It is stated that "the goal of this exercise is to evaluate your ability to write in grammatical sentences that go together well."

In the case of the oral exercises, many of the foregoing points do not apply. Oral communication takes place in "real time", and does not allow for dictionary consultation or extensive revisions (with the exception of public speaking or speech-writing). Our biasing for best performance on these two tasks was limited to the preparation and directions given to students. For the group discussion, participants were given time to familiarize themselves with the topic before beginning the tape-recorded conversation. The instructions state that all students must participate, and that the topic is flexible. For the job interview, the "candidates" are provided with the list of the questions they will be asked ten minutes ahead of time, although they may not take the list into the actual interview. They are advised that it is to their advantage to make up some questions of their own.

Work for Washback

The final principle refers to the effect that a test has on teaching practices. It is natural that where standardized tests are used, teachers responsible for students who will have to take such a test will want to prepare them as well as possible. This occurs as much because of the responsibility felt by the teacher toward the students as because of the inevitable implications for judgments of teacher effectiveness.

This being a fact of life in current educational reality, we have decided to use the teacher's awareness of the testing unit to advantage. One feature of open-ended tasks such as those which comprise this testing unit is that there is really no way to cheat. There is nothing to memorize, no way to "cram". The only way a student can be successful in writing a letter to Eric is by knowing how to organize the form of a letter, knowing the grammatical structure of sentences, and having access to appropriate vocabulary. We would be happy if teachers explicitly taught these skills, as they are likely to be useful to the students during and far beyond their high school years. The same holds true for all the writing and speaking tasks in the package.

Swain (1983) has some insightful comments regarding the specific value of influencing the immersion curriculum toward the inclusion of skills such as those drawn on in this testing unit:

Immersion education has two goals: one is to foster the development of high levels of second language proficiency; and the other is to do this at no expense to mother tongue development, cognitive growth or academic achievement. These goals are accomplished essentially through the teaching of academic content in the second language. Although at later grade levels more class time is used for the teaching of French per se (Swain, 1981), the emphasis is on teaching content. The result, typical of many classroom settings, is that the teacher talks and the students listen. Student responses are typically short and elliptical. In other words, individual students are given relatively infrequent opportunities to make use of their second language, especially in extended discourse or in sociolinguistically variable ways. As might be expected in this situation, the students develop native-like comprehension skills (Swain and Lapkin, 1982), but their spoken French has many non-native features in it (Harley and Swain, 1978; Harley, 1982). We think that the sorts of materials and related activities that form the À Vous la Parole testing unit exemplify teaching units which may help students to overcome these weaker aspects of their second language proficiency.

The project team felt strongly that teachers should be involved at every stage of the test development, as it is ultimately teachers who will administer the testing unit to their students. Without their willingness to use the test, any pedagogical value the test might have would be wasted. The test is too time-consuming to administer and score without the direct cooperation of the classroom teacher.

Teachers participated in the advisory committee which provided guidance to the research team throughout the period of materials development and pilot testing. There were workshops organized for those teachers whose classes participated in the pilot testing. During the pilot testing phase, we asked teachers to assist in the supervision and administration of the tasks, and also solicited feedback from them on all aspects of the booklet, tasks, and administration procedures. Many of their comments on early drafts of the materials were incorporated into the final version of the materials. Finally, the administration guide is oriented toward the classroom teacher and is intended to eliminate guesswork and needless effort in both administration and scoring of the test.

The scoring procedures were also finalized in the last phase of the project. Initially, through the use of a computer analysis of student results, measures which distinguished between the performance of French native/non-native speakers and second language learners of French were selected. In the final stage only those measures which were considered to be salient indicators of overall performance on the specified areas of second language competence (grammatical, sociolinguistic, discourse, and strategic) were retained.

Four procedures were used to score students' written and oral productions: counts of elements (such as calculation of the number of nouns or verbs in a given portion of the test or discourse), error counts (such as errors in the use of auxiliary être and avoir) check lists for presence of required features, and rating scales (such as a 4-point judgment of approximation of French pronunciation to that of a native speaker). A chart showing the actual parameters scored for this evaluation unit is shown in Table 1 (reproduced from Lapkin and Swain 1984).

In conclusion, the materials we have described here have built on existing tests and developments in psycholinguistic theory and have yielded a set of testing materials reflecting the state of the art. The process has been a rewarding one, as the materials produced show themselves to be workable in the field, acceptable to students and teachers, and capable of providing meaningful information about the productive skills of high-school level students in the French immersion programs. Swain's four principles (start from somewhere, concentrate on content, bias for best and work for washback) encapsulate many of the ideas that came together in the minds of the project team members in the process of developing these materials. We hope that the experience we have gained through this work will serve as points of reference for others involved in similar projects of creating assessment instruments. Likewise, we are sure that there are other principles yet to be discovered which will enable researchers and materials developers in future to create still more efficient, comprehensive, and expedient tests of communicative language proficiency.

NOTES

1. The projects discussed in this paper were funded by the Official Minority Languages Office, Saskatchewan Ministry of Education, by contract to the Ontario Institute for Studies in Education, Modern Language Centre and by the Office of Field Services and Research, O.I.S.E. The principal investigators on the projects are Jim Cummins, Sharon Lapkin and Merrill Swain. The Research Officers who have worked on the creation of the materials are Valerie Argue, Suzanne Bertrand, Daina Green, Jill Kamin, Laurette Lévy, Joyce Scane and Greta Shamash.

226

REFERENCES

British Columbia Ministry of Education, Learning Assessment Branch. 1978. The B.C. assessment of written expression. Vancouver: British Columbia Ministry of Education.

Canale, M., and M. Swain. 1980a. Theoretical bases of communicative approaches to second language teaching and testing. Applied Linguistics 1: 1-47.

Canale, M., and M. Swain. 1980b. A domain description for core FSL: Communication skills. In The Ontario Assessment Instrument Pool: French as a Second Language, Junior and Intermediate Divisions, Ontario Ministry of Education, pp. 27-39. Toronto: Ontario Ministry of Education.

Harley, B. 1982. Age related differences in the acquisition of the French verb system by Anglophone students in French immersion programs. Unpublished Ph.D. thesis, University of Toronto.

Harley, B., and M. Swain. 1978. An analysis of the verb system used by young learners of French. Interlanguage Studies Bulletin 3: 35-79.

Lapkin, S., and M. Swain. 1984. Final Report on the Evaluation of French Immersion Programs at Grade 3, 6 and 9 in New Brunswick. Toronto: The Ontario Institute for Studies in Education.

Odell, L. 1977. Measuring changes in intellectual processes as one dimension of growth in writing. In Cooper, C., and L. Odell (eds.), Evaluating Writing, pp. 107-132.

Stern, H., M. Swain, L. McLean, and R. Friedman. 1976. Three approaches to teaching French: Evaluation and Overview of studies related to the federally-funded extensions of the Second Language Learning (French) Programs in the Carleton and Ottawa School Boards. Toronto: Ontario Ministry of Education.

Swain, M. 1981. Immersion education: Applicability for non-vernacular teaching to vernacular speakers. Studies in Second Language Acquisition 4: 1-17.

Swain, M. 1983. Large scale communicative language testing: A case study. Language Learning and Communication 2(2).

Swain, M., and S. Lapkin. 1982. Evaluating Bilingual Education: A Canadian Case Study. Clevedon, Avon: Multilingual Matters Ltd.

TABLE 1 À vous la parole (Grade 9) Scoring Categories

		GRAMMATICAL COMPETENCE		SOCIOLINGUISTIC COMPETENCE	DISCOURSE COMPETENCE	STRATEGIC COMPETENCE
		Vocabulary Items	Rules of grammar and pronunciation			
WRITTEN	Composition	-sophisti-cation of vocabulary (verb count)	-use of prepo-sitions (error count)		-tense sequence (error count)	
	Technical Exercise		-word formation & grammatical spelling ("oral" error count)			
	Note			-appropriateness of style (check list)	-basic task fulfilment (check list)	
	Letter			-appropriateness of style (check list)		
ORAL	Group Discussion					-communica-tive strategies (3-point scale)
	Interview		-pronunciation (4-point scale)			

14.
Designing Oral Proficiency Tests in EFL for Hong Kong Secondary Schools

Peter Tung

As the communicative language teaching movement gains momentum in second-language education, traditional tests focusing mainly on learners' competence in grammatical elements are no longer adequate. In an attempt to assess the outcomes of communicative language teaching programmes in Hong Kong secondary schools, two oral proficiency tests were designed for this study of Chinese students in their final stages of secondary education.[1] The tests incorporate specific tasks and scoring procedures related to sociolinguistic competence as well as grammatical competence. These two areas of competence have been proposed by Canale and Swain (1979) as possibly independent components within a framework of communicative competence. Besides meeting new theoretical demands, communicative tests can also produce desirable washback effects in the classrooms, especially in an examination-oriented context like Hong Kong, where anything outside the examination syllabus is often not taught or not practised.

Several considerations guided the construction of the tests in this study. First, a situation was created in which the examinee had something to say to someone for a well-defined purpose. That is, the testing situation involved a set of realistic and motivating circumstances. Secondly, procedures were devised to elicit and assess performance reflecting various aspects of the theoretical constructs of communicative competence. Thirdly, efforts were made to ensure a reasonable degree of consistency in the administration of the tests. These deliberations will be evident in the description of the tests below.

THE TESTS

Situation

The two tests simulated the following situation. A secondary school student in search of a summer job found an advertisement in a local newspaper offering summer employment to students as tourist guides. The advertisement instructed the student to phone for an interview appointment, and subsequently, the student was invited to attend an interview. The examinees were asked to imagine themselves to be in the position of the student. Test 1, therefore, consisted of the telephone call, and Test 2, the job interview.

Subjects

The examinees were fifty secondary school students from five schools representing various types of institutions at this level in Hong Kong. The sample was intentionally chosen to include as wide a range of ability within the school-leaving population as possible. For this purpose, five Form 4 (i.e., Grade 10) and five Form 6 (i.e., Grade 12) students from each school were asked to participate in the tests. At the time of taking the tests, candidates had from 10 to 12 years of instruction in English as a foreign language.

Raters and Examiner

An examiner and a rater were present at each testing occasion. The examiner assumed a role appropriate to the testing situation and conversed with the candidates accordingly. The rater was responsible for administrative matters, such as distributing instruction sheets to the candidates and directing them to their seats at the beginning of the tests. During the tests, the rater sat unobtrusively behind the candidates and performed the scoring. At each school, the rater was a senior member of the English language-teaching staff, who also aided in the selection of the students for the tests. As five schools were involved, there were five raters. The author acted as the examiner in all the cases. Each of the raters knew the examinees, while the examiner was not familiar with anyone of them. Before the tests, all the raters were briefed on the contents, administration and scoring of the tests, and were given an opportunity to practise marking a recording of a mock candidate to become acquainted with the scoring system.

Administrative Notes

A set of notes was prepared for the examiner and the raters to make explicit their responsibilities and the procedures of the tests so that the candidates would receive approximately the same treatment. To this end, the examiner's questions, occasional comments, and answers to likely enquiries of the candidates were specified in the notes in the order that they might occur. Suitable prompts for the weaker candidates, to direct or restore communication, were listed. In addition, the points in the tests where responses from the testees would be expected were also indicated. There was also a diagram of the layout of the examination room. One end of the room would be arranged for conducting the telephone conversation, while the job interview would be held in another end of the room to effect a change of setting between the two tests.

Procedure

Ten minutes before the tests, the rater would sit a candidate at a quiet spot outside the examination room and give him or her an instruction sheet to prepare for the tests. On the instruction sheet, candidates were informed that there would be two tests, a telephone conversation and a job interview, and that they would be asked to make the telephone call first. Candidates were told that there were no set answers and that they should speak naturally as required by the situation. To make the circumstances uniform for all candidates, each of them was asked to assume a common name, either John Choi or Mary Choi, and was given a home address and a telephone number. An attractive advertisement for English-speaking Form 4 and Form 6 students to work as tourist guides in the summer was then presented to the candidates on the instruction sheet.

Test-takers were asked to apply for the job, and they were advised to spend the next five minutes of their time preparing mentally for what they were going to say when they telephoned the tourist agency and when they attended the interview. To limit the amount of information candidates were expected to convey in the tests, they were asked to consider (a) the reasons why they wanted to get the job, (b) the qualifications required for the job, (c) what the job would entail, and (d) the salary they expected. During the tests, the examiner would ask questions around these points.

To make the situation realistic and to reduce the memory load of the candidates, they were told that they could refer to the instruction sheet during the telephone conversation, but it would be removed from them before the interview. To introduce an element of negotiation into the telephone conversation, candidates were also issued a schedule of their future engagements together with the instruction sheet and told it would be useful when arranging a time for the interview. Similarly, to encourage two-way communication and to allow candidates to initiate conversations, they were given an opportunity during the interview to ask questions about the job. Again, hints on the kinds of things to ask were provided on the instruction sheet. For example, they could ask about the number of hours they had to work per week.

On the instruction sheet, candidates were also warned that they would be asked to imagine it was time for the interview immediately after they had completed the telephone call. In the actual testing situation, the rater tried to smooth the transition by leading the candidate to a different area of the room and reminding him or her of the change in time. Candidates were also told that they were free to improvise new information as long as it was consistent with the instructions already given. This provision was added to make the tasks easier and perhaps more personal for the candidates.

After a candidate had had ten minutes to read the instruction sheet, the rater would invite the examinee to enter the examination room and sit in front of a telephone. The rater would also instruct the examinee to treat the telephone as a real one and start making the phone call. The examiner, acting as the manager of the tourist agency, would answer the phone, ask a few questions about the identity of the caller, and arrange a time for him and the candidate to meet for an interview. After the telephone conversation, the rater would ask the candidate to imagine a change of place and time for the interview. Again, the examiner greeted the candidate as the manager of the tourist company and conducted the interview. The telephone conversation generally lasted less than three minutes, and the interview about six minutes. When the tests were over, the rater would ask the candidate to fill in a questionnaire about the testing experience and to provide other background information about himself or herself.

Scoring

Two types of scales were used to estimate the candidates' grammatical and sociolinguistic competence. Grammatical competence was taken to include all the areas assessed in a conventional test, namely, sentence-level grammar, the amount of relevant information communicated, pronunciation, fluency, and vocabulary. It was thought that performance in each of these areas could be measured with a graded scale, provided that the categories of the scales were clearly defined and few in number. Scales with six divisions were uniformly adopted so that marking could be done quickly and consistently.

The scales were adapted from various sources. The grammar scale was based on the **Foreign Service Institute Oral Interview Test** and related to sentence structures (see, for example, Oller 1979: 322). The scale for the amount of relevant information conveyed was based on one constructed by Bartz (see, for example, Valette 1977: 151). The pronunciation scale employed Brown's (1977) notions of intonation, assimilation and elision of speech sounds. Similarly, Brown's (1977) idea of fillers in speech and Crystal and Davy's (1975) connective features were used to build the fluency scale. The vocabulary scale was adapted from one designed by Clark (see for example, Valette 1977: 161).

A graded scale which was based on one used in the 1979 Hong Kong Certificate of Education Examination was also constructed to record the raters' overall impression of the candidates' performance. The scale is reproduced here as an example of the graded scales.

Overall Grade
1. Able to converse with ease; native-like.
2. Able to converse fluently with only occasional errors.
3. Able to convey meaning in spite of some inaccuracy.
4. Has difficulty in expressing his or her meaning in accurate English.
5. Unable to express himself or herself accurately in spite of frequent prompting.
6. Shows difficulty in understanding the questions put to him or her; response virtually non-existent even after constant prompting.

As exemplified by this scale, only brief descriptions were provided for each category of the graded scales. The principle guiding the division of the scales was the effectiveness of communication, whether information was conveyed or whether misunderstanding was caused. The threshold level of comprehensibility and acceptability was deliberately set at point 3 for all the scales. Below point 3, that is, for points 4, 5, and 6, the message would be distorted. To make marking simple, there was a separate mark sheet for each candidate. It was only necessary for the rater to circle the assigned grade of each area of the candidate's performance on the mark sheet.

Sociolinguistic competence was assessed in the tests in terms of behaviour observing some "sociocultural rules of use". Canale and Swain described a knowledge of these rules to be "crucial in interpreting utterances for social meaning, particularly when there is a low level of transparency between the literal meaning of an utterance and the speaker's intention" (1979: 55). They further stated that "primary focus of these rules is on the extent to which certain propositions and communicative functions are appropriate within a given sociocultural context depending on contextual factors such as topic, role of participants, setting, and norms of interaction" (1979: 55).

In formulating sociocultural rules of use for the tests, native informants were obviously important, but guidance was also obtained from the literature. For example, in Test 1, after the candidate had dialled the phone, he or she was expected to wait for a response from the other party before speaking. The corresponding rule, that the person being called should speak first, was studied in detail by Schegloff (1972). Schegloff treated the telephone ring as a summons. The summons and its response together formed a summons-answer (SA) sequence, which had at least two essential properties. First, an answer was guaranteed to follow the summons in ordinary circumstances. Secondly, the summoner was obliged to speak upon the completion of the first SA sequence. In Test 1, the acceptable consequent behaviour was for the candidate to either identify himself or herself or state the purpose of the call.

It was thought that specific behaviour required by the sociocultural rules of use was either displayed or not displayed by the candidates, and therefore a checklist of appropriate behaviours, ten for Test 1 and six for Test 2, was drawn up to assess the candidates' sociolinguistic competence (see Appendix A for some examples). Obviously, only a small sample of the behaviour which would be expected of native speakers in the testing situation could be listed. During the tests, the rater ticked off the behaviour demonstrated by the candidates on the checklist. As the examiner only evaluated the candidates' performance from recordings of the telephone conversations and the interviews, he did not use the checklist.

RESULTS

In general, the scores for the various aspects of grammatical competence given by each rater and the examiner correlate highly with one another. This is true for both Test 1 and Test 2. The interesting correlations, however, seem to be those between the global scores and the scores for each category of grammatical competence. Table 1 indicates the correlations of each rater's overall impression grades with the grades for individual areas of grammatical competence. In Test 1, all but three correlations are significant at the 5 per cent level with typical values between 0.7 and 0.8. Similar results are obtained for Test 2 as shown in the same table. In fact, the same pattern is obtained for the examiner's scores.

TABLE 1 Correlations between Raters' Global Ratings
and Grades for Individual Areas of
Grammatical Competence

Area	RATER				
	1	2	3	4	5
Test 1					
Grammar	.75*	.67*	.78*	.80*	.70*
Communication	.67*	.26*	.88*	.80*	.76*
Pronunciation	.67*	.67*	.72*	.80*	.61*
Fluency	.52	.77*	1.00*	.93*	.80*
Vocabulary	.56	.80*	.81*	.67*	.69*
Test 2					
Grammar	.77*	.72*	.86*	.75*	.58*
Communication	.72*	.73*	.83*	.87*	.70*
Pronunciation	.80*	.47	.83*	.79*	.32
Fluency	.75*	.81*	.85*	.72*	.70*
Vocabulary	.60*	.72*	.90*	.94*	.36

Note: Each rater evaluated 10 subjects.
*$p \leq$ .05.

A moderate degree of consistency exists between the scores of the two tests. The first two columns of Table 2 show the correlations between the global grades for the two tests for each rater and the examiner. Except for the rater from School 1, the correlations indicate that the judgment of the performance of particular candidates did not vary a great deal from Test 1 to Test 2 in the given circumstances. When the scores of the raters are compared with those of the examiner for each of the tests, the inter-rater reliability does not seem to be satisfactory for Test 1 and is only partially satisfactory for Test 2. The last two columns of Table 2 display the correlations between the global grades of the examiner and the raters.

TABLE 2   Correlations of Global Ratings

School[a]	Rater[b]	Examiner[c]	Rater and examiner[d] Test 1	Test 2
1	.20	.74*	.36	.56*
2	.55	.63*	.39	.57
3	.67*	.65*	.60*	.85*
4	.68*	.88*	.83*	.82*
5	.76*	.80*	.44	.84*

a n = 10 for each school.
b Correlations between each rater's ratings of Test 1 and Test 2.
c Correlations between the examiner's ratings of Test 1 and Test 2.
d Correlations between each rater's ratings and the examiner's ratings for each test.
*$p \leq$ .05.

When the sociolinguistic scores are correlated with the global ratings representing grammatical competence, results are irregular, and low and negative correlations seem to predominate. Table 3 summarizes this state of affairs.

TABLE 3 Correlations between Global Ratings and Sociolinguistic Scores

School	Test 1		Test 2	
	Rater	Examiner	Rater	Examiner
1	.16	−0.15	.52	.53
2	−0.53	−0.36	.66*	−0.09
3	.73*	.64*	.16	.38
4	.80*	.57*	.09	.21
5	.41	.21	−0.07	−0.18

n = 10 for each school.
*$p \leq$ .05.

As the two tests are by themselves of rather short dura-
tion, analysis is also performed by considering the two tests
as one unit, hereafter referred to as the combined test. The
results as shown in Table 4 indicate that the global ratings
strongly correlate with every aspect of grammatical competence
for the raters. A similar case exists for the examiner. The
inter-rater reliability for the combined test is now more acceptable (see Table 5). However, the sociolinguistic scores still
do not correlate with the grammatical scores in a regular
manner as shown in Table 6. Table 7 presents the distribution
of the global and sociolinguistic scores given by each rater
and examiner.

TABLE 4 Correlations between Rater's Global Rating and Grades for Areas of Grammatical Competence for Combined Test

Area	Rater				
	1	2	3	4	5
Grammar	.67*	.86*	.93*	.81*	.67*
Communication	.62*	.74*	.90*	.90*	.79*
Pronunciation	.81*	.83*	.79*	.80*	.56*
Fluency	.60*	.92*	.96*	.85*	.78*
Vocabulary	.61*	.88*	.94*	.87*	.74*

Note: Each rater evaluated 10 subjects.
*$p \leq$ .05.

TABLE 5 Inter-rater Reliability for the Combined Test

School	Reliability
1	.57*
2	.61*
3	.86*
4	.85*
5	.75*

$\underline{n}$ = 10 for each school.
*$\underline{p} \leq .05$.

TABLE 6 Correlations between Global Ratings and Sociolinguistic Scores for the Combined Test

School[a]	Rater	Examiner
1	-0.05	.23
2	.18	-0.10
3	.76*	.61*
4	.61*	.70*
5	.20	-0.01

a $\underline{n}$ = 10 for each school.
*$\underline{p} \leq .05$.

TABLE 7 Mean Global Ratings and Mean
Sociolinguistic
Scores (SS)

School[a]		Test 1			Test 2		
		Global Rating[b]			Global Rating[c]		
		Rater	Examiner	SS	Rater	Examiner	SS
1	M	5.1	5.3	5.2	4.6	4.9	2.9
	$\overline{SD}$	0.3	0.7	1.8	0.7	0.7	1.1
2	$\overline{M}$	4.2	3.8	6.2	4.4	3.3	2.8
	$\overline{SD}$	0.6	0.6	0.8	0.7	0.5	0.9
3	$\overline{M}$	3.3	3.8	5.8	3.6	4.0	3.5
	$\overline{SD}$	1.1	0.6	1.8	1.0	0.8	0.7
4	$\overline{M}$	4.6	3.9	7.3	4.4	4.1	3.0
	$\overline{SD}$	0.7	0.9	1.6	0.8	0.7	1.4
5	$\overline{M}$	4.2	4.4	6.4	4.2	4.3	2.8
	$\overline{SD}$	0.8	0.7	1.8	1.0	1.0	0.9

Note: The global ratings have been transformed
such that the highest grade is 6 and the
lowest 1.
Only the raters awarded sociolinguistic scores.
a n = 10 for each school.
b The maximum score is 10.
c The maximum score is 6.

DISCUSSION

First of all, it may be mentioned that the testing situation
and the tasks involved were considered to be realistic by
practically every candidate who had taken the tests. The
tasks and the situations were originally conceived on the basis
of the author's familiarity with the secondary school students in
Hong Kong. After the tests, the candidates were asked in a
questionnaire if they considered it probable that they would
encounter situations comparable to those of the tests. Ninety-
eight per cent of the candidates indicated that it was likely or
more than likely for them to make a similar telephone call and
all of the candidates replied that it was at least likely that they
would attend a similar interview. It seems that the tests have,
minimally, a prima facie claim to face and perhaps content
validity.

The results of the tests indicate that global ratings on a graded scale account for a sizable proportion of the variance of the scores for each aspect of grammatical competence on an identical scale. This might signify that markers tend to be influenced by a single aspect of the candidates' performance if graded scales are used to assess different components of their behaviour in the same test. One way to reduce this "halo effect" is to employ distinctly different systems of scoring for assessing independent traits or by specifying clearly the expected behaviour. The checklist of appropriate behaviour apparently provides a different scoring system from the graded scales, as evidenced by the incongruity of the grammatical and sociolinguistic scores. These findings are comfirmed by combining the scores of the two tests, in effect lengthening the tests. The consequent significant correlations between the sociolinguistic scores and the grammatical scores for two of the five schools could mean that some schools are more successful than others in implementing the communicative language teaching programmes intended to bring about a higher degree of sociolinguistic competence. Further investigations in this direction may be revealing. In all events, it seems that this study has lent support to the current thinking that grammatical and sociolinguistic competencies could be independently developed in second-language learners and consequently should be assessed separately on their own terms.

NOTES

1. The data in this study were first reported in an M.A. thesis submitted to the University of Hong Kong in September, 1980. An earlier draft of this paper was presented at the Fifth Annual Language Testing Research Colloquium held at the University of Ottawa in March, 1983.

REFERENCES

Brown, G. 1977. Listening to Spoken English. London: Longman.

Canale, M., and M. Swain. 1979. Communicative approaches to second language teaching and testing (Review and Evaluation Bulletins, Volume 1, Number 5). Toronto: Ontario Ministry of Education.

Crystal, D., and D. Davy. 1975. Advanced Conversational English. London: Longman.

Oller, J. 1979. Language Tests at School: A Pragmatic Approach. London: Longman.

Schegloff, E. 1972. Sequencing in conversational openings. In J.J. Gumperz, and D. Hymes (Eds.), Directions in Sociolinguistics: the Ethnography of Communication. N.Y.: Holt, Rinehart and Winston.

Valette, R. 1977. Modern Language Testing (2nd ed.). N.Y.: Harcourt Brace Jovanovich.

242

APPENDIX A

Examples from the "Checklist of Expected Examinee Behaviour"
(Scoring procedure: Put a tick against the behaviour correctly
exhibited by the student.)

Test 1 : Telephone Conversation

1. Student dials the phone   _____

2. Student waits for someone to answer the phone
   and greet him or her   _____

3. Student identifies himself or herself (before
   being prompted to do so).   _____

4. Student uses the appropriate self-address form
   "This is (NOT I am)... speaking."   _____

5. Student states the purpose of his or her call
   (before being prompted to do so).   _____

6. Student says good-bye or similar expression at
   the end of the call.   _____

Test 2 : Interview

1. Student responds to examiner's greeting and
   invitation to sit by sitting down and saying
   "Good morning/afternoon", "Thank you", or
   similar expression.   _____

2. Student responds to examiner's remark "You're
   a bit far over there, aren't you?" by moving
   his or her seat closer to the examiner.   _____

3. Student acknowledges/confirms examiner's
   statements about his or her student status
   and intention to work for the tourist
   agency during the summer.   _____

4. Student prepares to leave when the examiner
   says "(Well,) this seems to be it."   _____

5. Student thanks the interviewer.   _____

6. Student says good-bye.   _____

15.
Deux tests faits sur mesure

Marie-Claude Tréville

Au cours de l'année 1981, la direction du Centre national des Arts (CNA) d'Ottawa décidait de faire élaborer un test de français langue seconde qui serait utilisé dans le cadre de la procédure de sélection des candidats à un emploi. Fondé en 1967, le CNA est un organisme à vocations multiples : danse, opéra, théâtre, variétés, etc., subventionné par le gouvernement fédéral.

Jusqu'alors, lorsqu'il s'agissait de pourvoir un poste désigné "bilingue", le CNA avait recours à l'une ou l'autre de deux méthodes, alternativement ou successivement, qui consistaient soit à faire appel aux tests de la Fonction publique, soit à insérer quelques questions en français dans le cours de l'entrevue d'usage.

Le recours au personnel et aux tests du Service des tests, de la mesure et de l'évaluation de la Commission de la fonction publique pour l'évaluation des connaissances en langue seconde des candidats à un poste au CNA avait d'abord semblé naturel à cause des liens administratifs entre cet organisme et le gouvernement fédéral. À l'usage, cependant, cette solution ne s'était pas révélée satisfaisante pour des raisons pratiques d'abord : les agents administrant les tests ne pouvaient recevoir les candidats que sur rendez-vous, parfois plusieurs semaines après que la décision concernant le poste à remplir devait être prise. D'autre part, si on pouvait étendre l'usage des tests destinés aux employés de la fonction publique à certains agents d'administration du CNA, cela ne correspondait pas aux besoins spécifiques de la majorité d'entre eux et ne permettait pas d'évaluer la maîtrise de savoirs correspondant aux exigences réelles des multiples fonctions à remplir dans chaque département du Centre.

Dans certains autres cas, selon l'importance du poste à pourvoir, le candidat, pré-sélectionné d'après son curriculum vitae, était convoqué pour une entrevue par un comité composé de trois ou quatre personnes (responsables de l'embauche du personnel et représentants du service intéressé). Lors de l'entrevue, menée traditionnellement en anglais, un des membres du comité posait quelques questions anodines en français au candidat qui s'était préalablement déclaré lui-même bilingue, ou du moins apte à exercer les tâches requises dans les deux langues. La "connaissance" en français du candidat était donc jugée d'après l'idée préconçue qu'elle était suffisante et d'après quelques répliques données en français pendant l'entrevue. Il s'agissait donc plutôt de l'impression générale reçue par un examinateur improvisé. Bien que cette impression générale ait été souvent assez juste, en particulier dans les cas limites, c'est-à-dire quand le verdict était franchement positif (capacité évidente à communiquer) ou franchement négatif (incapacité évidente à communiquer), une telle procédure n'était pas sans poser des problèmes de conscience au service du personnel du CNA quand, parmi des candidats ayant les mêmes qualifications professionnelles, le critère linguistique devenait déterminant pour l'attribution du poste.

C'est ainsi que la direction générale du CNA en vint à vouloir un test qui serait sa propriété, qui serait simple, qui pourrait être administré et corrigé rapidement, même par des non-spécialistes du testing, et qui, fait sur mesure, permettrait de décider d'une façon systématique, juste et constante si une personnne avait ou n'avait pas la compétence suffisante pour exercer ses fonctions en français en présence de francophones. Les pages qui suivent décrivent nos différentes interventions dans cette entreprise.

La première étape de l'élaboration du test a été de déterminer les objectifs du test, c'est-à-dire de décrire les besoins réels en français ressentis par les employés du CNA déjà en place aux divers échelons de l'organigramme. Nous nous sommes familiarisés avec la structure interne du CNA, nous avons consulté les descriptions des postes (en ne nous intéressant qu'aux postes désignés "bilingues"). Nous avons ainsi appris que le CNA est composé de dix grands services : musique, théâtre, danse et variétés, finances, administration et personnel, relations publiques, Festival Canada, opérations, restauration et entretien. Devant la multiplicité des postes, nous avons fait un choix, approuvé par le CNA, des fonctions nous semblant les plus représentatives dans chaque division. Nous avons ensuite étudié ces fonctions sur un double plan, le plan institutionnel (descriptions détaillées des tâches faites par le service du personnel) et le plan pratique (en allant rencontrer les gens sur les lieux mêmes de leur travail).

À l'aide d'un questionnaire (que nous remplissions nous-mêmes au cours des entrevues), nous avons dressé un inventaire des actes de communication en français les plus fréquents et de tous les paramètres entourant ces actes, c'est-à-dire le type de discours, le but de l'interaction, le registre, les savoirs requis et les aspects situationnels pouvant influencer le comportement linguistique tels que le rôle des interlocuteurs, leurs relations, etc.

En plus d'une description des actes de communication, il nous fallait des échantillons, des modèles d'actes authentiques. Nous avons donc glané un grand nombre de documents écrits (que nous avons utilisés tels quels dans le test), mais nous n'avons recueilli aucun document sonore, à l'exception d'enregistrements de communiqués radiophoniques (que nous pouvions difficilement utiliser tels quels dans le test). Malgré des promesses répétées, le CNA, en effet, n'a malheureusement pas pu fournir d'enregistrements de communications téléphoniques ni de conversations prises sur le vif, pour la raison bien compréhensible que ces pratiques sont tout simplement illégales, à moins que les interlocuteurs n'en aient été avisés à l'avance et n'aient exprimé leur accord, ce qui fausse considérablement "l'authenticité" de l'échange verbal. En conséquence, nous avons pris note de tous les paramètres des communications orales typiques ayant lieu dans les divers services et avons nous-mêmes reconstitué et joué des conversations calquées sur les modèles authentiques.

Dans la sélection du matériel effectuée pour constituer un corpus et dans l'analyse des besoins visant à spécifier les objectifs du test, nous avons donc procédé intuitivement, en nous familiarisant avec les situations de travail au CNA et en nous inspirant, sans entrer dans leur complexité, des modèles de Munby (1978), de Richterich (1978) et de Carroll (1980). C'est ainsi que nous avons dégagé deux grandes catégories d'emplois dits bilingues au CNA et qu'il est devenu évident qu'à ces deux catégories bien distinctes, il faudrait faire correspondre deux tests différents dans leurs objectifs et dans leurs procédures.

Voici une description schématique de la situation rencontrée. La première catégorie d'emplois regroupe les services qui n'ont pas ou qui ont peu de relations avec le public : danse et variétés/ musique/ théâtre/ Festival Canada/ production/ personnel/ finance/ entretien, ainsi que le service des relations publiques, qui a surtout des rapports à sens unique avec le public (communiqués de presse et de radio). En résumé, les fonctions langagières recensées dans ces services sont celles mises en jeu lors des échanges suivants :

TABLEAU 1

Catégories	Fonctions langagières recensées dans les services de la première catégorie
Peu ou pas de relations avec le public	– contact téléphonique ou direct avec des artistes francophones (invitation, proposition, confirmation, installation, accueil) – contact téléphonique avec des impresarios francophones (rarement en français) (négociation, acceptation, rejet) – rédaction de contrats d'engagement avec des artistes francophones – contact avec les fournisseurs québécois ou franco-ontariens (commande d'équipement, réclamation, demande de services) par téléphone confirmé par lettre
Relations à sens unique	– publication de biographies, dépliants, communiqués – conférences de presse, messages publicitaires

La deuxième catégorie d'emplois regroupe les services qui sont en rapport direct avec le grand public. Les fonctions langagières qu'on y retrouve correspondent aux actes suivants :

TABLEAU 2

Catégories	Fonctions langagières recensées dans les services de la deuxième catégorie
Gestion des salles	– indication de directions, d'emplacements, etc. (ouvreuses, placeurs, surveillants des garages)
Guichets	– indication de prix, d'horaires et de programmes (vente aux guichets et par téléphone)
	– information et prise de renseignements pour réservations et abonnements (directement et par téléphone)
Restauration	– prise des commandes, explication, service à table et au bar, prise des réservations
	– information, enregistrement de plaintes

Pour la catégorie I, nous avons proposé un test de compétence générale en cinq parties : deux parties correspondant aux deux savoirs "lire" et "écouter" et comprenant des questions exigeant une compréhension globale, plus deux parties intégrant plusieurs savoirs d'expression et de compréhension au niveau du discours et consistant en un texte à trous et une entrevue, et enfin une composition écrite.

Pour la catégorie II, nous avons recommandé un test de performances spécifiques portant exclusivement sur des tâches à accomplir en français et sur les savoirs langagiers mis en cause lors d'échanges bien délimités. Le contenu, approprié à des situations de communication différentes, est donc différent pour chacun des trois services intéressés, mais la forme et la procédure sont les mêmes dans les trois cas.

Voici une description détaillée des deux tests.

TEST DE FRANÇAIS POUR LA CATÉGORIE I
(Personnel administratif du CNA)

Présentation matérielle

- un cahier de l'examinateur avec une description complète du test, toutes les instructions utiles concernant l'administration et la notation du test et la transcription des enregistrements;

- un cahier du candidat contenant les instructions utiles, les passages à lire, les questions à choix multiples et les réponses;
- une bande magnétique;
- trois feuilles de réponses correspondant aux différents sous-tests;
- deux grilles d'évaluation à l'usage des examinateurs;
- deux grilles perforées pour une notation rapide des sous-tests comprenant des questions à choix multiples.

But

Le candidat doit prouver qu'il peut comprendre des énoncés oraux et écrits et qu'il peut s'exprimer efficacement en français dans des situations langagières vraies, le tout ne requérant pas d'autres connaissances que celles faisant partie de l'activité professionnelle du candidat.

Format et procédures

Le test est composé de quatre parties intitulées respectivement expression orale, compréhension auditive, compréhension de la lecture et expression écrite, ce qui maintient la division opératoire "classique" en quatre domaines de savoirs langagiers sans exclure leur interdépendance, en particulier dans la partie "expression orale", qui consiste en une entrevue, et dans le test de closure.
La partie "compréhension auditive" dure moins de quinze minutes. Le candidat écoute deux enregistrements suivis de questions et de réponses à choix multiples (au total, huit questions). La deuxième partie consiste à lire quatre textes suivis chacun de trois questions à réponses à choix multiples (durée totale : vingt minutes). Pour ces deux parties, le candidat indique ses réponses en noircissant des cases sur sa feuille de réponses. La partie "expression écrite" comprend deux sous-tests que l'examinateur peut omettre s'il sait que l'employé éventuel dans le poste sollicité n'aura jamais à écrire en français. Le sous-test A est une composition écrite d'une dizaine de lignes à rédiger sous forme de note de service, à l'aide des renseignements donnés. La durée prévue est de vingt minutes. Un "texte à trous" constitue le sous-test B. Il s'agit d'un contrat réel entre le CNA et un artiste. Le texte est à compléter à l'aide d'une liste de mots ou d'expressions donnée. Le candidat indique ses réponses directement sur cette liste qui est sa troisième feuille de réponses et dispose de vingt minutes pour le faire.

L'expression orale est évaluée au cours de l'entrevue que le candidat doit subir devant un comité de trois ou quatre personnes du service du personnel et du service intéressé à retenir ses services. Deux de ces personnes au moins doivent être capables de juger de la compétence en français du candidat. Plusieurs questions sont suggérées à titre d'exemples aux examinateurs, qui peuvent les faire varier et les adapter à la situation exacte, le rôle des examinateurs consistant non seulement à poser des questions, mais aussi à nourrir la conversation par des réactions, des commentaires, etc. On devrait poser au moins quatre questions demandant des réponses élaborées. La procédure de l'entrevue peut s'avérer difficile quand, comme c'est le cas ici, elle ne s'inscrit pas dans un processus d'apprentissage c'est-à-dire quand le candidat n'est pas entraîné pour ce genre de test et quand les examinateurs n'y sont pas préparés non plus. Nous avons donc fortement recommandé une période d'initiation des examinateurs ou la présence d'un spécialiste (de l'enseignement des langues ou du testing) à l'entrevue.

Notation

La notation de la compréhension auditive et de la lecture se fait instantanément à l'aide de deux grilles perforées fournies aux examinateurs. Il en va de même pour la correction du "texte à trous".

La correction de l'expression orale et de la composition écrite est plus délicate. Pour mieux juger de l'efficacité de la communication, les examinateurs, qui ne sont pas des linguistes ni même des professeurs de langue, peuvent se fonder sur des impressions spécifiques structurées à l'aide d'échelles (allant de "faible" à "excellent" ou de un à dix) correspondant à la correction linguistique (aspect grammatico-structural, facilité d'élocution, correction phonologique ou orthographique), à l'adéquation de l'expression (compréhension de l'interaction) et à la performance pragmatique (efficacité de la transmission des messages quant au fond et à la forme).

TEST DE FRANÇAIS POUR LA CATÉGORIE II
(Personnel des services directs au public : gestion des salles/ guichets/ restauration)

Présentation matérielle

- un cahier de l'examinateur comprenant la description du test, toutes les instructions concernant l'administration

et la notation du test et la transcription intégrale des enregistrements;
- un cahier du candidat contenant les instructions utiles et les données à utiliser dans les jeux de simulation;
- trois bandes magnétiques, chacune contenant deux dialogues appropriés à chacun des services, suivis de questions et de réponses à choix multiples;
- une feuille de réponses;
- une grille d'évaluation de l'expression orale dans les jeux de rôles.

But

Le candidat doit prouver sa compétence fonctionnelle dans des situations de communication orale propres à l'accomplissement de ses tâches en tant qu'employé du guichet, du bar, du restaurant, du garage ou en tant que placeur, le test de langue ne requérant pas d'autres connaissances que celles nécessaires pour l'accomplissement des tâches inhérentes au poste sollicité par le candidat.

Format et procédures

Ce test est administré pendant et après l'entrevue du candidat par le service intéressé à l'engager. La forme et la procédure du test sont les mêmes pour les trois services, mais les thèmes exploités sont différents.
La partie "compréhension auditive" consiste en deux dialogues enregistrés suivis chacun de quatre questions et de réponses à choix multiples; elle se déroule en quinze minutes.
La partie intitulée "expression orale" consiste en jeux de simulation ou jeux de rôles dans lesquels le candidat et l'examinateur sont les protagonistes d'une petite scène dont la trame est proposée à l'avance. Deux jeux de rôles sont proposés pour chaque division (Guichet-Gestion des salles-Restauration). L'examinateur peut les utiliser tels quels ou les orienter différemment en jouant son propre rôle. Il est conseillé à l'examinateur de "bavarder" un peu en français avec le candidat pour le mettre à l'aise, puis de lui expliquer en quoi consistent ces jeux de rôles, enfin de lui soumettre les sujets en lui laissant le temps d'y réfléchir (quelques minutes). Il s'agit donc d'une simulation de situations authentiques dans laquelle sont données des consignes contraignantes portant sur le contenu. Ces consignes sont données en anglais et en français dans le cahier du candidat (il faut noter qu'il est

parfois difficile de donner les consignes en français sans fournir une aide indue au candidat qui peut se contenter de les
répéter avec le minimum de transformations grammaticales).

Idéalement, au lieu de ces jeux de rôles, l'examinateur
devrait suivre le candidat dans le lieu de travail et vérifier s'il
est capable d'offrir les services requis en français. Comme cela
n'est pas réalisable, l'examinateur s'improvise "acteur", mais
cette fonction s'improvise-t-elle, même si une liste de modèles
d'intervention est fournie? L'examinateur non préparé ou peu
doué pour le théâtre risque de remplacer le dialogue par une
conversation à propos du dialogue qui devrait avoir lieu. Par
exemple, au lieu de jouer le rôle du client mécontent au
restaurant qui devrait dire quelque chose comme : "Garçon!
Vous vous êtes sûrement trompé de table, je n'ai pas commandé
le steak-frites!", il va employer le style indirect en s'adressant au candidat et lui dire : "Qu'est-ce que vous me répon-
driez si j'étais votre client et si je vous disais que vous vous
êtes trompé de commande?". Ne recevant pas le stimulus réel,
le candidat va être tenté de répondre, lui aussi, de façon indi-
recte : "Je vais dire que je m'excuse et que je vais retourner
le steak à la cuisine..." La scène n'a alors plus rien d'authentique et ne renseigne guère sur le savoir-faire du candidat
placé dans une situation réelle. C'est un des dangers des
jeux de simulation quand ils sont administrés par des pro-
fanes; là encore, il serait souhaitable qu'un professeur de
langue puisse initier l'examinateur éventuel, ou du moins
l'assister pendant quelque temps.

Notation

La correction de la première partie se fait instantanément à
l'aide d'une grille perforée qu'il suffit de placer sur la feuille
de réponses. L'évaluation des jeux de rôles se fait à l'aide
d'une grille mettant en évidence les différents aspects de
l'efficacité de communication. Nous avons recommandé que
cette évaluation, de même que celle de l'expression orale en
entrevue (catégorie I), soit faite par deux personnes au moins
et que toute l'épreuve soit enregistrée, afin d'approcher le plus
possible des meilleures conditions d'objectivité et de fiabilité.
Or, par principe, le magnétophone n'est jamais utilisé au CNA
pendant les entrevues, de crainte d'augmenter la tension
nerveuse des candidats. C'est une raison de plus pour que
deux personnes soient chargées de l'évaluation de la langue.
Elles doivent le faire pendant ou immédiatement après l'entrevue, en prenant un à un les critères d'adéquation de l'expression, de correction linguistique (aux niveaux phonétique,

grammatico-structural et lexical) et d'efficacité de la communication et en les situant sur une échelle allant de "faible" à "excellent".

La notation de l'expression, comme l'administration du test d'expression, reste un problème : elle est faite par des gens qui sont francophones, certes, et qui peuvent juger approximativement de la compétence du candidat, mais qui n'ont, comme formation en matière de testing, que leur bonne volonté. C'est pourquoi, dans nos directives aux examinateurs, nous insistons sur l'importance de se familiariser à l'avance avec les procédures de notation et de se concentrer sur la performance langagière, en faisant abstraction, si possible, de l'imagination du candidat, des traits de sa personnalité, de sa culture générale, etc.

Avant que nos deux tests ne soient mis en pratique, nous avons procédé à leur évaluation. Nous avons soumis le premier à une trentaine d'employés du CNA occupant des postes bilingues de la catégorie I et le deuxième test à une vingtaine d'employés occupant des postes bilingues de la catégorie II. Les buts de ce pré-testing étaient les suivants :

- valider les résultats obtenus en les comparant avec les résultats d'un autre type d'évaluation des mêmes candidats (appréciation des employeurs ou auto-évaluation des candidats);
- faire une analyse statistique des différentes parties pour éventuellement les modifier (quand elles se sont avérées, par exemple, trop faciles ou trop difficiles);
- recueillir les réactions des utilisateurs et leurs suggestions concernant les procédures du test;
- établir la note de passage d'après la note moyenne obtenue par des employés en place remplissant efficacement leurs tâches en français;
- contrôler le fonctionnement de nos grilles d'évaluation de l'expression en demandant aux examinateurs de donner, avant même de procéder à la notation guidée par la grille, une note d'impression générale. Si cette note correspond à la note totale obtenue en décomposant la performance langagière, on pourra présumer que "l'intégrativité" a été préservée malgré le découpage de l'acte de communication.

Les résultats de l'analyse statistique se sont avérés globalement positifs et ont montré une bonne corrélation entre les sous-tests. Les épreuves mises à l'essai représentent une gradation des difficultés qui permet une discrimination adéquate. Cependant, le nombre des sujets ayant participé à l'expérimentation est insuffisant; le seul critère qui permette, pour l'instant, de juger véritablement de la valeur des tests est la satisfaction des utilisateurs, qui ont, depuis lors, commandé à l'Institut de langues vivantes deux tests parallèles à ceux décrits ci-dessus pour mesurer la compétence en anglais de leurs futurs employés non anglophones.

BIBLIOGRAPHIE

Carroll B. 1980. Testing Communicative Performance. Oxford: Pergamon Press.

Munby J. 1978. Communicative Syllabus Design. Cambridge: Cambridge University Press.

Richterich R., et J. Chancerel. 1978. Identifying the Needs of Adults Learning a Foreign Language. Strasbourg: Conseil de l'Europe.

16.
Ateliers sur divers aspects de l'évaluation de la performance linguistique des candidats inscrits aux programmes de formation linguistique de la Fonction publique canadienne / Workshops on aspects of second language performance evaluation for language training candidates in the Canadian Public Service.

1. Présentation
   Renée Proulx-Dubé

2. From needs to construct
   Gérard Frey and Angie Todesco

3. La mesure de la compétence en français langue seconde : une expérience de correction
   Anne-Marie Henrie et Gérard Monfils

4. The advanced language training program experience
   Huguette Laurencelle and William Cahill

5. FRANCOMER: le français au collège et en mer
   Lise Séguin-Duquette

1. Présentation
Renée Proulx-Dubé

Les tests de <u>performance</u> en langue seconde ne s'improvisent pas, même si, en apparence, ils ont l'air naturels et spontanés. De fait, lorsque cette situation se produit, c'est que tout le travail préliminaire a été bien fait. Au Service des tests, mesure et évaluation, nous avons été appelés à franchir chacune des étapes susceptibles de contribuer à l'élaboration d'un bon test de performance et il nous est apparu intéressant de faire état de nos travaux dans un atelier à composantes variables où nous procéderions d'abord à un exposé général de la situation avant de permettre aux participants de poursuivre dans l'une ou l'autre de quatre directions plus spécifiques couvertes par un nombre correspondant de présentations simultanées. Nous avons ainsi voulu expliquer les diverses étapes d'une enquête de besoins et les résultats qui sous-tendent l'élaboration de tout système d'évaluation conçu au Service de tests, mesure et évaluation de la Direction générale du programme de la formation linguistique de la Commission de la fonction publique canadienne ainsi que le construit qui se trouve à la base de chacun des systèmes.

La Direction générale de la formation linguistique étudie présentement ses programmes. Elle veut utiliser des approches communicatives/fonctionnelles qui permettent aux étudiants d'être davantage responsables de leur propre apprentissage. Notre mandat est de produire des systèmes d'évaluation qui tiennent compte des aspects pédagogiques et administratifs de l'apprentissage. Nous commençons chaque projet par une analyse de besoins qui est essentielle pour les raisons suivantes :

pour connaître les besoins de chaque groupe (étudiants, professeurs, élaborateurs, gestionnaires, etc.);

pour saisir les problèmes présents et futurs;

pour se familiariser avec les différents groupes qui utili-
seront le produit (système, instruments, etc.);

pour préparer les futurs utilisateurs aux changements
apportés et faciliter ainsi l'implantation des recommendations (système, etc.).

Pour réaliser ces enquêtes de besoins, nous procédons :

1) à l'étude du mandat de l'organisation, du milieu et du fonctionnement de la population étudiée;
2) à l'élaboration d'un plan d'action qui consiste à définir les
   objectifs du projet, l'échantillon et les instruments à
   utiliser;
3) à l'élaboration des questionnaires et des plans d'entrevues;
4) à la réalisation des entrevues individuelles ou de groupes;
5) à l'analyse des résultats des entrevues;
6) à la validation de ces résultats auprès des interviewés
   (cette étape est cruciale dans le processus);
7) à la préparation de la proposition du cadre du système
   d'évaluation basé sur les résultats de l'enquête de besoins;
8) à la validation du cadre auprès des utilisateurs;
9) à la présentation du cadre au comité de gestion concerné
   pour approbation officielle ou finale.

Même si une telle analyse de besoins implique beaucoup de
temps et d'argent, elle est essentielle. A première vue, les
objectifs d'évaluation des différents programmes d'enseignement
paraissent semblables (tests de progrès, tests diagnostiques et
besoins administratifs). Il faut tenir compte également du fait
que les programmes doivent être évalués à tous les niveaux
après l'implantation des systèmes d'évaluation. Jusqu'à maintenant, après avoir fait les analyses de besoins concernant les
instruments de mesure, les approches, les façons de les mettre
en pratique et les contraintes organisationnelles, nous avons
noté des différences majeures entre les besoins des programmes
d'enseignement. C'est ce que nous avons voulu expliquer dans
les quatre ateliers. Ceux-ci sont résumés dans les quatre
courts textes qui suivent cette présentation.
   L'objectif du premier atelier (Frey et Todesco) était
d'impliquer les participants dans l'élaboration d'un construit
pour un système d'évaluation pour l'anglais langue seconde. Le
programme d'anglais de la Direction générale de la formation
linguistique est actuellement à revoir le contenu des cours à la
lumière des nouvelles approches communicatives/fonctionnelles
afin de rapprocher les situations d'apprentissage et les situations du travail. Une analyse de besoins a été menée et validée
et les résultats ont été présentés au comité de direction. Les

présentateurs ont illustré, au moyen des résultats de leur analyse, comment ils ont élaboré le construit.

Le deuxième atelier (Henrie et Monfils) a permis aux participants d'évaluer la compétence linguistique des étudiants de français langue seconde à partir de critères de la compétence à communiquer tels que conçus et élaborés pour le Nouveau programme de formation linguistique (NPFL), qui est axé sur la communication. Suite à une enquête de besoins effectuée en vue d'élaborer un système d'évaluation qui permettrait de mesurer l'apprentissage de l'étudiant aux niveaux de compétence A (minimum), B (intermédiaire) ou C (avancé) du Nouveau programme de formation linguistique, le domaine de la communication orale a fait l'objet d'une attention particulière. Une grille ayant pour but de mesurer la performance à communiquer est déjà entre les mains des utilisateurs. Les critères d'évaluation de la communication orale sont les suivants : la transmission du message, la stratégie de communication, la compréhension, l'aspect sociolinguistique, l'aspect grammatical et le débit. Cette grille peut être utilisée avec différents contenus. Les animateurs ont présenté les critères d'évaluation et ont montré aux participants comment, au moyen d'enregistrements d'étudiants, on en fait l'application.

Dans le troisième atelier (Laurencelle et Cahill), les participants ont pu faire l'étude de divers outils d'observation proposés dans le système d'évaluation pour un programme où la formation linguistique, tant en français qu'en anglais, est différente des autres programmes : elle vise à rendre les participants capables de fonctionner à un haut niveau de bilinguisme. Pour ce faire, le programme est constitué, pour la première année, d'une phase scolaire suivie d'affectations dans le milieu de travail. La deuxième année sert de suivi. Les présentateurs ont donné les résultats de l'analyse de besoins, ont fait part de leur expérience et ont demandé aux participants leurs réactions face à différentes grilles qu'ils espèrent utiliser.

Le dernier atelier (Séguin-Duquette) avait comme but de permettre aux participants de travailler à l'établissement d'un plan pour des tests qui serviront à la certification des cadets de la Garde côtière. Francomer (Français au collège et en mer) est un programme de français langue seconde élaboré par la Direction des services linguistiques à la demande de Transport Canada. Ce programme offert aux élèves-officiers consiste en un cours d'un an situé entre deux tranches d'affectation sur les navires et au collège.

Les deux composantes principales du programme de formation portent sur la compréhension auditive et l'expression orale. Une enquête de besoins a permis d'élaborer un système d'évaluation qui consiste en des instruments d'auto-évaluation du progrès de l'étudiant ainsi que des tests qui mesureront le rendement et la performance des étudiants. Le genre et le contenu des instruments de mesure reflètent l'approche communicative-fonctionnelle du programme Francomer. L'atelier a permis aux participants de discuter de la planification de deux tests, de l'élaboration des items et de la détermination du critère maîtrise/non-maîtrise.

Les textes qui suivent ne se veulent rien d'autre qu'une réflexion un peu plus approfondie sur la complexité d'une démarche comme celle que nous avons entreprise. On ne devrait donc pas s'attendre à y trouver toutes les solutions mais plutôt des descriptions de situations, de conditions, d'instruments, voire même de formulaires qui ont constitué des outils valables dans notre contexte. Il appartiendra à l'élaborateur éventuel d'ajuster à sa propre situation ce dont il a besoin.

2. From needs to construct
Gérard Frey and Angie Todesco

In this workshop, participants were asked to engage in a construct-building exercise for tests being developed for francophone public servants learning English. The exercise was designed to illustrate the process employed by the test developers in arriving at a construct derived from the testing needs expressed by the respondents in an extensive needs analysis conducted among the potential users of the system of evaluation. In this needs study that covered three regions, Ottawa, Montreal and Quebec City, 282 persons were surveyed, including 41 administrators and program specialists, 40 teachers and 201 students. The major guidelines for the program and for the system of evaluation were provided by three major policy orientations: testing was to be communicative and job related, and was to take into consideration the increasing responsibility of students in managing their own training and evaluation.

In a process which paralleled that of the needs study, participants in the workshop were asked to list the language elements that they considered to be part of language proficiency as well as the criteria by which these elements were to be evaluated. As in the needs study, the workshop leaders organized the participants' answers into a construct that would account for the requirements of the potential users. In this way, the process of developing a construct based on an analysis of needs was demonstrated.

The workshop focused on the results of the needs analysis but in particular on the outcomes which were listed under the heading of Nature of Evaluation. With respect to content three major elements were identified in the study: communicative ability, language knowledge, and ability to perform specific tasks. The ability to communicate was considered by respondents to be most important, with language knowledge also given a prominent place in language training. The ability to perform specific tasks was also given considerable importance since language training was to be related to job performance. With respect to criteria the five mentioned in order of frequency were: comprehensibility, fluency, correctness, complexity, and appropriateness. These, then, were the components and the criteria that had to be reflected in our language testing construct.

Responses with respect to the desired content of the evaluation - communicative ability, language knowledge and ability to perform specific tasks - suggested a componential model of language to us, one which could account for grammatical competence and the ability to use language to fulfill certain functional or job related needs. This direction was further emphasized upon examination of such criteria as correctness, appropriateness, and fluency. One further outcome of the needs analysis was that the evaluation would have to be made at two levels. While respondents were obviously concerned that the various components of language proficiency be accounted for, it was necessary that a global level be added to account for such a criterion as comprehensibility. Thus our model also took this factor into consideration.

The construct that was finally developed was also influenced by the Canale and Swain model of communicative competence (as revised by Canale). This model also underlies another major system of evaluation in the Language Training Program Branch called the Nouveau Programme de Formation Linguistique. In the model designed for the English program, language proficiency is viewed as communicative competence which comprises the following four components:

grammatical competence
The knowledge and use of rules governing phonology, morphology, syntax and vocabulary;

sociolinguistic competence
The knowledge and use of rules governing forms or functions with respect to such contextual parameters as topic, role, status, attitude, situation, register;

discourse competence
Knowledge and use of rules or devices permitting the organization of a text with respect both to form and to meaning;

strategic competence
Awareness and use of coping mechanisms or strategies in communicative situations when performance variables threaten to impair communication.

At the global level, where all four components merge, we view communication as the ability to convey messages, intentions, feelings etc., either orally or in writing to others, and to comprehend messages, intentions, feelings etc., conveyed either orally or in writing.

Both at the global and at the componential level a number of evaluation criteria related to the principal and essential characteristics of the components have been identified. These criteria had for the most part been selected by the needs analysis participants. At the global level comprehensibility and comprehension are the major criteria by which students are to be evaluated. Other possible criteria are effectiveness, ease and size of output. At the componential level, correctness and complexity were selected for the grammatical component, unity and fluency for the discourse component, appropriateness for the sociolinguistic component and flexibility, independence and resourcefulness for the strategic component. (See Appendix A for the model of the construct.)

While the focus of this workshop was to show the link between the process determining needs and the development of a construct, it should be recalled that the needs analysis served other purposes as well. Most importantly, the responses permitted us to design a framework for the evaluation system comprising the categories of evaluation purpose, responsibility and timing for all language training program components.

The link between the needs expressed by our needs-study respondents and the resulting model of communicative competence was, we feel, evidenced in the positive reactions of these respondents to the model during feedback sessions. They demonstrated their satisfaction that what we had proposed reflected what they had asked for, and this in a continous integrated and comprehensive system that corresponded to the new policy orientations and to the context and approach of the training program.

APPENDIX A Communicative Competence Construct

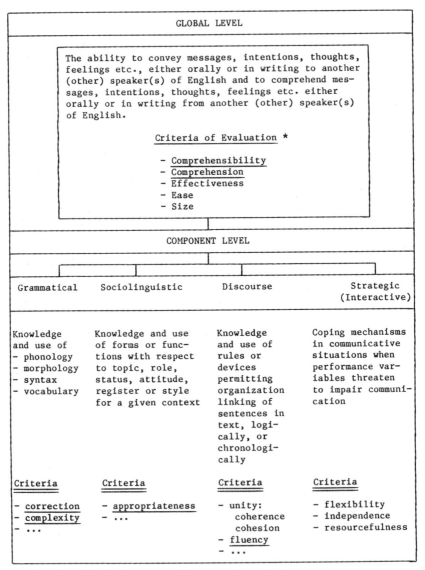

GLOBAL LEVEL

The ability to convey messages, intentions, thoughts, feelings etc., either orally or in writing to another (other) speaker(s) of English and to comprehend messages, intentions, thoughts, feelings etc. either orally or in writing from another (other) speaker(s) of English.

Criteria of Evaluation *

- Comprehensibility
- Comprehension
- Effectiveness
- Ease
- Size

COMPONENT LEVEL

Grammatical	Sociolinguistic	Discourse	Strategic (Interactive)
Knowledge and use of - phonology - morphology - syntax - vocabulary	Knowledge and use of forms or functions with respect to topic, role, status, attitude, register or style for a given context	Knowledge and use of rules or devices permitting organization linking of sentences in text, logically, or chronologically	Coping mechanisms in communicative situations when performance variables threaten to impair communication

Criteria
 	
- correction
- complexity
- ...
	Criteria
	
	- appropriateness
	- ...
		Criteria
		
		- unity:
		  coherence
		  cohesion
		- fluency
		- ...
			Criteria
			
			- flexibility
			- independence
			- resourcefulness

* Underlined Criteria derived from needs analysis

3. La mesure de la compétence en français langue seconde : une expérience de correction
Anne-Marie Henrie et Gérard Monfils

CONTEXTE D'ÉLABORATION DES TESTS DE PERFORMANCE EN COMMUNICATION ORALE

Le test de performance en communication orale fait partie du système d'évaluation élaboré pour le Nouveau programme de formation linguistique qui est axé sur la communication.

Le système a été élaboré suite à une analyse de besoins auprès des utilisateurs : professeurs, étudiants, élaborateurs, consultants et gestionnaires. Cette analyse a orienté nos décisions quant aux outils considérés nécessaires, leur genre et leur utilisation. De là les aspects retenus : l'auto-évaluation, l'évaluation de l'étudiant par le professeur, l'évaluation des connaissances linguistiques et l'évaluation de la communication orale et écrite, ainsi qu'une gamme d'outils complémentaires.

PRÉSENTATION D'UN TEST DE COMMUNICATION ORALE

La mesure de la compétence à communiquer oralement est effectuée à l'aide de tests de performance.

Ces tests de performance exigent que les apprenants accomplissent une tâche langagière à l'intérieur de mises en situation à partir d'un thème basé sur des fonctions et des sous-fonctions langagières. Les apprenants doivent montrer jusqu'à quel point ils peuvent se débrouiller dans des situations de communication authentiques.

CONTEXTE D'ADMINISTRATION

. L'entrevue orale, d'une durée maximale de quinze minutes, s'effectue individuellement, en interaction avec un natif de la langue et de façon spontanée.

. L'entrevue est enregistrée au magnétophone pour une correction ultérieure.

. L'examinateur doit être la personne qui corrigera l'entrevue puisque l'interprétation des critères de correction dépend largement des connotations contextuelles de l'entrevue d'évaluation.

. L'examinateur doit ignorer la progression grammaticale, le contenu et le vocabulaire cumulatif des leçons que l'apprenant a vues afin de se rapprocher le plus possible de la réalité d'une communication authentique.

. L'examinateur doit éviter de reformuler et doit demander à l'étudiant de préciser sa pensée, de reformuler, d'expliquer ou d'illustrer ce qu'il veut dire de façon à faciliter la mesure de la transmission du message. L'examinateur doit expliquer à l'apprenant que ce dernier :

   . aura à jouer différents rôles dans des situations variées;
   . aura à converser avec différents personnages dont l'examinateur assumera le rôle;
   . aura un scénario global pour chaque situation;
   . peut apporter des modifications aux scénarios proposés afin de rendre la communication plus authentique à condition de respecter les fonctions, les sous-fonctions et le thème;
   . doit déterminer ou préciser avec l'examinateur les paramètres de chaque situation ou activité d'évaluation pour éviter toute ambiguïté lors de l'activité;
   . aura le temps de réfléchir avant d'entreprendre chacune des activités d'évaluation;
   . choisira à chacun des tests deux activités de communication parmi les cinq activités proposées dans son livret de test.

TABLEAU 1 Une des activités proposées à l'étudiant

SUMMARY You are home making a telephone call.			RESUME Vous êtes chez vous et faites un appel téléphonique.		
You dial a bookstore, music store, or any other shop to order a book, a record or...			Vous appelez chez une librairie un disquaire ou autre pour commander, soit un livre, soit un disque...		
FONCTION	SOUS-FONCTION	THEME	CANAL	AGENTS	SITUATION
obtenir action	commander	commande	au téléphone	statut: client/ commis atti- tude polie	à la maison

PRÉSENTATION DU BARÈME ET DES CRITÈRES DE CORRECTION

Les fondements théoriques qui sous-tendent notre conception de la compétence de communication, inspirés du modèle théorique de Canale et Swain, comprennent quatre sous-compétences : la compétence stratégique, la compétence socio-linguistique, la compétence grammaticale et la compétence discursive. Nous mesurons ces diverses compétences à l'aide de six critères observables : la transmission du message, l'aspect stratégique, la compréhension, l'aspect sociolinguistique, l'aspect grammatical et le débit.

Ces critères d'évaluation sont cotés sur une échelle quali-tative allant de un à cinq. Les cotes additionnées donnent une note globale en pourcentage pour chaque activité d'évaluation. Le résultat de l'étudiant peut être comparé aux résultats de l'ensemble des apprenants qui ont subi le test à l'aide de la moyenne cumulative.

En plus de la notation sur une échelle qualitative, l'exami-nateur doit faire des remarques diagnostiques se rapportant à chacun des critères d'évaluation. Ces remarques diagnostiques permettent d'illustrer les forces de l'apprenant de façon à identifier les besoins d'apprentissage qui en découlent.

La production de l'apprenant est jugée selon son degré d'exactitude ou sa conformité à un critère de performance qui est, dans ce cas-ci, la production d'un locuteur natif à la langue cible dans la tâche langagière et selon l'activité choisie.

Les critères sont cotés sur une échelle qualitative où les mots clés sont : toujours, la plupart du temps, souvent, quelquefois, rarement.

toujours :
dans la totalité du temps considéré; complet, pas le moindre écart, sans exception; constance et persistance dans la qualité;
- une seule erreur et ce n'est plus considéré comme étant toujours correct;
- le contraire de "jamais";

la plupart du temps :
presque toujours, à quelques exceptions près; correct le plus souvent, dans la plupart des cas; la plupart du temps, le plus grand nombre de fois;
- le contraire de "rarement";

souvent :
d'ordinaire, généralement, dans l'ensemble; plusieurs fois, à plusieurs reprises, en de nombreux cas; fréquemment dans un laps de temps limité;
- le contraire de "quelquefois";

quelquefois :
parfois; plus souvent mal que bien;
- s'oppose à "souvent";

rarement :
exceptionnellement; très peu;
- s'oppose à "la plupart du temps";

jamais :
s'oppose à "toujours"; cette cote est exclue du barème car on estime que tout individu qui a fait plus de cent heures d'apprentissage devrait avoir fait quelque progrès...

Les critères de correction

Transmission du message
Définition : la transmission du message se réfère à l'intelligibilité du message, des idées, que l'apprenant essaie de transmettre à son interlocuteur.

Barème de correction :
5 points : L'étudiant transmet <u>toujours</u> un message compréhensible du premier coup.
4 points : L'étudiant transmet, <u>la plupart du temps</u>, un message
compréhensible du premier coup.
3 points : L'étudiant transmet <u>souvent</u> un message compréhensible du premier coup.
2 points : L'étudiant transmet <u>quelquefois</u> un message compréhensible du premier coup.
1 point : L'étudiant transmet <u>rarement</u> un message compréhensible du premier coup.

Stratégie de communication

Définition : La compétence stratégique se réfère à l'habilité de
l'apprenant à utiliser des moyens verbaux et non
verbaux compensatoires pour exprimer sa pensée.
C'est la capacité d'utiliser des stratégies pour faire
face aux "faux départs", pour contourner les
formes grammaticales qu'il ne peut encore maîtriser
ou pour s'adresser à un interlocuteur dont l'apprenant ne connaît pas le statut. C'est l'utilisation de
moyens pour éviter les bris de communication dus à
un manque de compétence grammaticale ou de
compétence sociolinguistique.

Barème de correction :
5 points : L'étudiant utilise <u>toujours</u> de bonnes stratégies de
communication.
4 points : L'étudiant utilise <u>la plupart du temps</u> de bonnes
stratégies de communication.
3 points : L'étudiant utilise <u>souvent</u> de bonnes stratégies de
communication.
2 points : L'étudiant utilise <u>quelquefois</u> de bonnes stratégies de
commnication.
1 point : L'étudiant utilise <u>rarement</u> de bonnes stratégies de
communcation.

L'examinateur doit commenter les stratégies de communication de l'apprenant de façon à lui faire développer les bonnes
et à lui faire abandonner les moins bonnes.

Les bonnes stratégies de communication sont celles utilisées
par l'individu qui "réussit", qui communique en langue
seconde. Ayant développé une sensibilité à l'autre langue qui le
rend apte à deviner juste, voulant communiquer à tout prix
quelle que soit la situation, recherchant les occasions de ré-
utiliser ses acquis, il se sent à l'aise dans l'incertitude et essaie
volontiers ses intuitions, en utilisant tous les indices que le

contexte peut lui fournir. Pour faire passer son message,
l'apprenant dispose de plusieurs techniques telles que la péri-
phrase, la circonlocution, la description, le mime, la définition,
le mot équivalent, le synonyme, l'antonyme, le néologisme,
l'analogie, la redondance, la répétition, la reformulation, l'allé-
gorie, la demande d'aide du genre "comment dit-on telle
chose?"...
Par contre, l'utilisation de trop de moyens compensatoires peut
finir par masquer le message ou nuire à la communication, voire
même par impatienter l'interlocuteur. Parmi les stratégies à
éviter par l'apprenant, on trouve l'utilisation abusive de toutes
les techniques énumérées plus haut. Il en est ainsi des
réponses évasives, des digressions vers des sujets plus connus,
des répétitions fréquentes pour gagner du temps ainsi que du
"remplissage" par des mots ou des expressions inutiles au
message, mais qui donnent à l'apprenant l'illusion de
converser.

Compréhension

Définition : Dans la compréhension, on vérifie la capacité de
l'apprenant à comprendre son ou ses interlocuteurs; c'est la rapidité avec laquelle l'apprenant
saisit d'emblée et de façon non équivoque ce que
son interlocuteur essaie de lui dire.

Barème de correction :

5 points : L'étudiant comprend <u>toujours</u> l'interlocuteur du
premier coup.

4 points : L'étudiant comprent <u>la plupart du temps</u> l'interlocuteur du premier coup.

3 points : L'étudiant comprend <u>souvent</u> l'interlocuteur du
premier coup.

2 points : L'étudiant comprend <u>quelquefois</u> l'interlocuteur du
premier coup.

1 point : L'étudiant comprend <u>rarement</u> l'interlocuteur du
premier coup.

L'examinateur veut savoir si l'apprenant peut comprendre un
locuteur natif de la langue cible dans les situations normales de
communication, dans un contexte le plus réel et le moins
scolaire possible, avec des bruits et des distractions, des hési-
tations et des reprises dues à la spontanéité de l'échange. Un
contexte hors de la salle de classe implique que le locuteur ne
connaît pas la progression grammaticale des leçons, qu'il ignore
à quelle leçon l'apprenant est rendu et qu'il utilise donc indis-
tinctement tous les éléments de la langue sans se soucier de la
complexité grammaticale de ce qu'il utilise.

Aspect sociolinguistique

Définition : L'aspect sociolinguistique recouvre l'utilisation appropriée du discours selon les facteurs contextuels tels que le sujet discuté, le statut des interlocuteurs, le rôle des participants, la situation dans l'espace et dans le temps, les normes d'interaction, le ton, l'attitude, le style, les niveaux et les registres de langue, le canal utilisé, l'intention des locuteurs (fonctions et sous-fonctions) et le genre (sérieux, humoristique). C'est ce qu'on appelle le respect des paramètres de la situation langagière.

Barème de correction :

5 points : L'étudiant tient toujours compte des paramètres de la situation langagière.

4 points : L'étudiant tient la plupart du temps compte des paramètres de la situation langagière.

3 points : L'étudiant tient souvent compte des paramètres de la situation langagière.

2 points : L'étudiant tient quelquefois compte des paramètres de la situation langagière.

1 point : L'étudiant tient rarement compte des paramètres de la situation langagière.

La langue est toujours utilisée en situation, dans un contexte donné, de sorte que personne ne parle de la même façon constamment. Les variations de styles, de dialectes, de registres ou de niveaux de langue d'un même individu sont fonction des circonstances, comportent des connotations sociales et culturelles différentes et provoquent des effets particuliers chez les interlocuteurs.

Bien que les variations sociolinguistiques soient régies par des règles d'usage tacites communes aux usagers de la langue d'une communauté donnée, il n'existe pas de taxonomie de ces variétés d'une langue donnée, si bien qu'on ne peut pas donner de règles de correction bien précises. Sous cet aspect, la compétence à communiquer devient l'habilité d'un individu à choisir, parmi la totalité des expressions qui s'offrent à lui, celle qui reflète de la façon la plus appropriée les normes sociales régissant le comportement dans un échange verbal spécifique. Ainsi, à l'intérieur d'un répertoire langagier, le locuteur fera un choix en vue d'exprimer le respect, la réciprocité, la camaraderie, l'intimité, la joie, l'impatience, la courtoisie...

Aspect grammatical

Définition : La compétence grammaticale recouvre tous les aspects que l'on retrouve habituellement sous "grammaire". Sous l'aspect grammatical, on vérifie si l'apprenant s'exprime correctement aux points de vue lexical, morphologique, syntaxique et phonologique.

Barème de correction :
5 points : L'étudiant s'exprime toujours correctement.
4 points : L'étudiant s'exprime correctement la plupart du temps.
3 points : L'étudiant s'exprime souvent correctement.
2 points : L'étudiant s'exprime quelquefois correctement.
1 point : L'étudiant s'exprime rarement correctement.

Débit

Définition : Par débit, on entend la facilité de l'apprenant à s'exprimer couramment, avec une certaine aisance, avec fluidité.

Barème de correction:
5 points : L'étudiant s'exprime toujours couramment.
4 points : L'étudiant s'exprime couramment la plupart du temps.
3 points : L'étudiant s'exprime souvent couramment.
2 points : L'étudiant s'exprime quelquefois couramment.
1 point : L'étudiant s'exprime rarement couramment.

Bien que le débit se mesure habituellement en termes de quantité ou de volume par unité de temps, il est mesuré ici de façon globale en termes de facilité d'élocution, de manière d'énoncer. En effet, on évite de comptabiliser les idées, les mots ou les groupes de souffle par unité de temps pour s'en tenir plutôt à ce qui paraît être un débit normal pour un locuteur natif de la langue cible. Ainsi, on évite le piège qui consiste à dire que tel apprenant est lent en français parce qu'il est lent dans sa propre langue.

L'examinateur doit plutôt se demander si le débit de l'apprenant est acceptable en français en termes de seuil de tolérance. S'agit-il d'une élocution laborieuse et limitée? Ce manque de facilité d'expression, de fluidité du discours est à ne pas confondre avec les pauses normales de la conversation alors que le locuteur cherche ses idées.

4. The advanced language training program experience
Huguette Laurencelle and William Cahill

The purpose of this workshop was to examine a model of a linguistic evaluation system designed for a cooperative school-work location program, that is, the model for the Advanced Language Training Program (ALTP). The background of the program was given, and particular emphasis was placed on the differences between this program and other Language Training Program Branch (LTPB) programs. In addition to looking at the model, the participants were asked to examine various evaluation tools and observation grids either proposed for or already used in the ALTP evaluation system.

INTRODUCTION AND BACKGROUND

The advanced Language Training Program represents an effort to divide the responsibility for all aspects of language skill development and maintenance among the individual participants, the LTPB and the participant's department. Until the advent of the Advanced Language Training Program, the only pattern available in LTPB was one within which the department was responsible for language needs identification; LTPB, for training; and Official Languages Division - Staffing Branch (OLD-SB), for certification. ALTP has attempted to reach this shared responsibility pattern by moving the whole of the language training undertaking outside the staffing process of the Public Service. This is the first and major difference between ALTP and the other LTPB programs.

Within ALTP, very capable and highly motivated candidates are sponsored by their own departments to undertake a program consisting of classroom development and on-the-job immersion in the second language. For the first time in its almost twenty-year history, LTPB has embarked on a training program where the lines of responsibility between training institute and job supervisory personnel are formally drawn.

The first candidates for this cooperative school-work location program were accepted in January, 1982.

The Tests Measurement and Evaluation Service (TMES) was given the mandate to produce a linguistic evaluation system for ALTP in February 1982. Between that date and August/September 1982, we developed the following system.

THE SYSTEM

The system we provided consists of different data bases in order that the three-way division of responsibility among the individual, the department and LTPB might be carried out. The first and most important data is gathered from observation grids designed for three purposes: candidate self-observation or self assessment, teaching personnel observations, and department supervisors' observations. The second data collection mechanisms are proficiency/achievement tests imposed and/or chosen by participants, their teachers/tutors and the administration, and finally there are committee reviews of candidate performance at set points throughout the program.

The primary purpose of this workshop was to examine a variety of observation grids which are used within the ALTP Linguistic Evaluation System. Because of space restrictions, however, only one of those listed below can be fully displayed here (see Appendix).

1) Grille d'auto-évaluation du participant au programme supérieur de formation linguistique en phase académique

Participant self-assessment grid for use during academic phase.

2) Grille d'auto-évaluation à l'usage du participant en phase d'affectation (Voir Appendice)

Participant self-assessment grid while on assignment (See Appendix)

3) Synthèse de l'évaluation de la performance du participant au PSFL par le personnel enseignant

Synthesis appraisal of the ALTP participant performance by the teaching personnel

4) Évaluation par le surveillant

Supervisor's evaluation

APPENDIX

Version provisoire
Preliminary version

GRILLE D'AUTO-ÉVALUATION
À L'USAGE DU PARTICIPANT
EN PHASE D'AFFECTATION

PARTICIPANT
SELF-ASSESSMENT
GRID WHILE ON
ASSIGNMENT

Nom du participant
Participant's name _____

Ministère/Department _____

Surveillant/Supervisor _____

Phase du programme PSFL
ALTP program component

N.B.: cocher les cases appropriées
N.B.: check required boxes

Affectation protégée
Protected assignment ☐

Affectation non protégée
Unprotected assignment ☐

Suivi
Follow-up ☐

Indiquez le temps consacré
par le participant à tra-
vailler dans la langue
cible.

Indicate the
amount of time
the participant
spent working
in the target
language

1 à/to 50% _____
51 à/to 75% _____
76 à/to 100% _____

A. Dressez la liste des tâches que vous avez eu à accomplir depuis le début de l'affectation et qui ont exigé l'utilisation de la langue cible. Puis indiquez sur l'échelle de 1 à 5 points – où 1 = performance pauvre et 5 = performance excellente (sans bavure, sans hésitation, avec complète maîtrise des éléments...) – votre appréciation de la réalisation de chacune de ces tâches. Dans la troisième colonne, indiquez avec un crochet (✓) les éléments que vous voulez approfondir davantage.

Establish the list of tasks you have accomplished since the beginning of the assignment and which required the use of the target language. Indicate on the scale of 1 to 5 where 1 = poor performance and 5 = excellent performance (without gross mistakes, without hesitation, with complete mastery of the elements...) your appreciation of your performance for each one of these tasks. In the third column indicate with a check-mark (✓) those tasks you intend to give further attention.

Tâches Tasks	Évaluation Evaluation – 1 2 3 4 5 +	Besoin d'apprentissage Need for emphasis (✓)
a)		
b)		
c)		

B. Dans cette section, évaluez   Evaluate in this section your
    globalement votre performance   performance for each of the
    pour chacun des savoirs.   skills from a global point
    Consultez l'explication de   view. Use the scale
    l'échelle donnée en A.   described in section A.

            Évaluation globale par savoir
            Overall evaluation by skill

            Lire/Reading   1 2 3 4 5

            Écrire/Writing   1 2 3 4 5

            Comprendre/Listening   1 2 3 4 5

            Parler/Speaking   1 2 3 4 5

C. Appréciez l'effort que vous   Check the effort you have
    avez mis dans la poursuite de   put in the attainment of
    vos objectifs au travail.   your objectives in the work
                                         situation.

    Très peu d'effort   Effort exceptionnel
    Very little effort   1 2 3 4 5   Exceptional effort

D. Évaluez votre progrès sous   Evaluate your progress from
    les deux aspects de   the two aspects, those of
    l'apprentissage linguistique   linguistic training and of
    et de l'acquisition de   self-learning techniques.
    techniques
    d'auto-apprentissage.

    Progrès linguistique
    Linguistic progress

    Très peu de progrès   Progrès exceptionnel
    Very little progress   1 2 3 4 5   Exceptional progress

    Techniques d'auto-apprentissage
    Self-Learning techniques

    Très peu de progrès   Progrès exceptionnel
    Very little progress   1 2 3 4 5   Exceptional progress

E. Commentaires/Comments

5. FRANCOMER: le français au collège et en mer
Lise Séguin-Duquette

Le cours Francomer a été élaboré à la demande de Transport Canada, dans le cadre de ses plans ministériels touchant les langues officielles. Il vise l'enseignement du français langue seconde à des anglophones possédant une base de connaissance du français telle qu'acquise durant un an du programme d'études secondaires. C'est un cours modulaire, c'est-à-dire composé de modules autonomes, lesquels ont été élaborés suite à une étude systématique du milieu et des besoins de la population à laquelle il s'adresse, c'est-à-dire les élèves-officiers du Collège de la Garde côtière à Sydney, en Nouvelle-Ecosse.

En même temps que l'entente sur l'élaboration du cours, on a signé une entente sur l'élaboration du système d'évaluation intégré au cours. Ce système d'évaluation comporte un test de rendement par module ainsi que des tests "d'étape" dont le but est de vérifier les acquisitions portant sur des ensembles de modules.

Le système d'évaluation, tout comme le cours, adopte une approche communicative-fonctionnelle dans la vérification d'objectifs spécifiques tels qu'apparaissant dans chacun des modules. Dans Francomer, on parle plutôt d'opérations que d'objectifs, les objectifs étant considérés comme des sous-catégories des opérations. Les opérations deviennent donc le centre de l'enseignement et la capacité d'effectuer une opération, le couronnement de cet enseignement. Les opérations, il va de soi, constituent le foyer à partir duquel sont élaborés les tests.

Le système d'évaluation Francomer est "fait sur mesure" pour la population cible et en fonction du contenu et de l'approche du cours. Il en découle presque naturellement que les jugements évaluatifs sont de nature critériée plutôt que normative.

C'est en effet la technique propre aux tests critériés qui a guidé l'élaboration des tests, en passant par l'identification des domaines de performance jusqu'aux barèmes de correction appropriés.

À titre d'exemple, le module 1, intitulé "Le Collège" (voir l'appendice A), vise à habiliter l'élève-officier à accueillir adéquatement tout visiteur qui se présente au Collège. Il est fréquent, en effet, qu'un visiteur ait besoin d'aide pour trouver un endroit ou une personne. Cette fonction est ressortie comme étant très importante, lors de l'enquête de besoins et les sous-fonctions se sont révélées comme suit :

1. Orienter un visiteur qui veut téléphoner
2. Orienter un visiteur qui cherche un endroit
3. Renvoyer un visiteur à qui de droit
4. Donner des renseignements à un visiteur qui cherche quelqu'un.

Le module apprend donc à comprendre diverses demandes sur différents thèmes avec intonation, prononciation, lexique et niveau de langue propres à divers échantillons de personnes. L'élève-officier apprend également à répondre efficacement à cette variété de demandes en donnant des indications, en renvoyant à la personne compétente ou en offrant d'accompagner le visiteur et ce dans une langue correcte, familière ou soutenue en fonction des interlocuteurs.

Le test, pour sa part, évalue la performance des étudiants en rapport avec les exigences de départ et les savoirs enseignés. C'est ainsi que dans un premier temps sera évaluée la capacité de reconnaître la nature d'une série de demandes. Par exemple, l'étudiant entend : "Excusez-moi, je cherche la cantine, pouvez-vous me dire où ça se trouve?"

Sur sa feuille de réponses, l'étudiant doit signifier qu'il a compris la demande en indiquant s'il s'agit d'une personne, d'un endroit, du téléphone ou de l'heure :

	Place	Person	Phone	Time
1.				
2.				

L'usage de l'anglais est possible dans le contexte du Collège de la Garde côtière : il est même souhaitable si l'on veut obtenir sans détour des mesures unidimensionnelles, c'est-à-dire libres de contamination relevant d'autres savoirs.

La performance active de l'étudiant est ensuite vérifiée à l'aide d'une simulation (au laboratoire de langues) dans laquelle on situe l'élève-officier à un endroit précis du Collège (point de départ), puis on le soumet à diverses demandes de directions.

Les réponses sont alors prévisibles et habilitent le correcteur à déterminer si l'étudiant est capable d'orienter ou non un visiteur qui a besoin d'aide.

Les directives données à l'étudiant précisent entre autres : "You are posted at the bell in the parade square..."

Viennent ensuite les demandes de renseignement : "Pourrais-tu me dire où se trouve le bureau du gardien?"

Une réponse type jugée acceptable pourrait se formuler comme suit :

> "Le gardien...c'est facile. Prenez la porte là, devant vous, tournez à droite et marchez jusqu'à l'entrée principale. C'est là."

Il est entendu que le gestuel (là, devant vous) peut faire partie intégrante de la réponse verbale parce que le correcteur étant familier avec le milieu physique est en mesure d'en juger la pertinence.

En ce qui touche le barème de correction de l'expression, plusieurs essais nous ont amenés à la considération de trois critères principaux : le message, la qualité et la prononciation. Francomer est une approche communicative-fonctionnelle; c'est donc le message qui prime sur tout autre critère. Concrètement, c'est l'aspect "message" qui est d'abord évalué et qui influence l'évaluation au niveau des deux autres critères, un message étant défini comme une réponse logique par rapport à la question ou à la situation.

Ainsi, si l'élève bredouille une réponse incompréhensible ou donne une réponse illogique par rapport au stimulus, on juge qu'il n'y a pas de message; il devient donc impossible d'en juger la qualité tant grammaticale que lexicale ou d'énonciation.

Les critères "message" et "qualité" sont évalués sur une échelle de 4 points (3-2-1-0) et appliqués à chacun des items, alors que le critère "prononciation" est évalué sur une échelle de 3 points (2-1-0-) et appliqué à la fin de chaque sous-test seulement.

Conscients que la qualité d'un message peut être influencée par la longueur de celui-ci (plus un élève parle, plus il risque de commettre des erreurs), nous analysons chaque type d'item pour déterminer s'il donne lieu à une réponse simple et directe ou à une réponse planifiée comportant plusieurs éléments.

La correction est alors adaptée à ces deux possibilités distinctes et le critère "qualité" est appliqué en fonction de R.C. (réponses courtes) ou R.L. (réponses longues), ces dernières bénéficiant d'un niveau plus généreux de tolérance aux erreurs.

Les items de chacun des tests seront soumis à une analyse selon le modèle de Rasch (Wright and Masters 1982) à l'aide des résultats obtenus par les étudiants. Nous aurons ainsi une meilleure idée de la précision des mesures et de la compétence véritable des étudiants.

Le but ultime de ces analyses est de permettre au professeur d'effectuer un diagnostic des faiblesses des étudiants et de procéder à un enseignement correctif. Ce but est commun à tous les tests de modules.

Toutefois, avec les données issues des analyses statistiques et avec le jugement des experts-professeurs, il nous sera possible de fixer un seuil de réussite/échec à utiliser en fonction des besoins administratifs.

On présume que ce jugement sera porté lors des tests touchant des ensembles de modules, ceux-ci étant statutairement administrés aux examens de synthèse de Noël et de fin d'année.

Le programme Francomer (modules et tests) est dans sa première année d'implantation; les données recueillies à ce jour laissent apparaître certains besoins d'ajustement. Cela nous semble normal dans la mesure où les modèles d'enseignement et de tests "sur mesure" ne nous ont pas précédés en nombre suffisant pour nous paver un chemin sans embûche. Il reste que Francomer représente à beaucoup d'égards une première dans le domaine de l'enseignement des langues secondes.

BIBLIOGRAPHIE

Cahill, W., and G. Frey. 1982. Linguistic program evaluation in the Testing, Measurement and Evaluation Service: an overview. MEDIUM. 7.2.

Canale, M. 1981. From communicative competence to communicative language pedagogy. In Richards, J., and R. Schmidt (eds.), Language and Communication. New York: Longmans.

Canale, M., and M. Swain. 1980. Theoretical bases of communicative approaches to second language teaching and testing. Applied Linguistics 1.1.

Carroll, B. 1980. Testing Communicative Performance. Oxford: Pergamon Press.

Courchêne, R., and J. de Bagheera. 1981. Testing communicative competence: problems and perspectives. MEDIUM 6.4.

Grenier-Henrie, A-M., G. Monfils, et H. Robineau-Laurencelle. 1980. La mesure de la compétence de communication à la direction générale de la formation linguistique : Les tests de performance en communication orale. MEDIUM 7.2.

Mackay, R., and J. Palmer (eds.). 1981. Languages for Specific Purposes Rowley, Mass.: Newbury House.

Monfils, G. 1982. La mesure de la compétence de communication à la direction générale de la formation linguistique : fondements théoriques. MEDIUM 7.1.

Oller, J. 1979. Language Tests at School. London: Longman.

Oskarsson, M. 1978. Approaches to Self-Assessment. Oxford: Pergamon Press.

Palmer, A., P. Groot, and G. Trosper (eds.).1981. The Construct Validation of Tests of Communicative Competence. Washington, D.C.: TESOL

Popham, W. 1978. Criterion - Referenced Measurement. Englewood Cliffs, N.J.: Prentice-Hall.

Richterich, R., and J. Chancerel. 1977. Identifying the Needs of Adults Learning a Foreign Language. Oxford: Pergamon Press.

Séguin-Duquette, L. 1982. La théorie du trait latent. MEDIUM 7.2

Sheppard, L. 1978. Norm-referenced vs criterion-referenced tests. Educational Horizons 58.

Todesco, A. 1982. What's in a name: the problem of construct validation. MEDIUM 7.2.

von Elek, T. 1982. Tests of Swedish as a second language: an experiment in self-assessment. Work Papers from the Language Teaching Research Center. No. 31.

Wesche, M. 1981. Communicative testing in a second language. Canadian Modern Language Review. 37. 3.

Wright, B., and G. Masters. 1982. Rating Scale Analysis: Rasch Measurement. Chicago: MESA Press, University of Chicago.

APPENDIX A

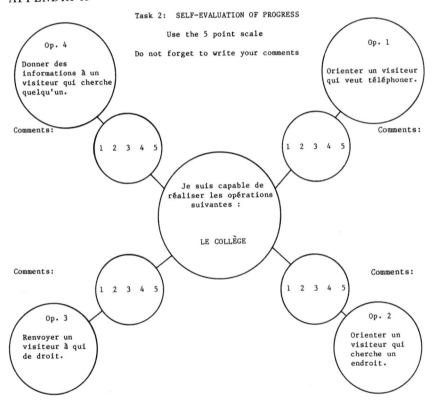

Task 2: SELF-EVALUATION OF PROGRESS

Use the 5 point scale

Do not forget to write your comments

Op. 4

Donner des informations à un visiteur qui cherche quelqu'un.

Op. 1

Orienter un visiteur qui veut téléphoner.

Comments:

1 2 3 4 5

1 2 3 4 5

Comments:

Je suis capable de réaliser les opérations suivantes :

LE COLLÈGE

Comments:

1 2 3 4 5

1 2 3 4 5

Comments:

Op. 3

Renvoyer un visiteur à qui de droit.

Op. 2

Orienter un visiteur qui cherche un endroit.

17. Le testing de performance en langue seconde : une perspective canadienne

Raymond LeBlanc
(avec la collaboration de Renée Proulx-Dubé, Mireille Voyer, Diane Pruneau, Pascal-André Charlebois et Marjorie B. Wesche)

Du fait de sa politique nationale de bilinguisme, le Canada présente une situation où l'évaluation de la performance langagière est particulièrement importante. En effet, dans un grand nombre de milieux divers, l'obtention ou la conservation d'un poste, les promotions, la certification, etc. peuvent être intimement liées à l'habileté à employer la langue en situation normale de communication. Face à la lourde responsabilité, à cause des ramifications sur le plan humain, d'évaluer l'habileté à communiquer, les spécialistes de ces milieux ont dû, après un constat d'échec des tests composés d'items portant sur des points discrets, se mettre à l'oeuvre pour tenter de produire des instruments répondant mieux à des besoins spécifiques.

Les éléments de solutions proposés ont été nombreux et diversifiés. La "perspective canadienne" dont il est question dans le titre de la présente contribution ne veut donc prétendre à aucune exhaustivité, la tâche étant beaucoup trop complexe. Ce que cette expression recouvre est une description des instruments et des modes d'évaluation de la performance en langue seconde utilisés par un ensemble d'organismes jugés représentatifs de la situation canadienne. Il sera ainsi question à tour de rôle d'un ministère fédéral (Commission de la fonction publique du Canada), de deux sociétés de la Couronne (Air Canada et Canadien National), d'un organisme provincial de promotion linguistique (Office de la langue française du Québec), d'une compagnie privée pan-canadienne (Canadien Pacifique) et d'une institution bilingue de haut savoir (Université d'Ottawa). Les renseignements qui suivent ont été surtout tirés des présentations faites par les différents représentants de ces organismes lors d'une table ronde dans le cadre du Symposium de l'Université d'Ottawa et de Carleton University sur le testing de performance en langue seconde, de même que des notes et des textes fournis par le présentateur et les présentatrices. Les noms de ces collaborateurs apparaissent à tour de rôle dans le texte lorsqu'il est question de leur organisme. On peut obtenir des renseignements supplémentaires en s'adressant directement à ces spécialistes, dont on trouvera les coordonnées en fin de volume. Toute erreur d'interprétation qui aurait pu se glisser dans les lignes qui suivent reste cependant la responsabilité du présent rédacteur.

COMMISSION DE LA FONCTION PUBLIQUE DU CANADA
(Renée PROULX-DUBÉ)

Le Gouvernement du Canada, par l'intermédiaire de la Commission de la fonction publique, offre, depuis 1964, des cours de langue à ses fonctionnaires. Ces cours ont pour but d'aider les employés des divers ministères à atteindre leurs objectifs en matière de langues officielles, en particulier de pouvoir répondre adéquatement à toutes demandes de services venant tant du public que des fonctionnaires fédéraux, dans la langue officielle de leur choix, le droit à ce service ayant été reconnu par la loi sur les langues officielles votée en 1969.

Les programmes d'enseignement des années 60 répondaient, selon les croyances de l'époque, à des besoins langagiers généraux tout en respectant le mieux possible quelques styles d'apprentissage. Vers le milieu des années 70, une nouvelle tendance est apparue : l'apprentissage linguistique devait de plus en plus être orienté sur les besoins de l'organisation, donc vers des besoins langagiers axés sur les tâches. En novembre 1974, le président du conseil du Trésor annonçait la mise en marche d'une étude indépendante sur les programmes de formation linguistique de la Fonction publique du Canada sous la direction de Gilles Bibeau. Suite à la portion de cette étude portant sur les facteurs pédagogiques (LeBlanc 1976), il était recommandé dans les conclusions du Rapport synthèse (Bibeau

1976) que soit adoptée une démarche de type andragogique qui comporterait trois phases essentielles, la phase d'enseignement formel, la phase d'auto-apprentissage et la phase d'activité de communication. En 1978, la direction générale de la Formation linguistique décidait de modifier ses programmes d'enseignement. Elle définissait les orientations majeures en précisant l'approche et la démarche qui allaient sous-tendre les nouveaux programmes de formation linguistique. Cette dernière devait désormais répondre à des besoins langagiers reliés aux exigences langagières des postes, s'inscrire dans une démarche andragogique et favoriser avant tout l'apprentissage de la langue comme moyen de communication. Le mandat du service de Tests, mesure et évaluation de la direction générale de la Formation linguistique, face à ce changement, fut de concevoir, d'élaborer, d'expérimenter et de mettre en place un système d'évaluation du rendement des étudiants inscrits dans les programmes de formation linguistique. Le système adopté est constitué de différents instruments obligatoires et complémentaires. Les instruments obligatoires sont l'auto-évaluation, les tests de rendement, l'évaluation par le professeur et les tests de performance. C'est sur ces derniers qu'il convient maintenant de s'arrêter plus en détail afin de mettre en lumière les problèmes rencontrés ainsi que certaines des solutions apportées.

Dans la préparation des tests de performance, il importait 1) de prendre en considération les nouvelles orientations en fonction d'une population adulte-fonctionnaire qui devait pouvoir travailler dans la langue seconde une fois de retour au travail; 2) de tenir compte des besoins langagiers de l'étudiant, du contenu et de l'approche du programme; 3) de penser à la fois à la mesure du code linguistique et à celle de la compétence de communication; 4) d'assister le professeur dans la planification de son enseignement en fonction des besoins langagiers de ses étudiants; 5) d'aider l'étudiant à déceler ses forces et ses faiblesses.

Au sujet des tests de performance orale adoptés, Proulx-Dubé déclarait :

> ... les apprenants ont une tâche langagière à accomplir comme, par exemple, annuler un rendez-vous, dans le cadre d'une mise en situation réaliste à partir d'un thème basé sur des fonctions et des sous-fonctions langagières. L'entrevue s'effectue de façon interactive et spontanée, de sorte que le contenu est imprévisible et varie d'un individu à l'autre selon le vécu de chacun.
>
> La correction se fait à un double niveau : celui de la transmission du message et celui des composantes de la communication orale. Ces composantes sont l'aspect stratégique, la compréhension, l'aspect socio-linguistique,

l'aspect grammatical et le débit. Ces aspects sont cotés sur une échelle de 1 à 5. Les cotes additionnées donnent une note globale pour chaque situation simulée. Le principal problème a été la création d'un barème de correction qui puisse s'appliquer à tous les niveaux d'apprentissage, indépendamment des contenus, et mesurer globalement et simultanément toutes ces composantes. Nous avons donc décidé d'affecter certains éléments d'un coefficient de pondération qui permet de tenir compte du niveau d'apprentissage de l'étudiant au moment où il subit le test. Par exemple, la transmission du message compte pour 50 % des points au tout début de l'apprentissage alors qu'au niveau le plus élevé, ce critère vaut 10 % des points. (1983)

Les composantes de la communication qui constituent la théorie de base sous-tendant cette conception de la performance de communication orale sont inspirées de Canale et Swain (1980) et cette conception se retrouve dans tous les tests de performance du service de Tests, mesure et évaluation, à tous les niveaux et dans tous les projets.

Suivons à nouveau Proulx-Dubé :

Nous croyons que la transmission du message est une composante très importante de la communication car elle représente l'aspect global de la communication. Cette transmission se réfère à l'intelligibilité du message, des idées que l'apprenant essaie de transmettre à son interlocuteur et elle est à la base de toute interaction significative.

En ce qui concerne la compréhension, le degré de compréhension que le locuteur a de son interlocuteur joue un rôle assez important pour qu'on en tienne compte. Nous avons inclus, par conséquent, l'aspect "compréhension" dans le barème de correction. Cette compréhension, qui se retrouve à l'oral, tient compte de ce que Widdowson (1978) appelle la "réciprocité" qui existe dans un échange verbal interactif. Il n'y a pas d'échange sans une certaine compréhension et, dans une conversation normale, toute ambiguïté est éclaircie par une rétroaction immédiate. Il y a simultanéité entre écouter et parler et ces activités sont évaluées dans le même test de performance.

L'aspect stratégique est l'habileté qu'a l'apprenant à utiliser des moyens verbaux et non verbaux pour s'exprimer. Il utilise des moyens compensatoires tels la description, la reformulation, la mime, la répétition, et ce, pour éviter les bris de communication.

Sous l'aspect <u>sociolinguistique</u> ("appropriateness"), on mesure l'utilisation appropriée du discours selon les facteurs contextuels tels le statut des interlocuteurs, le ton, l'attitude, les niveaux et registres de langue : c'est ce qu'on appelle le respect des paramètres de la situation langagière.

L'aspect <u>grammatical</u> recouvre tous les aspects que l'on retrouve sous le terme grammaire, à savoir le lexique, la morphologie, la syntaxe et la phonologie.

Le <u>débit</u> se définit comme la facilité de l'apprenant à s'exprimer couramment, avec une certaine aisance, avec fluidité. Il est mesuré, chez nous, de façon globale en termes de facilité d'élocution, de manière d'énoncer. On ne le mesure pas en termes de quantité ou de volume par unité de temps. (1983)

Pour ce qui est de la mesure de la performance de la communication par écrit, elle s'effectue à l'aide de mises en situation où l'étudiant est amené à rédiger une lettre, une note de service ou un compte rendu selon les objectifs du programme ou du module. La correction se fait à deux niveaux : celui de la transmission du message et celui des composantes de la communication écrite : l'aspect sociolinguistique, l'agencement du contenu, la forme de la phrase et la compréhensibilité. Ces aspects sont cotés sur une échelle de 1 à 5. Les cotes additionnées donnent une note globale pour chaque situation. Les éléments du barème de correction de la communication écrite ne sont pas affectés d'un coefficient de pondération. A l'écrit, la difficulté de la tâche est fonction du moment où l'étudiant en est dans son apprentissage et va, par exemple, de la transmission du message court à la note de service.

Quant aux tests de compréhension auditive, ils mesurent aussi la performance en ce sens qu'ils présentent des documents variés tant au point de vue des thèmes que des niveaux de langue. L'étudiant doit accomplir des tâches semblables à celles qu'il a à accomplir au bureau lorsqu'il est en situation d'écoute, par exemple prendre des notes sur ce qu'il a entendu. La correction varie selon la tâche à accomplir mais est toujours basée sur le fond (message) et non sur la forme.

Pour les tests de compréhension de l'écrit, c'est la technique "cloze" qui est utilisée à partir de la lecture d'un document de travail comme, par exemple, une lettre circulaire.

Comme on aura pu le constater, les tests de performance ont été élaborés en fonction d'une tâche ou d'un certain nombre de tâches à accomplir dans un milieu réel de communication et ceci, dans les quatre savoirs. Cette élaboration est cependant tout juste terminée et ce n'est qu'à la fin de l'année qui vient que les données recueillies permettront d'effectuer les analyses

statistiques et de faire les réajustements éventuels. En attendant, il y a tout lieu de croire que cette nouvelle approche
vers la mesure de la performance de la langue seconde devrait
produire la majorité des résultats escomptés vu qu'elle tient
compte d'un nombre représentatif des composantes de la
communication.

AIR CANADA et CANADIEN NATIONAL (Mireille VOYER)

Au moment où ces lignes sont écrites, les programmes
d'évaluation linguistique d'Air Canada et du Canadien National
ont été séparés, ce qui n'était pas encore le cas plus tôt dans
l'année; c'est pourquoi ils sont ici présentés ensemble, placés
qu'ils étaient sous la même direction. Air Canada est une soci-
été de la Couronne dont la principale activité est le transport
aérien. Le Canadien National jouit du même statut, mais cette
fois au niveau du transport terrestre.

La variété des occupations possibles dans des compagnies
de transport peut être surprenante. Pour en mentionner
quelques-unes : mécanicien, préposé au stationnement, ven-
deur de billets, agent de bord, mécanicien de locomotive,
secrétaire, barman, équipage de traversiers, sans oublier les
cadres intermédiaires et supérieurs, les ingénieurs, les infor-
maticiens, etc.

Or, comme le note Voyer :

Par suite de l'obligation, pour certaines catégories
d'employés, de fournir au public voyageur des services
dans les deux langues officielles, on a dû créer pour eux
des cours maison axés sur des situations de communication
en contexte de travail. Ces cours avaient pour cadre les
trains, les gares, les avions, les soutes à bagages, les
aéroports, etc. Les situations langagières de ces occupations étant faciles à circonscrire, répétitives et assez
brèves, elles se prêtaient bien à l'enseignement de la
langue de spécialité. Très vite, nos formateurs et nos
conseillers pédagogiques devinrent très adroits et très
audacieux dans l'approximation de l'authenticité dans le jeu
de rôle et la simulation. Les cours se donnaient sur les
lieux mêmes du travail : gares, aérogares, etc. A Ottawa,
par exemple, la salle de classe se trouvait à un moment
donné dans une voiture désaffectée. Des instruments de
travail authentiques faisaient partie de l'équipement de la
salle de cours : billets, horaires, plateaux de service,
bouteilles, verres, cartes d'embarquements, formules, etc.
On n'hésitait pas à se rendre aux guichets ou dans les
voitures pour simuler des situations de travail. (1983)

Il n'est donc pas étonnant que les professeurs aient pu être mal à l'aise lorsqu'ils faisaient subir aux étudiants des épreuves de rendement élaborées sur le modèle des tests de rendement objectifs de la méthode Dialogue Canada, une méthode d'enseignement du français langue seconde, de type structuro-global, mise au point et utilisée par la Fonction publique du Canada. Les rapports de correction de tests arrivaient de Vancouver, Toronto, Winnipeg, Moncton, avec des mentions comme : "Ne rend pas justice au candidat.", "Le candidat communique mieux en conversation familière.", etc. Les conseillers pédagogiques durent donc se rendre à l'évidence : les tests, qui mesuraient la connaissance du code, défavorisaient grandement certains employés, en particulier les moins scolarisés.

C'est en visionnant, sur vidéo-cassettes, des enregistrements de scénarios improvisés par les étudiants dans leur cadre de travail et sur des situations de travail, ou bien en assistant en personne à des séances de fin de cours qu'on pouvait constater les progrès réels accomplis dans la capacité de communiquer dans les cadres restreints des fonctions de chacun. Mais la nécessité de gérer des dossiers de contrôle du progrès à l'intention des administrateurs sous formes quantifiables perpétuait l'utilisation des tests, si rassurants par leur prétention à l'objectivité et à la rigueur scientifique. Cependant, le malaise s'amplifiant, certains agents de bord et agents passagers contestaient le niveau d'habileté à utiliser la langue parlée qu'ils s'étaient vu reconnaître sur la foi des tests en vigueur. Il fallait donc, à tout le moins, trouver un deuxième instrument de mesure pour valider le premier jugement en cas de contestation officielle.

Le groupe des normes et des tests linguistiques de la Commission de la fonction publique du Canada accepta que le préposé au testing d'Air Canada/Canadien National participe à ses travaux d'élaboration de nouveaux instruments de mesure au niveau supérieur. Ce préposé put ainsi acquérir par la pratique les connaissances docimologiques nécessaires à une éventuelle adaptation du test de connaissance de la langue déjà existant aux besoins des clientèles. La validation de ce test fut ainsi faite et le tout fut mis sous clé pour ne servir que dans les cas où un grief syndical au sujet d'un niveau de connaissance de la langue serait porté jusque devant les tribunaux. On n'a jamais eu à s'en servir.

Lors de son séjour à Ottawa, le préposé s'était aussi intéressé à un test-entrevue auquel travaillaient ses hôtes pour mesurer l'expression orale. Ce test semblait être, à première vue, la réponse aux doutes entretenus au sujet des tests de type objectif (points discrets). Partant du schéma de l'équipe d'Ottawa, on élabora le test-entrevue utilisé maintenant de façon systématique. Depuis 1979, un test de ce type a été employé avec plusieurs centaines de candidats, à la fois comme instrument de mesure de la performance en compréhension et expression orales en français et aussi comme test de classement dans les programmes.

Comme le décrit Voyer :

Le test se compose de trois parties d'une durée de cinq minutes chacune : 1) l'intervieweur pose des questions au candidat sur son travail et sur sa formation dans la langue cible; 2) le candidat prend une carte au hasard sur laquelle il lit cinq opinions possibles sur des sujets d'intérêt général. Il en choisit une et fait part de son point de vue sur le sujet à l'intervieweur; 3) le candidat parle de ses loisirs.

L'épreuve comporte les caractéristiques suivantes : 1) en face à face (intervieweur/candidat); 2) enregistrée sur cassette; 3) durée totale de quinze minutes; 4) maximum de six entrevues par jour par intervieweur; 5) cinq à dix minutes de repos après chaque entrevue pour l'intervieweur; 6) administrateur reposé car il peut avoir une influence négative sur le résultat; 7) entrevue sur le ton d'une conversation courtoise : les interventions de l'intervieweur sont courtes.

Pour ce qui est de la correction, elle comporte les caractéristiques suivantes : 1) les intervieweurs sont formés aux techniques de l'entrevue; 2) le test est corrigé par un jury de deux personnes, autres que l'intervieweur, qui sont tirées d'une équipe permanente de cinq personnes, toujours les mêmes, qui corrigent toutes les cassettes acheminées de tous les coins du Canada; ces cinq personnes ont intériorisé par l'écoute fréquente, de façon globale, la qualité de l'expression des niveaux 1, 2, 3 et 4. De plus, elles ont l'occasion d'écouter des enregistrements modèles de spécimens authentiques de la performance de plusieurs candidats déjà jugés à chacun des niveaux; 3) ces spécimens ont été au préalable classés à l'un des quatre niveaux par un jury de dix personnes composé de quelques gestionnaires des deux compagnies, d'administrateurs de l'enseignement des langues, de conseillers pédagogiques et de professeurs de langue; 4) d'autre part, l'équipe de correcteurs sait que le niveau 3, par exemple, est le niveau exigé d'un agent de bord d'Air Canada pour pouvoir exécuter son travail pendant le vol. Elle sait également qu'on exigera un niveau 4 d'un cadre intermédiaire ou d'une secrétaire de direction. Elle sait aussi à quoi correspond chaque niveau dans le programme de cours de langue; 5) c'est donc par un jugement qualitatif et global, sans passer par l'analyse détaillée, qu'on accorde un niveau 1, 2, 3 ou 4. Les résultats sont le plus souvent très clairs et il y a rarement conflit. Seuls quelques cas frontières sont difficiles à trancher : quelle est en effet la ligne de démarcation entre un 3+ et un 4?; 6) les correcteurs accordent une attention particulière aux éléments suivants : a) compréhension par l'intervieweur des messages émis par l'interviewé et vice-versa; b) rapidité et fluidité du débit; c) correction du code. Dans les cas douteux, les deux membres du jury procèdent à une analyse plus détaillée et la cassette peut être recorrigée par un jury de deux autres personnes de l'équipe qui ignorent le premier jugement; 7) en cas de contestation par le candidat ou son supérieur, on fera réévaluer la cassette par deux nouveaux correcteurs. Il arrive, exceptionnellement, qu'un candidat soit jugé à un niveau plus élevé lors de cette deuxième correction. (Voyer 1983)

L'équipe d'intervieweurs et de correcteurs d'Air Canada et du Canadien National peut maintenant mettre à profit son expérience avec le test-entrevue pour concevoir, administrer et corriger selon le même principe de nombreux tests de rendement qui mesurent la performance des étudiants inscrits dans de nouveaux cours maison élaborés suivant une approche communicative fonctionnelle-notionnelle. Il s'agit, en fait, de courtes simulations sur des sujets tirés de la vie professionnelle.

Pour la responsable des programmes dont il vient d'être question, la conclusion est claire : après quatre années d'utilisation intensive du test-entrevue en français, on peut affirmer qu'il s'agit d'un instrument valable d'évaluation de la performance en langue seconde de sujets de toutes sortes : peu ou très scolarisés, issus de milieux géographiques et sociaux divers, connaissant plus ou moins la langue seconde, etc. La confiance au test et la crédibilité acquise aux yeux des administrateurs se fondent sur le fait qu'il y a eu très peu de contestation des jugements et qu'aucun cas n'est allé jusqu'à l'arbitrage. En outre, lorsque certains cadres qui connaissent le français demandent des renseignements sur le test, il est intéressant de les rendre juges des spécimens enregistrés pour pouvoir comparer leurs jugements à ceux de l'équipe. En pratique, les résultats concordent le plus souvent, ce qui montre bien que ces jugements sont le reflet de l'évaluation linguistique instinctive du milieu.

OFFICE DE LA LANGUE FRANÇAISE DU QUÉBEC
(Diane PRUNEAU)

L'Office de la langue française est un organisme gouvernemental québécois chargé par le Charte de la langue française de définir et de conduire la politique québécoise en matière de recherche linguistique et de terminologie et de veiller à faire le plus tôt possible du français la langue de communication du travail, du commerce et des affaires dans l'administration et les entreprises.

L'article 35 de la Charte de la langue française énonce que "les ordres professionnels ne peuvent délivrer de permis au Québec qu'à des personnes ayant de la langue officielle une connaissance appropriée à leur profession". Le règlement qui en découle stipule que la connaissance appropriée à l'exercice de la profession s'évalue selon un ensemble de cinq critères : compréhension du français oral, compréhension du français écrit, expression orale en français, expression écrite en français, connaissance et capacité d'utilisation de la terminologie française de la profession.

Sont exemptées de l'examen, entre autres, les personnes qui ont suivi trois années d'enseignement à temps plein en français à compter du secondaire, ce qui pourrait être interprété comme le niveau de performances souhaité pour l'admission à la pratique d'une profession au Québec. De fait, il n'en a jamais été ainsi, le niveau exigé à l'examen se situant plus bas que ce à quoi on serait en droit de s'attendre après trois ans d'études générales ou professionnelles en français.

Au début de son activité, l'Office de la langue française n'utilisait qu'un seul test de connaissance générale de la langue pour tous les candidats. Cependant, après quelques années de ce régime, on en était venu à déceler un certain nombre de problèmes qui rendaient la création de nouveaux tests inévitable. Une question fondamentale demeurait, cependant : comment mesurer la connaissance du français appropriée à chaque profession (il y a trente-neuf ordres professionnels au Québec) en tenant compte du niveau de formation des candidats et des cinq critères de connaissance énoncés plus haut sans pour autant multiplier indûment les instruments?

Un premier élément de réponse consista à regrouper, là où la chose était possible, certaines des professions selon des critères d'affinité de formation et de niveau de scolarité. On put ainsi réunir les trente-neuf professions en dix-huit blocs dont on peut retrouver la composition au Tableau 1. On peut y voir qu'une seule profession, celle d'infirmier ou infirmière auxiliaire, requiert le niveau de scolarité de fin de secondaire. Il y a onze professions qui ont des exigences scolaires de niveau collégial tandis que les autres demandent une formation universitaire.

Le problème le plus évident auquel devaient faire face les spécialistes de l'Office était qu'en utilisant le test général, on observait un fort taux d'échecs chez les infirmières auxiliaires de même que chez les infirmières. Comme ces deux clientèles constituaient plus de 40 % des candidats, un remède s'imposait. Pruneau décrit la première démarche :

Nous décidâmes de réunir une équipe de spécialistes de français langue seconde bien sensibilisés à ces deux clientèles afin d'essayer de résoudre ce problème.

L'équipe fut constituée comme suit : un professeur en provenance d'un Centre d'orientation et de formation des immigrants (COFI), une personne responsable de la formation à l'hôpital Royal Victoria et anciennement responsable des langues secondes à la Direction générale de l'enseignement aux adultes du ministère de l'Education du Québec, la responsable des langues secondes à la Commission des écoles catholiques de Montréal, un conseiller pédagogique d'un Collège d'enseignement général et professionnel anglophone (Dawson College) et la responsable de l'évaluation à l'Office de la langue française. (1983)

Plusieurs possibilités s'offraient aux spécialistes de l'Office. La formule retenue fut celle d'examens comprenant deux parties générales (compréhension de l'oral et expression écrite) et deux parties se rapportant à la profession (compréhension de l'écrit et expression orale).
Suivons à nouveau Pruneau :

L'examen de l'Office demeure un examen de langue seconde. Il mesure la capacité de communiquer en français. Nous estimons qu'un professionnel qui a une connaissance appropriée à l'exercice de sa profession doit d'abord avoir une maîtrise de la langue générale nécessaire à la communication avec des francophones.

Le premier changement fondamental qu'a subi l'examen est que, si nous tenons compte du code dans la transmission du message, le premier critère n'est pas grammatical ou formel; il est de l'ordre de la connaissance. En d'autres termes, nous nous posons la question "Le message passe-t-il?" plutôt que "La langue est-elle correcte?" Par contre, il n'y a ni structure, ni temps de verbe, ni notion linguistique à exclure. Tout ce qui est d'usage courant, tout ce qui remplit une fonction précise dans la langue est susceptible de se retrouver dans l'examen.

Selon notre approche, il était aussi important que les situations de langue que nous allions utiliser dans l'examen ressemblent le plus possible à des situations de communication réalistes, susceptibles d'être rencontrées dans la vie quotidienne. Ainsi, nous avons demandé aux rédacteurs d'enregistrer les dialogues destinés à la compréhension de l'oral avant de les écrire pour qu'ils ressemblent le plus possible à des situations de communication réalistes tandis qu'à la compréhension de l'écrit, nous avons demandé aux ordres professionnels de nous fournir des textes de première main que les candidats sont susceptibles de lire dans leur travail. De cette façon, nous avons voulu éviter de défavoriser les candidats ayant appris le français hors du cadre scolaire.

L'examen comprend quatre parties qui se répartissent selon les "habiletés" et les valeurs suivantes :
- compréhension de la langue orale   40 points
- expression orale   30 points
- compréhension de la langue écrite   20 points
- expression écrite   10 points

Il y a autant de questions que de points, sauf pour l'expression écrite, où l'on alloue deux points par question.

Les professionnels, quelle que soit leur profession, ont tous à utiliser davantage la langue orale que la langue écrite et l'examen doit refléter cette situation. On a aussi accordé plus d'importance aux "habiletés" de compréhension qu'aux "habiletés" d'expression. (Pruneau 1983)

En compréhension de l'oral, quelques messages sont plus longs pour les candidats de niveau universitaire. Le type de questions varie et il y a plus ou moins d'images selon le cas. Le débit utilisé dans les textes est plutôt lent (pour tous les niveaux). Les structures, quant à elles, sont de types dont la compréhension ne dépend pas du niveau de formation scolaire.

En expression orale, habileté mesurée en entrevue indivi-duelle, le candidat est maître du terrain et du niveau où l'entrevue se déroule. L'ajustement au candidat s'y fait donc automatiquement.

A la compréhension de l'écrit, les trois niveaux sont traités différemment : complexité des textes, présence de divers niveaux de langue, etc. On a tenté de se rapprocher du niveau intellectuel généralement attendu des candidats (par exemple, moins scolarisés par rapport à plus scolarisés). Cette volonté, réelle au point de départ, ne se concrétise pas tou-jours dans la réalité : ce sont les ordres professionnels qui ont choisi les textes et plusieurs ajustements ont dû être faits au cours de la production du test. Ainsi, certains types de questions proposés faisant appel à l'analyse, à la comparaison et à l'argumentation, jugés trop difficiles, ont été éliminés.

TABLEAU 1 Regroupement des professions pour fins
d'évaluation de l'habileté en français
langue seconde

Professions	Scolarité
1. Infirmiers et infirmières auxiliaires	Secondaire
2. Infirmiers et infirmières	Collégial
3. Hygiénistes dentaires	Collégial
4. Techniciens en radiologie	Collégial
5. Podiatres Technologistes médicaux Audioprothésistes Techniciens en sciences appliquées Chiropraticiens Opticiens Denturologues Techniciens dentaires	Collégial
6. Ingénieurs	Universitaire
7. Ingénieurs forestiers	Universitaire
8. Médecins Vétérinaires Pharmaciens	Universitaire
9. Comptables agréés Comptables généraux licenciés Comptables en administration industrielle Administrateurs agréés	Universitaire
10. Avocats Notaires Conseillers en relations industrielles	Universitaire
11. Physiothérapeutes Ergothérapeutes	Universitaire
12. Travailleurs sociaux Psychologues Conseillers d'orientation	Universitaire
13. Architectes	Universitaire
14. Dentistes	Universitaire
15. Chimistes	Universitaire
16. Diététistes	Universitaire
17. Orthophonistes et audiologistes	Universitaire
18. Agronomes Arpenteurs-géomètres Évaluateurs agréés Urbanistes	Universitaire
Optométristes	Universitaire

Pour les deux blocs généraux qui présentent très peu de candidats (cf. Tableau 1, groupes 5 et 18), on a choisi de mesurer la compréhension écrite par le biais de textes généraux. Un spécialiste de la profession est invité à l'entrevue pour mesurer l'aspect connaissance et capacité d'utilisation de la terminologie française de la profession.

L'administration des examens se fait de façon collective, sauf pour l'expression orale, qui est mesurée en entrevue individuelle. Les directives sont données en français, car, dans la vie quotidienne, la communication inclut les directives. Pour ce qui est de la note de passage, elle a été fixée à 60 %, ce qui correspond au seuil fixé dans les collèges et universités. Ce pourcentage s'applique à chacune des parties de l'examen.

Dans ses efforts d'évaluation de la performance en langue seconde, l'Office de la langue française doit faire face à des conditions particulières : trop petit nombre de candidats dans plusieurs professions pour permettre les calculs de validité/fiabilité, non-disponibilité des populations représentatives des seuils à atteindre, etc. Malgré ce contexte, les nouveaux instruments réussissent à atteindre leurs objectifs.

CANADIEN PACIFIQUE LIMITÉE
(Pascal-André CHARLEBOIS)

Le Canadien Pacifique est une compagnie canadienne aux activités très diversifiées, dont les plus connues demeurent le transport ferroviaire, terrestre, aérien et maritime et les télécommunications. C'est vers 1969 que devaient débuter les premiers cours de langue seconde à l'intention des employés de cette compagnie, mais ce n'est qu'en 1978 que la formation linguistique au Canadien Pacifique a véritablement pris son essor. Ce changement a été le produit de cinq grandes étapes : 1) élaboration de la politique linguistique de la compagnie et distribution aux employés du texte des décisions sous forme de brochure; 2) inventaire des performances linguistiques des employés (environ 15 000); 3) définition des exigences linguistiques de tous les postes; 4) détermination du degré de formation linguistique requis par l'employé dans son poste; 5) établissement de programmes de formation linguistique.

Une bonne portion de la présentation de Charlebois était consacrée à montrer l'interrelation des programmes de formation et de l'évaluation de la performance en milieu de travail. Donnons-lui la parole.

L'emphase sur la performance nous a amenés à repenser nos contenus, nos stratégies pédagogiques et nos outils d'évaluation. Nous avons mis au premier plan le vécu professionnel des employés, la fonction sociale de la langue et le "savoir-faire".

Nous avons adopté une approche systémique. Les chefs de services se sont vu confier la mise en oeuvre de la politique linguistique de la Compagnie et le développement linguistique de leurs employés au même titre qu'ils étaient responsables de leur développement professionnel et technique. Le développement linguistique des employés fait ainsi partie intégrante de la réalité quotidienne de gestion des gestionnaires.

En termes de formation linguistique, notre approche est centrée sur l'apprenant. Nous faisons appel à sa curiosité, à sa créativité, à son sens de l'initiative et à son autonomie. L'apprenant devient ainsi le propriétaire de sa progression, ce qui est, à notre sens, la véritable source d'un testing de performance. Nous parlons avec l'apprenant d'objectifs d'intégration, c'est-à-dire d'objectifs qui visent à intégrer ses habiletés et ses connaissances afin de développer un individu normalement efficace dans son milieu de travail.

Comme le testing de performance est fonction des stratégies pédagogiques, nous articulons la formation linguistique autour de trois grands axes : 1) l'apprentissage du code; 2) les expériences éducatives délibérées; 3) les expériences éducatives spontanées. (1983)

La compétence de communication et la compétence linguistique ne s'excluent évidemment pas mutuellement. Pour cette raison, l'apprentissage du code demeure une des préoccupations dans les programmes linguistiques du Canadien Pacifique. Cependant, encore là, ce n'est plus le code pour le code qui présente de l'intérêt, mais bien le code en tant que porteur de signification. C'est la performance linguistique qui est aux commandes et les situations de communication dictent le choix des éléments de grammaire. Il importe d'ailleurs de bien distinguer entre la grammaire de la langue parlée et celle de la langue écrite.

Les expériences éducatives délibérées sont des expériences qui procèdent d'un modèle théorique prédéterminé et d'un plan d'action pensés par le professeur de langue, agent de formation dans le vrai sens de l'expression. C'est ici qu'on retrouve des activités comme le jeu de rôle, les études de cas et la simulation. L'agent de formation est aux commandes et les apprenants sont les acteurs.

Les expériences éducatives spontanées sont constituées par la somme des tentatives des apprenants pour utiliser la langue cible comme outil de communication dans les situations de la vie courante. C'est le domaine de l'imprévisible. L'apprenant est aux commandes et l'agent de formation n'est plus là pour le guider comme c'était le cas pour les expériences éducatives délibérées. En vivant de telles expériences éducatives spontanées, l'apprenant devient un vrai _performant_. Les expériences spontanées vécues avec des collègues de travail sont appelées à procurer une grande satisfaction personnelle et à développer l'estime de soi parce qu'elles correspondent à ce qui se passe dans la vie. Écoutons à nouveau Charlebois.

Notre défi en tant que formateur est de récupérer les expériences éducatives spontanées. Divers moyens s'offrent à nous : l'évaluation, la coévaluation et l'auto-évaluation. Au Canadien Pacifique, nous avons opté pour les trois modes d'appréciation. Le gestionnaire est au centre. Comme il est responsable du rendement professionnel et technique de ses employés, il est aussi responsable de leur performance linguistique. Le rendement linguistique s'inscrit dans le cadre de l'évaluation constructive du personnel au même titre que le rendement professionnel et technique. Le testing de performance en langue maternelle et en langue seconde s'articule autour des situations linguistiques décrites dans la fiche de fonction de l'employé.

Pour aider le gestionnaire à développer son personnel sur le plan linguistique, nous lui offrons deux formules : 1) la centralisation de la formation linguistique au siège social de la Compagnie; 2) les services d'un agent de formation linguistique en poste dans son unité de travail. Ce dernier aide les employés à faire face à leurs expériences éducatives spontanées. A titre d'exemple, il aidera un employé à préparer une présentation devant un groupe, à comprendre la teneur d'une lettre, à trouver un terme technique. Présentement, les employés font surtout appel à l'agent de formation pour de l'aide à la rédaction. Cette relation d'aide employé/agent de formation permet d'intégrer très rapidement l'agent de formation dans une unité de travail afin qu'il réponde aux véritables besoins des employés.

Cette approche d'un testing de performance en milieu de travail fait par les employés pour les employés et avec les employés paraîtra peut-être naïve et simpliste à certains. Nous lui trouvons cependant de grands avantages et elle nous sert fort bien. Elle a l'avantage de mettre au premier plan le vécu de l'employé, la dynamique des relations humaines et l'optimisation du potentiel de chaque employé. (1983)

UNIVERSITÉ D'OTTAWA (Marjorie B. WESCHE)

Au cours des dernières années, l'Institut de langues vivantes, organisme responsable des applications des politiques de bilinguisme à l'Université d'Ottawa, s'est trouvé de plus en plus impliqué dans l'élaboration de tests de langue seconde en français et en anglais. La majorité des tests produits à l'Institut vise des clientèles qui se retrouvent dans le cadre du contexte bilingue de l'université. Ce sont 1) des étudiants de premier cycle dans des facultés qui exigent un niveau fonctionnel donné dans la langue seconde comme condition d'obtention du diplôme; 2) des étudiants de deuxième et de troisième cycle de certains départements, Histoire et Géographie par exemple, où l'on a imposé des exigences de langue seconde reliées aux domaines d'études comme condition d'obtention du diplôme (Godbout 1980; DesBrisay et al. 1980); 3) des membres du personnel enseignant de la faculté des Sciences sociales dont le contrat exige la démonstration d'une certaine habileté fonctionnelle en langue seconde en rapport avec leur travail comme condition d'obtention de la permanence (voir à ce sujet l'article de Krupka dans ce volume). En outre, plusieurs autres tests doivent être préparés, soit en rapport avec des cours spécifiques offerts par l'Institut - on pense, par exemple, au cours de langue écrite en anglais langue seconde à l'intention des ingénieurs -, soit pour d'autres cours plus généraux. Ces tests peuvent servir au classement dans les cours, à la mesure du rendement ou à l'attestation que tel niveau donné a été atteint en rapport avec des habiletés fonctionnelles précises.

L'Institut accepte aussi, à l'occasion, des projets de tests pour des organismes de l'extérieur. Encore là, il s'agit parfois de la mesure de l'habileté générale mais, dans la plupart des cas, ce type de travail implique l'élaboration d'instruments permettant d'évaluer les savoirs langagiers face à des situations spécifiques d'étude ou de travail : par exemple, l'élaboration de tests en français et en anglais devant faire partie du processus de sélection des éventuels employés du Centre national des arts (voir à ce sujet l'article de Tréville dans ce volume). Tout récemment, des membres de l'Institut se sont intéressés au Ontario Test of English as a Second Language (OTESL), un projet interuniversitaire, logé à l'Institut, visant à développer un test d'anglais scolaire que les collèges et les universités pourront utiliser suite à l'admission de leurs étudiants (Cray et Wesche 1984).

Les tests préparés pour les départements d'Histoire et de Géographie, pour les professeurs de la faculté des Sciences sociales et pour le Centre national des arts de même que le projet OTESL en cours sont tous des produits, à des niveaux divers, d'une approche orientée vers la "performance" où le candidat doit faire la preuve de sa connaissance de la langue dans le contexte de tâches et de situations qui simulent celles pour lesquelles il se prépare à employer sa langue seconde. Dans chaque cas, les tests s'adressent à des clientèles ayant des besoins réels et des exigences qui peuvent être décrits en termes de types de discours et de situations d'emploi de la langue. Ces tests s'éloignent des premiers tests produits à l'Institut en ce qui a trait aux procédures d'élaboration, au contenu et à la forme et, en cela, ils sont le reflet de ce qui s'est passé dans le cas des tests d'habileté générale à l'intention des étudiants du premier cycle. Ces tests, portant sur les savoirs réceptifs et qui doivent être administrés à plusieurs milliers d'étudiants au cours de la première semaine de la session d'automne, sont toujours composés d'items à choix multiples. Cependant, avec le temps, ils sont devenus de plus en plus orientés vers ce que les candidats peuvent "faire" avec la langue seconde plutôt que vers ce qu'ils pourraient connaître de son système sous-jacent (DesBrisay 1982; Wesche 1983). Parmi les changements, on note l'abandon d'items indépendants au niveau de la phrase au profit d'items basés sur des textes oraux et écrits plus substantiels qui procurent de ce seul fait un contexte situationnel. Les items tentent d'obliger le candidat à interpréter la signification à l'aide de la langue d'une manière à peu près naturelle. Dans cette optique, les items mesurant des connaissances grammaticales spécifiques ont été abandonnés. On essaie aussi de respecter l'authenticité des textes et leur pertinence par rapport aux besoins de l'étudiant dans le contexte universitaire. Dans la préparation d'items à choix multiples, on formulera les distracteurs en fonction d'erreurs véritables faites par des usagers de la langue seconde dans des items semblables à réponse libre.

Comme le dit Wesche :

> Notre philosophie de base dans tout notre testing repose sur l'emploi de tâches pragmatiques - dans le sens où l'emploie Oller - qui demande du candidat de traiter de la langue en contexte avec les mêmes types de contraintes temporelles que celles qu'on trouve dans l'emploi normal de la langue (Oller 1979). En même temps, nous avons essayé de faire correspondre les types de discours, les contenus et les tâches le mieux possible avec les besoins ou les exigences en langue seconde de nos candidats, c'est-à-dire les sortes de situations et de types de discours qu'ils doivent pouvoir utiliser, qu'ils emploient la langue aux plans réceptif, interactif ou productif et que le canal soit audio-oral, écrit ou combiné. Nous tentons également de tenir compte de ces besoins dans nos critères de notation et de

pondération en mettant une emphase relative sur la correction par rapport à la communication, sur les niveaux de compétence et les aspects sociolinguistiques, etc. (1983)

Pour ce qui est des autres tests dont il a été question plus haut, ils diffèrent des tests à choix multiples en ce qu'ils s'adressent à des clientèles ayant des besoins langagiers relativement restreints et homogènes et qui peuvent être décrits en termes de situations où les candidats devraient pouvoir utiliser leur langue seconde, de types de textes avec lesquels ils devraient être à l'aise et d'opérations qu'ils devraient être capables de mener à terme. On peut ainsi créer des instruments critériés où les critères reflètent les objectifs de performance qui, eux, correspondent aux besoins langagiers des candidats. Dans tous ces tests, la question est de savoir si les candidats peuvent satisfaire aux objectifs de performance à un niveau acceptable, par exemple pour fins de certification. Dans chaque cas, la décision est déterminante en ce qui a trait au progrès du candidat dans ses études ou dans sa carrière. Il ne s'agit donc pas de classer des groupes de candidats les uns par rapport aux autres, mais bien d'établir si ces derniers rencontrent les exigences minimales établies pour tel objectif donné.

Il convient maintenant de s'arrêter sur les six étapes proposées par Wesche (1983) pour décrire la démarche suivie dans l'élaboration des tests à l'Institut, en illustrant certaines d'entre elles au besoin.

La première étape consiste à établir la raison d'être du test : quelles sortes de décisions doivent être prises suite à son utilisation et qu'elle est l'importance de ces décisions? On comprendra la différence qu'il y a entre le classement d'un étudiant dans un cours, l'octroi de crédits, l'admission à l'université et la poursuite d'une carrière.

Le but des tests développés à ce jour a été de donner une réponse affirmative ou négative quant à, par exemple, 1) la capacité d'étudiants au niveau des études supérieures d'effectuer de la recherche dans un domaine de spécialisation en employant les revues spécialisées sur le sujet et publiées en langue seconde et 2) l'habileté de membres du personnel enseignant à s'acquitter de leurs tâches professionnelles dans un milieu bilingue demandant des capacités réceptives de niveau fonctionnel mais des capacités productives restreintes.

La deuxième étape doit permettre d'identifier les comportements de base souhaités suite à une analyse de besoins. Cette question n'est pas résolue d'un seul coup mais implique plutôt un processus d'interaction entre les élaborateurs de tests et les usagers pendant un certain temps. C'est ce qui permet d'établir les caractéristiques générales du schéma du test, de même que ses composantes en termes de types de discours, de contenus, d'opérations, de contraintes sur la forme ou le mode de présentation (par exemple, sans bruit de fond, accent standard, etc.) et des objectifs des items ou des techniques en termes d'habiletés et de fonctions à mesurer. Dans le cas des tests pour les départements d'Histoire et de Géographie, cette étape a occasionné de nombreuses réunions et discussions avec des professeurs et des étudiants intéressés qui ont amené les départements impliqués à établir un consensus sur ce qu'il était légitime d'exiger de leurs étudiants. On passa par la suite à la description des besoins fonctionnels en lecture de ces étudiants des deuxième et troisième cycles, puis, à partir d'une sélection de documents appropriés faite par les professeurs en fonction du contenu, du style et du niveau de difficulté conceptuelle, on en arriva à préciser la forme du test, les types de textes et de tâches et les critères de notation à employer. Il devint alors possible d'établir un projet de test tenant compte à la fois des contextes où évoluaient ces étudiants et des contraintes administratives des départements.

Dans le cas du projet OTESL, on procéda à une enquête sur les besoins des étudiants en anglais langue seconde dans les institutions post-secondaires ontariennes par le biais d'entrevues avec des enseignants d'anglais, des responsables de programmes, des professeurs dans des départments à forte composante d'étudiants étrangers, des agents d'admission, etc. L'observation des comportements des étudiants étrangers et les discussions avec eux, qu'ils soient dans des programmes spéciaux ou dans des programmes réguliers d'anglais langue seconde, ont également été mises à contribution. Enfin, on fit aussi entrer en ligne de compte les renseignements recueillis sur les domaines de spécialisation que choisissent ces étudiants et ceux qui étaient disponibles dans d'autres études du même ordre. (Voir à ce sujet les articles d'Emmett et de Seaton dans ce volume.)

La troisième étape, en général parallèle à la deuxième, porte sur la cueillette de matériel pour le test. Cela ne va pas toujours sans difficultés. Ainsi, un des problèmes rencontrés par l'élaborateur de test face à l'emploi de documents authentiques est la compréhension même de textes spécialisés dans certains domaines, par exemple en psychologie clinique ou en stratigraphie. Également d'intérêt est le fait que certains textes publiés dans des revues spécialisées et proposés comme matériel éventuel par

les spécialistes du domaine sont mal écrits et beaucoup
d'enregistrements de cours ou de réunions donnent lieu à
du marmonnage, à des bruits incongrus, etc. Il devient
alors nécessaire de procéder à des modifications et à des
réenregistrements. L'objectif est de procurer aux candidats une version un peu améliorée et épurée des textes
tout en leur conservant autant de leur aspect naturel que
possible. On peut tirer de ce qui précède les inévitables
conclusions suivantes : une situation de test ne saurait
être tout à fait naturelle, elle cause toujours une certaine
quantité de stress et la présentation de matériel de test sur
ruban magnétique et même magnétoscopique amène une
perte considérable de fidélité par rapport au face à face.
Cependant, une telle technique permet la présentation
répétée et en même temps constante du matériel à des
groupes relativement importants et constitue le plus
souvent la seule solution pratique possible. Par contre,
dans les tests s'adressant à des petits groupes (par
exemple, celui des Sciences sociales ou celui du Centre
national des arts), c'est le dialogue face à face et le jeu de
rôle qui sont employés.

Dans le quatrième temps, on passe à l'élaboration de
l'approche et des items du test. A ce point, on doit
aborder la question des types de situations langagières
(dialogue, lecture intégrale, prise de notes, etc.) qui
peuvent être ou non reliés à certains modes et combiner ou
non les canaux de communication. On y détermine aussi la
façon de noter les différentes performances. On tente d'y
inclure des conditions semblables à celles à partir desquel-
les le candidat sera éventuellement jugé dans sa vie de tous
les jours. Par exemple, est-il suffisant qu'il comprenne
des renseignements généraux et puisse les interpréter
littéralement ou s'attend-on à ce qu'il reconnaisse l'ironie ou
l'humour? Quelle est l'importance relative de la précision
par rapport à des stratégies de communication efficaces?

Il est en outre vital que le contenu et les tâches d'un
test soient intéressants, pertinents, et qu'ils suscitent
l'implication du candidat. C'est là la seule façon d'obtenir
une performance valide qui reflète bien ce que le candidat
peut faire. L'expérience à l'Institut montre qu'une
approche basée sur la performance aide à élaborer des
tests qui sont perçus comme très pertinents, ce qui pro-
cure une bien meilleure chance d'une implication totale dans
la tâche à accomplir et d'une performance vraiment représentative des capacités véritables.

A mesure que les items sont créés, il importe de main-
tenir une interaction continue avec les spécialistes du sujet
ou de la situation de travail qui aident à les juger et à les

raffiner. On utilise aussi l'expertise des professeurs de langue à cause de leur expérience de la salle de classe et de leur familiarité avec les objectifs visés par l'enseignement.

La tendance, jusqu'à maintenant, surtout dans les cas où un niveau élevé de connaissance de la langue écrite était requis, a été de combiner des tâches moins directes comme des exercices de cloze avec des tâches orientées vers la performance. Ces deux solutions n'apparaissent mutuellement exclusives ni pour le test dans son ensemble, ni pour les tâches individuelles. Une telle approche fournit des points de repère mieux standardisés tant pour l'évaluation de composantes d'autres tests que pour l'établissement de niveaux de performance appropriés. Elle permet aussi d'"individualiser" certaines parties d'un test (lectures spécialisées, dialogues) tout en destinant les autres à l'ensemble des candidats. Enfin, il est possible d'y tenir compte des besoins spécifiques de même que des besoins généraux que partagent diverses clientèles (par exemple, le cas de l'économiste et du pharmacien qui tous deux doivent faire de la recherche dans des domaines spécialisés fort différents, mais qui doivent aussi comprendre les discussions dans les deux langues à leur Conseil de faculté).

La cinquième étape est celle de l'essai du test à divers moments de son élaboration. On voudra trouver des groupes présentant des caractéristiques aussi semblables que possible à celles de la clientèle visée, en plus de tester le test avec des professeurs de langue et des experts du sujet traité. Quand une version pilote du test est finalement complétée, le test au complet est mis à l'épreuve avec des groupes aussi nombreux que possible (par exemple, des étudiants au niveau des études supérieures en Histoire et en Géographie, des groupes représentatifs d'employés bilingues au Centre national des arts, etc.). Des renseignements additionnels sont aussi recueillis à l'aide d'autres types de tests, de jugements de professeurs ou de superviseurs et de procédés d'auto-évaluation. Vu que les techniques psychométriques telles l'analyse d'items et les mesures de validité interne fournissent moins de renseignements dans le cas de tests où les items ne sont pas indépendants, il est capital d'avoir accès à plusieurs autres types d'information provenant de validations externes en plus de ceux fournis par les analyses habituelles. L'utilisation de la technique "test-retest" et des mesures de fiabilité interévaluateurs est souvent essentielle dans l'établissement de la fiabilité de mesures de performance, en particulier lorsque des techniques interactives à réponses libres sont employées.

Un test qui est dans sa forme finale et que l'on emploie régulièrement devrait toujours être susceptible de révisions et d'améliorations basées sur les commentaires des usagers et sur des données cumulatives plus importantes. La satisfaction des usagers face aux décisions positives et négatives auxquelles le test contribue constitue, bien sûr, le critère ultime de validité. C'est à ce stade, le sixième dans la liste, que se trouvent les tests de performance élaborés à l'Institut. Les premiers commentaires sont unanimes à reconnaître que ces instruments constituent une amélioration importante sur les méthodes d'évaluation utilisées auparavant, que les approches employées plaisent mieux aux candidats et aux usagers et que les tests contribuent à des décisions justes quant au niveau de compétence en langue seconde. De plus, les tests de performance constituent un moyen très efficace pour faire comprendre à d'éventuels étudiants ou employés que ce sont des savoirs fonctionnels en langue seconde qui sont requis, non pas la connaissance de règles de grammaire ou l'adresse dans les items à choix multiples. C'est peut-être là la conséquence la plus importante d'une approche orientée vers la performance. Il y a donc place pour beaucoup d'enthousiasme face aux tests de performance là où ils sont utilisables et pertinents, c'est-à-dire quand les besoins des candidats sont homogènes, relativement limités et se prêtent à des descriptions fonctionnelles et quand le niveau critique des décisions à prendre justifie le coût relativement élevé d'élaboration, d'administration et de notation qu'une telle approche implique." (Wesche 1983)

Le domaine des tests de performance en langue seconde est fort jeune. Ce fait se vérifie dans les descriptions qui ont été données de l'état de leurs instruments par tous les participants à la table ronde. On n'aura cependant pas pu s'empêcher d'observer au passage que les premières réactions recueillies sont très positives et que, là où des résultats ont été enregistrés, ils sont également fort encourageants. Il reste des obstacles à franchir dont, en particulier, celui de la faiblesse relative des techniques docimologiques traditionnelles devant les types de tâches que les tests de performance proposent. Cette situation est encore souvent fort inconfortable pour ceux qui veulent défendre leurs nouvelles approches face à une certaine catégorie de l'establishment du testing; il y a donc fort à faire sur ce plan. Il y a peu de doute, cependant, que si une approche véritable de communication doit être employée pour un enseignement efficace de la langue seconde, son existence même est liée à la production d'instruments de mesure compatibles avec elle. Ce sont les tests de performance qui semblent le mieux en mesure de répondre à ce critère.

BIBLIOGRAPHIE

Bibeau, G. 1976. Rapport de l'Étude indépendante sur les programmes de formation linguistique de la Fonction publique du Canada - Volume 1 - Rapport synthèse. Ottawa : Imprimeur de la Reine.

Canale, M., and M. Swain. 1980. Theoretical bases of communicative approaches to second language teaching and testing. Applied Linguistics 1.1: 1-47.

Charlebois, P.-A. 1983. Le testing de performance en langue seconde dans le cadre du Programme de formation linguistique du Canadien Pacifique : une approche dynamique. Présentation faite lors du Symposium sur le testing de performance, Université d'Ottawa.

Cray, E., and M. Wesche. 1984. The Ontario test of English as a second language: A progress report. TESL Talk (forthcoming).

DesBrisay, M. 1982. A feasibility study of large scale communicative testing. Journal of Applied Language Study 1.1: 77-86.

DesBrisay, M., M. Wesche, D. Taylor, W. Feldberg. 1980. Report on the test of English proficiency for graduate students in history. Journal de l'ILV 22: 52-58.

Godbout, R. 1980. Un problème spécifique d'évaluation : la compréhension de l'écrit aux études supérieures en Histoire. Journal de l'ILV, 22.

LeBlanc, R. 1976. Rapport de l'Étude indépendante sur les programmes de formation linguistique de la Fonction publique du Canada - Volume 5 - Les facteurs pédagogiques. Ottawa : Imprimeur de la Reine.

Oller, J. 1979. Language Tests at School. New York: Longman.

Proulx-Dubé, R. 1983. Les tests de performance à la Fonction publique canadienne. Présentation faite lors du Symposium sur le testing de performance, Université d'Ottawa.

Pruneau, D. 1983. Le programme de testing de l'Office de la langue française du Québec. Présentation faite lors du Symposium sur le testing de performance, Université d'Ottawa.

Voyer, M. 1983. Le testing de performance au Canadien National et à Air Canada. Présentation faite lors du Symposium sur le testing de performance, Université d'Ottawa.

Wesche, M. 1983. Performance testing at the University of Ottawa. Paper read at the Colloquium on Performance Testing, University of Ottawa.

Wesche, M. 1983a. Communicative testing in a second language. The Modern Language Journal 67. 1: 41-55.

Widdowson, H. 1978. Teaching Language as Communication. London: Oxford University Press.